D0987443

NOV 0 6 2013

BIOG
SAITO,
WILLIAM
H.

An Unprogrammed Life

Adventures of an Incurable Entrepreneur

William H. Saito

WILEY

John Wiley & Sons Singapore Pte. Ltd.

Copyright © 2012 John Wiley & Sons Singapore Pte. Ltd.

Published in 2012 by John Wiley & Sons (Asia) Pte. Ltd., 1 Fusionopolis Walk, #07-01, Solaris South Tower, Singapore 138628

All rights reserved.

No part of this publication may be reproduced, stored in a retrieval system, or transmitted in any form or by any means, electronic, mechanical, photocopying, recording, scanning, or otherwise, except as expressly permitted by law, without either the prior written permission of the Publisher, or authorization through payment of the appropriate photocopy fee to the Copyright Clearance Center. Requests for permission should be addressed to the Publisher, John Wiley & Sons (Asia) Pte. Ltd., 1 Fusionopolis Walk, #07-01, Solaris South Tower, Singapore 138628, tel: 65-6643-8000, fax: 65-6643-8008, e-mail: enquiry@wiley.com.

This publication is designed to provide accurate and authoritative information in regard to the subject matter covered. It is sold with the understanding that the Publisher is not engaged in rendering professional services. If professional advice or other expert assistance is required, the services of a competent professional person should be sought. Neither the author nor the Publisher is liable for any actions prompted or caused by the information presented in this book. Any views expressed herein are those of the author and do not represent the views of the organizations he works for.

Other Wiley Editorial Offices
John Wiley & Sons, 111 River Street, Hoboken, NJ 07030, USA
John Wiley & Sons, The Atrium, Southern Gate, Chichester, West Sussex, P019 8SQ, United Kingdom
John Wiley & Sons (Canada) Ltd., 5353 Dundas Street West, Suite 400, Toronto, Ontario, M9B 6HB, Canada
John Wiley & Sons Australia Ltd., 42 McDougall Street, Milton, Queensland 4064, Australia
Wiley-VCH, Boschstrasse 12, D-69469 Weinheim, Germany

Library of Congress Cataloging-in-Publication Data

ISBN 978-1-118-07703-0 (Paperback)
ISBN 978-1-118-07742-9 (ePDF)
ISBN 978-1-118-07741-2 (Mobi)
ISBN 978-1-118-07727-6 (ePub)

Typeset in 11.5/14pt, Bembo by MPS Limited, a Macmillan Company, Chennai, India
Printed in Singapore by Markono Print Media

10   9   8   7   6   5   4   3   2

For Hitomi and Lisa

lecture 10/13 F30

Contents

Foreword

Entrepreneurs are often characterized as creative innovators with a higher propensity for risk-taking and achievement. They imagine solutions to problems by introducing new technologies, increasing efficiencies in productivity, or by generating new products or services. While certain entrepreneurial personality traits may be present from birth, research studies have revealed there is much more complexity in the interplay between entrepreneurial behaviors and environmental influences.

William Saito's story is an ideal example of that dynamic interplay between nature versus nurture. From his first computer programming job at age 10 to the sale of his company, I/O Software, to Microsoft at age 34, William has shown that entrepreneurship is not some magic formula or the result of any particular personality trait. Much like the story of Ewing Kauffman—a poor Missouri farm boy who started a company in his basement, created the foundation I'm privileged to lead today, and died a billionaire—William illustrates that anyone can succeed on the entrepreneurial journey, particularly if one has a passion for his or her work and the determination to persevere even amid the inevitable trials and failures.

I first met William after he won the 1998 Ernst & Young Entrepreneur of the Year (EOY) award, which continues to be sponsored by the Kauffman Foundation. William went on to become one of the most active judges for EOY award competitions—at the local, national, and global levels. We have also shared the stage at many events, most recently as speakers at the Milken Global Institute conference.

After selling his company in the United States, William moved to Japan and took on the roles of both educator and government adviser. Notably, since November 2009, together with the Honda Foundation, he has been instrumental in the planning for the Kauffman Foundation's Global Entrepreneurship Week (GEW) in Japan, a celebration of entrepreneurship that encourages people from across the world to follow the kind of example William sets in this book. GEW is now held in nearly 120 countries. At the Kauffman Foundation, our mission is to develop and fund programs to help entrepreneurs more easily start and grow their businesses; to contribute new research insights regarding the link between entrepreneurship and economic growth; and to help educate policymakers about how they can pave the way for a more entrepreneurial economy.

As an innovator, entrepreneur, venture capitalist, and educator, William Saito has been supporting startups in his business, in the classroom, in events organization, and now in the pages of this book. It is a worthy read, and offers encouragement for entrepreneurs everywhere.

—Carl Schramm
President and CEO, Ewing Marion
Kauffman Foundation
Founding board member, Startup America

Preface

FBI at the Door

I've always liked taking things apart. I'd see a gadget, a device, a new appliance in the family living room, and I'd start wondering how it worked. This might well be seen as an innate curiosity about the fundamental nature of things—not only *how* things worked but *why* they worked as they did. Sooner or later, I would grab a screwdriver and take my curiosity to the next level. This might be seen as a childlike death wish. You see, I was very good at taking things apart and finding out what made them run, but I was not very adept at putting them back together. Looking back, it certainly wasn't because I couldn't put them back together, but the thrill of discovery in deconstructing something was never matched by the tiresome process of trying to put it all back together. When I was very young I started with simple things like the family's stereo system or Dad's reel-to-reel tape deck, then it progressed to TVs, personal computers, and, finally, computer software. My parents got me a PC when I was very young, and I quickly learned to program on it. Within a short time I was actually making money from my programming ability (more on that later); that's about the time I discovered that it's even more fun to take software apart than to take a TV apart—and the great thing is that your parents don't get upset if you're not inclined to put it back together again.

When I was a kid, most software (especially programs that catered to teenagers) came with some level of copy protection. So one of the first real challenges—and by challenges I mean joys—in my life was figuring out how to break the copy protection. I think it's important to point out that this had nothing to do with making illicit copies; I had no use for the software whose copy protection I was trying to crack. I just did it because it was a challenge. Some people enjoy crossword puzzles or brain twisters, and others, like me, enjoy getting inside software to see how it works. That's all. Not to use it or resell it or damage it. Just to open it. To my 11-year-old mind, the newest corporate groupware program was just like a Rubik's cube: a puzzle to be solved. I didn't understand what something like Lotus 1-2-3 did or why anyone would want to use it, but I could see that someone had gone to a lot of trouble to lock the door, so to speak, and to me that was a challenge. A brain teaser. So I figured out how to pick the lock.

Over the years, software got bigger, more complex, and more expensive, and as you'd expect, the locks also became more sophisticated. Sometimes it was a complicated code, other times it was modification to the media itself, and eventually it became an external hardware device such as a USB-based key that acted as a lock to turn the program on. It's as if someone was inventing an endless series of new Rubik's cubes, each a little more difficult than the one before. I loved the challenge that each new program presented; something worthy of my time and effort (though in many cases it didn't take very much time or effort). Through programming, I figured out how to crack all kinds of software copy protection, just as I'd done years earlier, and I never found a lock that I couldn't pick one way or another. I could get into anything.

Eventually I created a small business with friends who shared my love for programming, and among various other projects, we decided to create our own security software. Of course, the only way to make bulletproof security software is to find out what's wrong with all the products already on the market—in other words, test them for weaknesses, see how people like ourselves can pick the locks of these commercial data encryption programs. Once we saw what was wrong with other people's security software, we could set about patching those holes to make something better.

So part of our work involved breaking all the security products on the market to discover their weaknesses, hunt for digital, or in some cases intentional, back doors left open when the house was supposed to be locked up tight. We naturally kept a big database with all our test results, showing exactly how to break any major security product on the planet. We'd improve on the best techniques we found, and then incorporate these innovative concepts into our own products. It was serious work, but I have to admit that it brought back lots of memories, and I was having a *great* time.

One afternoon in 1994 two big guys in suits came strolling into our reception area, and I mean big. One of them was a good 6′5″ and built like a tank. Neither of them looked like software engineers. Before our receptionist had a chance to ask what company they represented, the two pulled ominous-looking IDs and said in a booming voice that brought work in the office to a halt faster than a power blackout, "Federal Bureau of Investigation."

The bigger of the two agents announced, "We're looking for William Saito."

I was 23. I'd been breaking copy protection on software since I was in the fifth grade. I knew that this was technically illegal, but so what? I wasn't stealing the software or doing anything . . . you know . . . bad. I just wanted to test my skills against the team that made the software. No harm, no foul. Nothing I had done, nothing my company had done was going to come to the attention of the FBI.

Then I began to think about the dozens, no, hundreds of security programs we had successfully hacked into over the past couple of years. What if one of them was somehow tied to some government organization? What if purely by accident we'd got our hands on something we weren't supposed to, what if we'd cracked something that we shouldn't have touched? Maybe there was some government code out there masquerading as a commercial product, and. . . . For a fraction of a second I wondered if they had PCs in federal prisons.

Of course, all of that insanity came and went in a flash. I had done some routine work with our local city police department. Perhaps this visit had something to do with that. Or maybe my mom had figured out that going to medical school and running a software company were just clever ways to avoid those hated piano lessons, and she'd called the feds. Anything was possible.

I rose from my seat, I looked around the office. Of course, everyone was looking at each other, wanting to make some kind of hilarious joke, but no jokes were forthcoming. Was it my imagination or was one of our programmers eyeing the rear window that opened onto a fire escape out back?

Okay, that was enough. I faced the big fellow with the badge and said, "I'm William Saito. What can I do for you?"

His face showed not the slightest trace of emotion as he said in a practiced monotone, "Is there somewhere we could talk?"

I showed the two of them into the conference room right next to my office and closed the door. We talked for quite a while, but their whole discussion boiled down to something like this: "We're with the research facilities from Quantico. We hear from friends in the Los Angeles area that you guys know all about computers, that you're real good at solving 'problems,' and that you've been willing to help local law enforcement in the past. We're wondering if you could help us, too."

If it were 10 years later and we all had cell phones and instant messaging, I would have quickly typed, "Sorry, no one's getting arrested today. Go back to work!" and sent it to all of our undoubtedly curious staff. Instead, I smiled and said, "Sure. Just tell me how I can help."

Acknowledgments

Every successful entrepreneur stands on the shoulders of mentors, friends, family, role models, and business leaders who blazed their own paths to create standards and practices that others can follow. It would take too many pages to mention everyone who helped me along the way, but one mentor in particular walked through my door unexpectedly early in my career and that has made all the difference in the successes that followed.

In 1997, representatives from Ernst & Young came to my office and offered to help me apply for their Entrepreneur of the Year Awards Program, which I eventually won in 1998. I wrote about why I initially turned them down three times, and I remain grateful to this day for their persistence and determination. Because of that experience and the network it created early on, I was able to meet with start-up companies, CEOs, and venture businesses all over the world, but especially in the United States and Japan.

This book is written not only from my personal experience of running a venture business (lots of people have done that), but also from my many years of working with the Entrepreneur of the Year awards program. I am probably the only awardee who has been fortunate enough to judge all levels of the competition—local, national, Japan, and the world competition in Monte Carlo. I have personally reviewed thousands of business plans and proposals, talked to countless young company managers, and learned a great deal from them. I know what makes a company a winner, and I know what little things will hold back even a terrific company with a powerful technology from ever making it to the big time. This book is a thank you to all those shoulders I have stood on and all the entrepreneurs who shared their stories with me. I'd like to pass on some of what I've learned to any enterprising souls out there who are hoping their company will also hit it big someday.

While discussing the possibility of writing a book with my agent, Cindy Mullins, I wondered if I really had enough of a story to tell to warrant the time and effort required. I didn't have to wonder long, because a contract from John Wiley & Sons was soon on my desk, and I knew there was no turning back at that point. I am grateful to Cindy and to David Russell, both of Safari Universal Relations, for helping me keep the time and research commitment to a manageable level, and to our editor at Wiley's Singapore office, Nick Wallwork, for ushering the book through the publishing process. This has been a whole new challenge for me, but I've always liked to try new things at least once.

Chapter 1

Blame It on DNA

If I have ever seemed overly inquisitive, independently minded, impatient to see what comes next, and, yes, a bit headstrong, I came by it naturally. More than anyone else, I blame my grandmother. I sometimes say the real talent in my family came from her, and the rest of us have just been trying to catch up. Frankly, no matter what any of us achieves, I don't think we'll ever be as independent, strong-willed, and self-confident as she was way back when.

My grandparents were international travelers before World War II, a time when a majority of Japanese still lived and died within the small village where they were born. Almost nobody went overseas. But my grandmother was in motion from an early age. She came from a cold, northern prefecture called Yamagata, where farming has always been a major occupation. Women of her time had a pretty basic job description: keep your husband healthy, raise strong kids, and when you aren't helping with the work in the fields, get back home to cook, clean, wash, and sew. It was a routine that did not allow for much variation, and it could easily last half a century or more.

But one young girl by the name of Kimiyo knew from an early age that this job description just wasn't going to satisfy her. She wanted more, a lot more. The first step was education, and she threw herself into her studies. Many years later, a U.S. journalist would note matter-of-factly something that must have shocked her family and friends no end: "[Kimiyo] is one of the few women of her land who went on to study after high school." In fact, she continued her studies until the age of 22, which was rare enough for men, but unheard of for a woman, and then left Yamagata entirely. She got a job teaching home economics (one of the few things women were allowed to teach)—and not even in Japan but in Seoul (the capital of what is now South Korea). She had received a scholarship to the prestigious Nara Women's University, and a part of that scholarship included her teaching home economics abroad. Traveling as a single woman, she packed up and left her family and friends, boarded a ship, and traveled to another country and another culture. Looking at a map today, her journey might not appear very long, but in terms of the social norms she was tossing aside, she might as well have been going to the moon.

She settled into Seoul and threw herself into teaching. While there, she met an interesting fellow from Okinawa; an English teacher named Onaga who shared her interest in people and places far from home. They were married, had five children and continued to live and teach overseas for 18 years.

Her husband had become a renowned scholar of English literature, just as Kimiyo was earning fame as an expert on "home economics," which to her meant things such as nutrition, proper diet, healthy food preparation, and so on. After World War II, the Onagas received special permission from General Douglas MacArthur to move to Okinawa. In fact, right before the war ended, my grandfather had written directly to General MacArthur to requisition a ship to evacuate all the Okinawans from Seoul back to Okinawa. My grandmother hesitated initially, preferring Tokyo instead, but she decided that the more decimated Okinawa needed educators like her and her husband. With five children in tow, the couple left the frozen winters of Korea and settled in the Onaga family's native homeland, tropical Okinawa. There, amid the ruins of the war, they continued to do what they loved best, no matter what the hardship. "We taught school in tents," Kimiyo reflected later, but they kept on working. Eventually her husband landed a position in the English department at the University of the Ryukyus, the major academic institution in the region, and Kimiyo found a regular teaching position in home economics. To many of the repatriated Okinawans, my grandparents were considered saviors.

At the time, what passed for home economics in Japanese schools focused largely on serving tea, flower arranging, and other cultural pursuits designed to help proper young ladies find good husbands. Kimiyo Onaga would have none of that, not while so many Japanese children were seriously ill or malnourished, and all too few attended any kind of proper school. She was interested in the new science of nutrition, something that postwar Okinawans desperately needed to understand, and Kimiyo was always ready to teach. I'm sure she was seen by most Japanese men as having an unladylike concern for academic study and an even more unladylike willingness to speak her mind, but these characteristics served her well. Somehow, her work brought her to the attention of the U.S. Army.

It's important to remember that after World War II Japan was in very dire straits. Food was still extremely short, and many people were literally starving. Almost everything was rationed, if it was available at all, a situation that continued for years. Japan's industrial infrastructure was decimated, its largest city was firebombed, and little was left of prewar business or agriculture. Worse yet, the wartime government had imposed such harsh conditions on its own citizens that the postwar years would have been marked by widespread poverty and hunger even without the bombing. Difficult though it is to imagine today, postwar Japan was officially classified as a Third World country, a place without industry, commerce, or sufficient agriculture to feed its people.

Perhaps it was part of America's efforts to rebuild the country after the war, or because Okinawa was at that time a U.S. territory and home to thousands of American servicemen—whatever the reason—the military decided to take steps to improve the health of the local population. As one step, in 1952 the Army supported a research and study trip for five Japanese home economists to travel to the United States, cross the country, and learn first-hand about the American diet and American views on nutrition. After a stopover in Los Angeles, they would go to New York City, and then, having seen two of America's largest cities, they would visit a small college in Kentucky where they would study for five weeks, and next travel on to Lansing, Michigan, for another three weeks, and finally, visit San Francisco before returning to Japan. Kimiyo Onaga was one of the five they invited.

To us, this would seem a no-brainer, a fabulous opportunity for anyone to escape the dreary devastation and constant struggle in Japan and go see the wonders of America first hand. And yet, if we try to see the world through Japanese eyes of that time, it must have been a frightening prospect. For just as the war had decimated Japan, it had helped pull America out of the Great Depression, and the postwar years there were a boom time for business. To Japanese, American soldiers looked like giants, big and strong in their clean, new uniforms, and America itself was seen as a land of unimagined wealth and power. For any Japanese, much less a diminutive woman from Okinawa, a mother with five children under her care, to travel there at the invitation of the vanquishing army should have been an awesome, perhaps terrifying suggestion. I don't know for sure what went through my grandmother's mind when she received this invitation, but I'm willing to bet that she thought it over for at least a nanosecond or two before she started packing.

Even today I like to imagine my grandmother as part of this intrepid group of Japanese women, strapping parachutes on their backs and boarding a military plane (prop planes back then) for the long, cold, bumpy ride to Los Angeles. These five women were not just going far away from their homes or even from Japan, but were suddenly being whisked halfway around the world, from one of the most destitute nations to the single most affluent place on earth, where they would see things they had never even dreamed of and try to make sense of it all through a U.S. government interpreter.

I never had any doubt which of the five women was destined to become the leader of this group, the one who wanted to see more and ask more questions and happily step up and talk to strangers. So I was not at all surprised when I discovered an old newspaper clipping about her trip in which the United Press referred to her as, "Mrs. Onaga . . . a sort of unofficial spokesman for the five." The purpose of the trip was to study American eating habits "so they can teach the people on the islands about health through food." All the same, the women seemed equally interested in the panoply of gadgets in American kitchens and

the somewhat shocking fashions (including
shorts!). My grandmother noted the importan
in the American diet, and she saw the results:
big!" she told the *New York Times*. She notec
and could not afford to eat meat very oft
would teach them the importance of including p.
soon as she returned.

As important as studying nutrition, my grandmother got to see the
United States up close, to meet people, and see a world that only a
handful of Japanese at that time really understood. America was not just
the invincible industrial, commercial, and military giant that it appeared
to most people in postwar Japan, but a land of great social freedom, both
legal and cultural, and unlimited opportunity that was almost unimag-
inable to people in Tokyo or Okinawa at that time. Those few months
she spent in America had a profound effect on her, and that is
undoubtedly why I was born in the United States and not in Japan. But
now I'm getting ahead of myself.

My grandfather eventually became the Dean of English at the
University of the Ryukyus and my grandmother continued to teach in
the home economics department. She became well known for her
knowledge of nutrition and her passion for talking about it and putting
her lessons to practical use—in the kitchen. She opened an important
cooking school in the capital city of Naha, and anyone who wanted to
get a license to cook in a commercial kitchen in that area had to take her
course, so in a sense, she helped to train all the chefs in the region. She
also wrote several popular books about cooking, she had a cooking show
on NHK, Japan's government-sponsored TV network, and she continued to teach and study about nutrition all her life. I've seen university
research reports on the nutritional analysis of lunches served in institu-
tional kitchens in Okinawa that she helped write in the late 1960s.

While her travels in America no doubt made a deep and lasting
impression on her, Kimiyo had no intention of uprooting her family and
moving to the United States. She felt her mission was to teach people in
her homeland, and she certainly enjoyed that. She and her husband
loved Okinawa and were fascinated by the old Ryukyu culture. They
made a good home for their kids, and starting from the widespread
poverty of postwar days, they built very successful lives in the decades

owed. In fact, they acquired a very large amount of land and
tely lived quite well.

One result of that growing affluence was that her five children also
ved well and certainly by the time the youngest, a girl named Yoko,
was growing up, the kids were being spoiled. I think that in many ways
Yoko was a lot like her mother. Even from an early age she was
headstrong, energetic, smart, and motivated. Life in Okinawa was great,
but she grew up in increasing affluence and the child of local celebrities.
Her father was a dean at the university, which was prestigious enough,
but her mother was a public figure—a writer and teacher, a promoter of
local culture, and even a TV personality. Yoko didn't want to simply
grow up in her parents' shadow, and more than that, she was growing
bored with her easy life in Okinawa. So this bright, headstrong girl
decided to get out of the islands where she was raised and make her own
way in the world. She went to school in Tokyo, quite a long way, both
emotionally and geographically, from her home. Of course, she was
anything but a typical Japanese college co-ed. She had inherited what
might be called an independent attitude and a strong will to do what she
wanted to do. She also had the financial wherewithal to support her
rebellious nature, so, for example, she lived in a private apartment in
Tokyo instead of in a girls' dormitory. That in itself was unusual. From
what I hear, she skipped classes to do much more important things—like
go to rock concerts (she went to hear Elvis and the Beatles when they
came to Japan). It all sounds so ordinary now, but back then it was
pretty radical.

Like her own mother, Yoko was as smart as she was strong-willed.
She studied veterinary medicine and worked as a vet in Tokyo. I'm
sure she was good at it, and she probably enjoyed it, but she was restless.
I think there's a restless-spirit gene in the family DNA, and she had
more than her share.

Although her mother had stayed in Okinawa all those years, she also
knew that in Japan opportunities for personal growth and success—
especially for women—were limited and perhaps always would be. So
she told her children what she had seen and heard in America, and she
told them about this strange but wonderful place across the ocean,
where even Japanese who didn't speak English could make a living and
raise their families in a very different, more affluent, and more socially

open environment. Yoko would have heard these things throughout the 1950s, from the time she was a young girl through her early teens. One by one, she saw her older siblings begin to follow Kimiyo's advice and move overseas, and by the late sixties, when Yoko was in her early twenties, out of school and working as a vet, a lot of things must have come together. Her restless nature, combined with her mother's stories about America, must have rung a bell, or perhaps she had already experienced the kind of frustration that awaited a smart, young, self-motivated woman in Tokyo, with its rigid, male-dominated social mores and sexist working environment. Whatever the reason, whether the pull of America or the push of her DNA and her low boiling point, she decided to go. She packed her things and bought a ticket on a liner sailing from Yokohama to Los Angeles.

My father came from Fukushima, a northern prefecture that has now become famous all over the world (unfortunately, not for the kinds of things people in Fukushima would like to be known for). Being the youngest of five brothers, Dad was left on his own a lot as a child, so he went off to fish. He became quite a good fisherman. And, since the youngest child had to cook for the family while they worked in the fields, he also learned to cook. The whole Saito family were good cooks; one of his oldest brothers had gone to Hawaii to work in a restaurant. Apparently, it was a way to make a living during winter, before rice planting commenced in the spring. I don't think Dad had any real plan to immigrate to America; he just wanted to check out the country he had heard so much about from family and friends alike. So one day he booked passage on a ship from Yokohama to Los Angeles.

My mom had very specific goals in mind when she bought her passage to the States. She wanted to (1) go to the United States, (2) take up residence there, and (3) find a husband. Mom grew up amid affluence and in a household where she was encouraged to be independent. She probably pushed the envelope on the last one, but she was certainly strong, self-confident, and ready to meet life on her own terms. She is also quite short, and she decided early on that she didn't want to have short children. So she did the only logical thing: she went looking for the tallest guy on the ship. After some searching around, she discovered a nice, easygoing fellow from Fukushima who stood 182 cm. (about six feet), reasonably tall for a Japanese man today, but unusual forty years ago.

Dad probably intended to stay in the United States for a week or two, but Mom had other ideas. She set up a series of dates, and suggested they get married (shyness was never her problem), and settle near the coast where they had landed. Neither of them could speak much English, but that was true of a lot of people in southern California. Their first home was a tiny, student-type garret of an apartment in a poor neighborhood in Boyle Heights, which they shared with another family, also from Okinawa and formerly well-to-do but now making do in the United States. My parents enjoyed cooking—Mom, of course, had learned from her own mother, who ran a cooking school, and everyone in Dad's family cooked, so he knew his way around a kitchen at an early age. They soon found jobs in restaurants; in fact, they both worked two jobs a day just to get by. The salaries weren't great, but it was work when they needed work, and one of the big advantages of working in restaurants was that they could bring leftovers home to feed their family.

First Encounter

In 1971 the beginning of a family was on the way. Their first child was a boy, a good omen. But how should they name this child? They decided on a typical compromise, a Western first name and a Japanese middle name, so that he could function easily in either society, at least in theory. Mom's father, Professor Onaga at Ryukyu University, died just three days before I was born, and she remembered his love of old English literature when she named me William after some sixteenth-century English playwright whose works my grandfather admired greatly, and my paternal grandparents added the male given name Hiroyuki. Sometime later came a younger brother and sister, although in true Japanese fashion, my parents focused all their energies, hopes, concerns, discipline, and much, much more on the eldest son.

Of course, because my parents could not speak much English when I was born, they knew they couldn't help me in one critical area where most American parents would naturally help their children—language learning. They worried that this would be a big handicap for their kids, and like everything else, their response was something like "focus on William and we'll worry about the other two later." Well, they were right to worry. All through elementary school I got called into parent–teacher meetings. My teachers seriously thought I was mentally retarded because my English grammar was so poor. I could not write a coherent sentence in English. My brain had a weird mixture of my mother's Okinawan speech, my father's Fukushima dialect, some standard Japanese, a splash of Spanish, and a lot of southern Californian English all scrambled together. There was no English as a Second Language (ESL) program or anything formal like that at my school, but my teachers used to spend hours with me after school each week, trying to help me get my brain and my tongue around this big, incomprehensible thing called English that I really needed to learn if I was going to get anywhere in school. (By the way, after I graduated from elementary school, my mom volunteered to help start a real ESL program there, so something good came of all this.)

One thing my parents could do for me in order to help compensate for my poor language skills was to teach me a universal language called math. So I started doing math when I was very young. In retrospect, my dad got a little carried away with it. I was doing multiplication drills when I was in the first grade. My grandmother in Okinawa, a willing participant in this conspiracy, sent over a Japanese math book, and my parents drilled me to the point where I could handle the problems in that text, too. Of course, they didn't mention that it was an advanced high school math text, and I was learning this stuff when I was in elementary school. My parents took turns drilling me, correcting my homework (not the school homework, that was too simple, but the homework *they* assigned each day). I can confidently say I studied a lot more than most kids my age, but not because I wanted to. Another sidelight is that Japanese textbooks are mostly memorization drills and repetition, so I discovered that my basic computational skills were great—I was really fast at multiplication or calculus—but most of the time I had no idea what I was doing or why, and when it came to word problems, I was stuck.

Before I'd even entered elementary school, my dad had hung up his apron and found work as a chemist, which is what he was trained for. He always said that was just another kind of "cooking" that he enjoyed. He specialized in high-temperature, lightweight ceramics (if I remember right, he helped design the tiles used on the space shuttle). Every morning he would go off to work, and sometimes on the weekends he'd take me along and let me play in the lab. Now, I was just a little kid, but I quickly learned a lot of the basics of a chemistry lab, and then I wanted my own chemistry set at home, which Dad was happy to oblige. I went through a lot of chemistry sets over the years, and I would borrow stuff from my dad's lab occasionally. As you can imagine, I cooked up all sorts of interesting experiments.

In fact, I approached chemistry a lot like I approached cooking in later years—I would scan the instructions, get the basic idea of what ingredients and what amounts were needed, then follow my instincts (and some serendipity) to make it come out right. For example, there were some bigger kids in our neighborhood who had a tree house near our home. I don't remember exactly why, but one day I decided that I'd had enough of these guys and thought how cool it would be to blow up their tree house. How to do that? Well, I'd need to make some nitroglycerin, like the stuff they used in the movies. How hard could that be? So I found some books in the library that gave me the basics— all I had to do was mix nitric acid and glycerin in specific amounts. What I didn't catch was that the *order* of the mixture was critical—you need to add glycerin into the nitric acid, not the other way around—and it's vital to keep the mixture cool. Fortunately, I used my Capsela robot to do the mixing for me. Unfortunately for the robot, it and everything in its immediate proximity was destroyed in the resulting explosion. This is how kids learn.

Some guardian angel, perhaps the same one that had convinced me to use a robot proxy in this experiment, was telling me that I shouldn't be a chemist. Cook, maybe; chemist, no. I needed to find something safer, like a software program that I could debug and recompile over and over until I got it right without taking out a whole room in the process.

Sure enough, as I was transitioning into junior high school, I met a teacher who had a profound effect on my life. His name was Tom Kardos and he was my science and math teacher in the sixth, seventh, and eighth grade. He was sort of a tech guy back then, the kind of person who is up to date on all kinds of products and specs, the kind of guy you ask before you buy something. He had arranged to get a personal computer for the school, and that one PC was a huge thing back then. I remember that he was very encouraging and supportive of kids and really wanted to help them develop. He once took me and another student aside and gave us an incredible motivating speech, telling us how special we both were and how we should not let anything stand in our way. Tom saw right away that I wasn't the best English speaker in the class, but he knew I had serious math skills and tons of curiosity, so he let me play with the school computer. It was there that I learned the rudiments of how to input data, how to make the system work, and other very simple stuff, which was pretty exciting. There wasn't really much you could do on a PC back then, but it was a whole new universe to me, a toy to make all other toys obsolete. Sometime around the sixth grade Mr. Kardos called my parents in for the usual parent-teacher conference, but this time he said we have a special problem: "We don't have any math left to teach your son." I had already gone through everything in the math courses, not just for elementary school but for the next few years, and I was totally bored in math class.

Then he told them about the school's computer, and how I was happily working away on that while the other kids were sitting in math class. He said something like, "These things called personal computers could be really good for him. With his math skills, he will find things to do on the computer that are both interesting and challenging. If you want to keep stretching his abilities and helping his mind to grow, I recommend you get him his own personal computer and see what happens."

Of course, my parents were Japanese, which means that anything a teacher said was the word of God. So they started looking around for a personal computer, whatever *that* was. This was around 1982, which in retrospect was very auspicious timing. For one thing, my father's job was going well, which meant that the family income had improved. We weren't living well, but we weren't dirt poor. In the years since I was born, we had moved twice, and I grew up in a nice suburban community outside of Los Angeles called Walnut. The other significant occurrence in the early 1980s was that this thing we take for granted today, the personal computer, was a revolutionary new product back then, just poised to take off commercially and change people's lives forever.

To a lot of people in the early 1980s, the word *computer* still conjured up images from TV and Hollywood movies of giant, room-sized monoliths with rows of giant tape reels and blinking lights, generally operated by people at NASA or some evil (and fabulously rich) criminal genius in a James Bond movie. The idea of shrinking the computer into a smaller format only began in the 1970s, right around the time I was born. Hewlett-Packard released a machine with a keyboard, a single-line display screen, and a small printer, all of which could just barely fit on the top of a big desk. Not only was it a big step forward in miniaturizing computer design, but it could actually program in BASIC, the lingua franca of PC geeks. Not to be outdone, in 1975, IBM released an even more powerful model in a more compact desktop format. The landmark IBM 5100 had a keyboard and a multiline CRT (cathode ray tube) display, which sat on top of an oblong box that housed the motherboard and related peripherals, plus a separate keyboard. It was a pretty sexy piece of hardware, and it would have made a fabulous personal computer, but at close to $20,000 per unit (and remember that a dollar back then was equal to roughly ten times what it is today), the machine was solely for business use.

Everything changed in that same year (I was four years old) when the famous MITS Altair 8800 PC kit appeared on the cover of *Popular Electronics*. That story basically said that anybody with a few hundred bucks, a soldering iron, and some spare time could put together a real, working desktop computer and start right in programming. That may not sound like big news today, but in 1975 the story was so revolutionary, so awe-inspiring that a scrawny kid named Bill Gates rushed across Boston to show it to his best friend, Paul Allen, who immediately quit his job at Honeywell and went to work for MITS. Gates dropped out of Harvard to join him in programming the Altair, creating a tiny business venture they called Micro-Soft.

Just one year later, in 1976, two kids working in a garage in Los Altos, California, created their own PC, but only sold about 200 of the clunky things. Soon they produced a second, much more functional model, and this one, called the Apple II, went on to sell *millions* of units. It almost single-handedly created legitimacy for the PC market, enough for the 800-pound gorilla in the computer industry to take this weird new concept of a "personal" computer seriously. In 1980, IBM started a project to build what it still referred to as a microcomputer, not a PC. It debuted in August of 1981, shortly after I'd turned 10 years old, and my math teacher was already trying to figure out what to do with me.

The new machine was officially called the IBM 5150 to make it sound like a slightly newer version of the venerable 5100 business desktop—an illusion to be sure, but a good piece of IBM marketing strategy. Of course, no one outside of IBM called it the 5150; it was almost instantly acclaimed the IBM PC and seen as the first serious entry-level machine to come along. Unlike every other PC on the market at the time, including the Apple, it used a 16-bit Intel CPU that most manufacturers considered too powerful and too expensive to waste on those "toy" computers being snatched up by hobbyists with thick glasses and white socks. This was some serious hardware.

Although it didn't cost $20,000, the base model was close to $2,000, which was still a heck of a lot of money back then, and it didn't even come with disk drives and other basic peripherals you'd need, all of which added to the bill. You could easily spend $5,000 or more just to get an IBM PC up and running with all the things you wanted to have in the package. To users, this modular structure was part of the appeal: you could add what you wanted as you wanted it, reconfigure certain things, and try different combinations of both hardware and software. To us, it was a fantastic way to express a certain kind of creativity, like Lego blocks (my favorite toys as a child) you could actually use for something. To my parents, it was still $5,000 (multiply that by several times if you're reading this in the twenty-first century) for a kid's educational toy. I'm sure the price tag hit them like a ton of bricks (and not the Lego kind).

Any normal parent with limited means would have said, "Let's wait until the boy is older" or something like that. Not my parents. They were determined that I was going to succeed in school. They knew that English literature was not going to be my strong suit, so if there was anything they could do to help me build my math skills, they wanted it. And so, not long after the IBM PC made its debut, my crazy parents took out a second mortgage on their new house and borrowed the money to buy my first computer. And they didn't skimp—it was a monster machine, complete with the 5.25″ floppy drive option, a whopping big 64 kB (yes, "k," not M, G, or T) of memory, running at a blistering 4.77 MHz (M, not G, and yes, the decimal point is in the right place), with a full-color display. My parents didn't understand exactly what a PC was all about, but they believed, in fact, they had literally bet the farm that this was the best tool on the planet to help their child learn a new language that might someday be just as important to him as English.

My Addiction Starts

I don't have to say it, do I? The very first thing I did when I got this fabulously expensive, complex new machine was to take it apart. Until then, I'd taken apart every electronic gadget in the house, and I almost never bothered to put them back together. This usually got my parents very upset (although I think my Dad secretly enjoyed it because it provided a good excuse to buy more new gadgets). I still remember how I took apart the family TV set and never put it back together. My folks went ballistic, and looking back on it, I can understand their feelings. They worked hard to make a little money and buy things, and then their oldest child quickly destroyed them all with a screwdriver. Fortunately, they never knew how many times I nearly electrocuted myself, or things would have been much worse. To put it mildly, I've had a much more personal relationship with 110 volt power than most people will ever experience. I survived my childhood and in the process learned a healthy respect for alternating current.

Still, AC power was nothing compared to my parents when they were angry, and God help you if both of them were angry at the same time. After they had mortgaged the house to get me a PC, and I immediately took the thing apart, you can imagine the fireworks. That was the last straw. I could tell they weren't putting on a show; they were really, *really* angry this time. And so, my IBM PC became one of the first things I ever put back together. In the process, my pre-adolescent brain discovered something interesting: it wasn't all that difficult (especially if your life is on the line). With the right parts, even the world's primo PC was basically a big, empty box, and it wasn't exactly rocket science to put the motherboard and other parts into their appointed slots, run some cables, attach the I/O ports, and hey, the thing was up and running, just like new. In other words, one of the first lessons I ever learned was that building PCs wasn't a big deal. That idea would germinate for a while and bear serious fruit later on.

Once I started working with a keyboard instead of a screwdriver, I discovered that the little white box on my desk could open up an interesting new world. I read any magazine that talked about PCs or software, of which there weren't many. There were no computer sections in the book stores back then. If I remember right, there was just one book that explained programming stuck somewhere in the math section of our local Waldenbooks, or maybe something buried way in the back of Radio Shack. This just wasn't something that normal people were interested in back then.

So I taught myself to program and started having fun. BASIC, assembler, Pascal—one programming language quickly led to another. It was pretty simple stuff, but it was exciting. So many different ways to write code, and once you figured it out, so much you could do with an automated number-cruncher in a box. My math textbooks looked boring in comparison, and rightly so. Here was a way to create complex mathematical problems and let the machine figure out the answers. I liked that. This was a real "aha!" moment. With just a simple keyboard, I could even create something useful, maybe even valuable. This was a new concept. Furthermore, in order to convert the mathematical problem into a computer program, I had to completely understand the underlying principles for the equation. This "programmed" me to understand not just how but why things worked the way they did—an important skill for later in life.

Next door, the older guys were tinkering with their cars, and their results were highly visible. You could see them (and hear them!) driving around, picking up girls, and looking cool. The kind of tinkering I was doing was invisible—it was hard to show it to anyone, and very few people would understand it in the first place—but for the first time I had a real sense that I could *create* something. That was huge for me. Not just to play with the computer, but to use it as a tool to make something that you show or give or sell to someone else. It was the difference between being a hobbyist (someone who plays with something for self-amusement) and a craftsman who produces something worthwhile that people can use.

Tom Kardos, the math teacher who told my parents that they should get me a PC, was naturally pleased to see my progress. Tom was well-known in the community as an all-around tech guy, a geek before we knew about geeks. People knew that he read all the electronics magazines and that he was up to date on whatever new technology was hot, and at that time it was computers. About six months after he'd had that life-changing talk with my parents, one of my teacher's friends approached him to ask if he might know anyone who could program a computer. The friend's company was regularly doing a series of computation-intensive steps on hand calculators, which prompted this fellow to wonder if computers could help to speed up the process, and if so, who could program a computer to do whatever was necessary. Sure enough, Tom knew an unusually talented student who had been programming the IBM PC since it first came out. Perfect guy for the job. Did he forget to mention that I was not quite in junior high school at the time?

It turned out that the company the friend had referred to was none other than Merrill Lynch, Pierce, Fenner & Smith, Inc., at that time, the largest stockbroker in the world. They had an office in Burbank, about an hour and a half's drive from our home in Walnut. One Saturday, following up on Mr. Kardos' introduction, my dad drove me over to their offices, and I had a meeting with a bunch of guys at Merrill. What they wanted seemed pretty straightforward—write a couple of programs that would perform various financial calculations on a series of numbers they would give me. Of course, I had no idea what any of this financial stuff meant, but I understood what they wanted, or at least I thought I understood what they wanted, and I was reasonably sure that I could figure out how to program it. I thought this was very cool, and I probably would have done it for free if they'd asked me to, but they offered to pay me some reasonable amount for every time I came to their office.

That was the beginning of my first consulting job. Actually, my first job of any kind. Since I didn't know who Merrill Lynch was, I didn't even enjoy the prestige of landing a big-name client. I was just excited that somebody would pay me to program on the computer, something I'd been doing at home on my own every night for fun. Of course, I had school on the weekdays, so every Saturday my dad would drive me over to their offices at 9 A.M., and I'd meet with the client for about two hours. Dad didn't want to come inside, so he'd just sit in the car in an empty parking lot or go to a donut shop and read the newspaper until I was done. Whenever I'd finish my work, he'd greet me with a smile, we'd drive back home, and I'd start programming whatever they'd asked for in just the way that I *thought* they wanted it done. Then the following Saturday, we'd go back again. This probably should have been some good father-son quality time, but now that I think back on it, my mind was totally absorbed with the project, and I think my dad understood that and let me sit for long stretches in silence, looking over the print-outs. Back then, computers printed out on endless stacks of wide, neatly folded paper with sprocket holes along both sides. I'd carry a stack of print-outs back to Merrill every Saturday, and all the way there I'd be looking through the printout of the source code, thinking, *How do I solve that problem? How do I fix the program here?* I was basically debugging the code in the passenger seat of my dad's car.

Some readers may already be scratching their heads, thinking, *Why not just take the computer to the client's office and do some of the work there?* Ah, a very good point. First, in spite of its relatively small size compared to other computers, the PC was anything but easily portable. The idea of disconnecting all the wires and cables, lugging it over to the client's place, and wiring it all back up again was not in the least attractive. Most of my two hours would have been spent setting up the machine, only to have to take it apart and pack it up again. Pointless.

There was another issue, one that I didn't think about consciously, but that somehow had insinuated itself into my brain. The work I was doing was my property. The code I was writing was my code. They set up the problems, I designed the solutions. I had no desire to show them the nuts and bolts of my programming, even way back then. Call it a precocious awareness of the value of intellectual property, but it served me well.

So every Saturday we'd drive over to Merrill Lynch, I'd go hand over my stack of neatly folded printouts, and they'd sit down and start to check it on their HP 12C handheld financial calculators. What took me maybe a second or two on the computer took 15 minutes to do on the calculator. I would sit there and wait while they checked everything, then one of the guys would say, "You got this part right, but in this part the numbers are coming out all wrong," or "You made a mistake on step 76 . . . it should be this. . . ." Sometimes it was, "You got this right and that right, but that's not really what we wanted at all." It was a learning experience.

What was I programming? I didn't much know or care. I now understand enough about financial transactions to see that I was computing pricing strategies for options trading, calculating parts of the famous Black-Scholes model, net present value, fair value, time value, and so on. They had a math guy who gave me all the necessary equations (most of which I didn't understand at the time), and I would input them in the computer during the week and be told the following week, "On step 33 you're supposed to multiply here instead of subtracting, and on step 99 you need to divide by 4 instead of divide by 6." I had to learn calculus via its discrete mathematical components. All that was fairly simple, and after a while I was getting pretty good at it. We finished the base product they wanted to build in about six months. Then I got my first lessons in what software developers call *feature creep*. Clients ask you to design something, and you give them exactly what they wanted. They're happy, but only for a while. Then they want more; couldn't you also do this or add that? Soon they're asking to have all sorts of new features added to whatever they'd initially requested. The Merrill guys were typical clients. Soon enough they started asking if I could make a certain data input produce a certain type of output. They'd say, "If we hit this "F" key, we'd like this data to come out, and have it formatted this way. Can you do that?" And foolish little me, I'd say, "Sure" (the beginning of a frequent habit) and go home and try to figure out how to do it. I now see that this became a pattern for me later in life.

I stayed busy with that project for about two years, which covered most of junior high school. Two years of Saturdays driving back and forth to their offices and two years of weekdays programming after school. After two years, I suppose I'd accomplished everything that they wanted done. The work just slowed, and then it stopped. We parted very amicably, because there just wasn't any more work for me. However, by that time I was a lot more skilled and a lot more confident of my programming abilities. I started doing simple programming jobs for all sorts of companies in the area. It wasn't anything interesting, but it produced steady cash, which I used to buy computer parts. That really started me on my PC addiction, because new machines were starting to become available, and I didn't want to be limited by the speed of the IBM PC I'd been using.

You'll remember my first "aha!" moment when my parents made me put the PC I'd disassembled back together again, and I discovered that it was really pretty easy? I took that to the next logical step and figured out how to build a PC from scratch with individual parts. In a short time I was building desktop computers, which was a very high-value item back then, and then adding even more value by installing my own custom software. Software installation was considered just short of witchcraft at the time, so this was a real pro package. I had no trouble selling the machines, which brought in more profit, which allowed me to buy more parts, and thus to keep ratcheting up both the value-added and economies-of-scale curves. More importantly to a 12 year-old boy, it meant that I had enough income to upgrade my own PC, buying whatever was the hottest item on the market and selling off my older machine.

In March of 1983, IBM released the XT, which came with a built-in hard drive (interesting concept, yes?), and later that year came the PCjr, which used something called floppy disks, and then in 1984 came the big, boxy AT, or "Advanced Technology." I bought them all, and I don't have to tell you that I took each one apart to see what it looked like inside and then put it back together (well, mostly back together). One important result is that I learned about computers from the inside out. As the years went by, more and more people began using PCs, and some people learned to do simple programming on them, but very few people learned how to put the machines together from the microchip level. When you did that, you really came to understand what a device was capable of, and what it was not. As the machines became more sophisticated, there were ways to boost the performance—if you knew what parts to buy, where to get them, and how to customize your hardware. Fairly soon, I'd get bored trying to tweak a few percent improvement in performance from whatever machine I was using, so I'd just sell the computer, preloaded with some software that I wrote, and buy a new one. It became my version of hot cars or teenage drug addiction. I always wanted to have the newest, fastest, coolest machine. Is that so strange? Other kids were learning how to supercharge their Mustangs; I was learning how to overclock the processor on my AT and developing my programming skills day by day, all of which I suspected would pay off one way or another down the road. Little did I know.

Study, Study, Study

I probably don't need to explain too much about why my parents were maniacal about education. Asian parents have a tendency to push their kids hard to succeed, and Japanese mothers are famous for what is still called the education Mom syndrome—driving their kids to study, study, study, and get into a top-name university. The generally accepted thinking is that an entire lost childhood is a small price to pay for a comfortable life later on. If living in America had in any way mellowed my folks' attitudes toward educating their children and steering them toward a predetermined goal line, there was no evidence of it in the way they raised me. Predictably, my younger brother and sister didn't get anywhere near the same treatment, but when it came to the eldest son, I might as well have been growing up back in Japan. The constant drilling with high-level math books when I was very young was just the start. When I was five or six, I think I wanted to be a fireman or a fisherman. "That's nice," my mother and even my grandmother would say, matter-of-factly, "But you're going to be a doctor." Just like that. Done. Decided. Don't even think about anything else, because this is what's going to happen. From about the age of six I was told again and again, by both my parents, that I was going to be a doctor. Nobody told my younger brother or sister that they were going to be doctors, but come to think of it, nobody pushed them to overachieve in school the way I was pushed. I guess I didn't think much about it; I just accepted it.

In other respects, my early school years were a lot like those of my peers—with the exception of numerous parent-teacher conferences, largely about my poor English ability. I joined the Boy Scouts, and I did a lot of the usual things that Boy Scouts do. I got a lot of merit badges and rose through the ranks; although I didn't stay in Scouting long enough to become an Eagle Scout. Too many other things were begging for my time and attention by that point. When I was quite young, I went fishing with my dad a lot on weekends. He bought a camping car, and it was my job to load it up with all our gear on Friday after school; then he'd come home from work, pack up the whole family, and drive to some place in the mountains where we'd camp, fish all day Saturday, then drive home on Sunday. When I was young, we went away almost every weekend. I used to love all that camping and fishing, and I still love to fish, although I don't have as much time for it as I'd like. But back then it was wonderful; it was a break from the school week, it was a chance to relax and just be with my family for a while, and most of all—and this is really important—*there are no pianos out in the woods!*

In case you don't know any Asian families, suffice it to say that mine was typical in many respects: one of the absolute musts for children was to learn to play an instrument. In my case, it was piano. My parents were as maniacal about piano instruction as math instruction. The big difference was that they could do the latter by themselves; the former required outside help. So at one point they hired two piano teachers. That's right, two. One was a rote Suzuki method instructor, and the other was supposed to be more general, to give me a proper feeling for the instrument and the music. If that teacher had any such ideas in mind, I'm sure a quick chat with my mother was all it took to refocus the instruction on drills, drills, and more drills. Asian educational theory (especially Asian mom theory) says you can't drill a child too much; you can't push too much; children don't like to study or do the things that are good for them, so you have to be strict and forceful. My folks fit that mold. Actually, many Asian moms are competitive. Sometimes they live vicariously through their children. I knew that if another Asian family had their kid playing piano, I had to learn, too, and practice enough to be even better.

I knew that my mother had learned to play the piano, perhaps when she was younger, but I never heard her play. She bought an upright for the house for only one reason: to be sure that her children learned. I wasn't antimusic. Actually, I was interested in the violin. It's portable, it becomes your instrument. But violins are expensive and my parents simply said, "No way. You're doing piano." End of story.

In almost any subject you can think of, the teacher makes all the difference. A good teacher can make a bad textbook seem interesting, and a great teacher can make a wayward child with neither interest nor aptitude in a subject somehow perk up and demonstrate talent no one thought he had. A bad teacher, on the other hand, can effectively kill any interest or desire students have for any subject. I did not have a bad teacher. I had two killjoys who (from my perspective at least) liked neither music nor children. Every week I had to go to separate lessons with these two different teachers, one of them a piano Nazi and the other an uninterested senior citizen, then come home and practice until I thought my fingers would crack and my elbows seize up.

There was no respite from piano. None. Math was easy. I got math early on, and eventually I could hold my own. But piano was infinitely painful. As soon as I would finally begin to master one piece, they would pluck out something more difficult and less interesting to play. I took these double lessons constantly for 10 years. Ten years in a child's life is a very long time, and the only thing it taught me, and I mean this sincerely, was to hate the piano. I do not use the word *hate* very often, and I do not use it lightly, but when I say I learned to hate those 88 keys and the sounds they made, that may even be a bit of an understatement. To this day I suffer from PTSD—Piano-Trauma Stress Disorder. I can't go near one, I can't even listen to it being played for long. If hell exists, for me there is no question that it has endless rows of black and white keys.

My trials at the hands of the piano torturers aside, I was a more or less normal kid. I attended public school in Walnut for both elementary and middle school. But when it came time for high school, my mother's Japanese DNA kicked in again. Our improved family circumstances made it just barely possible for them to consider sending me to a private school instead of the local public high school, and so that, too, became a goal.

In order to compensate for my still less-than-stellar verbal skills, my mother decided that I should go somewhere with a good debate program and learn how to make a point and communicate it effectively. Of course, it had to be a top-notch high school with the kind of academic reputation that would help my application to medical school. That went without saying. Also, it wouldn't hurt if we could find a school with a hint of a Catholic air to it—my grandmother was a devout Catholic, which meant my mother was raised as a Catholic, and so she was trying to raise me as a Catholic. But in addition to all these other things, the school needed to have a really good debate team. I thought I might wind up going to some snooty private school in Massachusetts or somewhere, but no, my parents found exactly what they were looking for right at home. Well, sort of. Their high school of choice was an hour away by car, and my mom, who had never sat behind a wheel, would soon learn to drive just to take me to school in the morning. In the afternoons, I would have to take a series of city buses to get home, a trip of well over two hours. But for the chance to have me spend three years at this special school, they felt it would all be worth it.

Damien High School in La Verne, California, is not exactly Ridgemont High. It's a private, all-boys Roman Catholic institution famous for producing two things: champion athletes and champion debaters. The school has lots of terrific sports teams, and it has turned out more than its share of professional baseball, football, basketball, and soccer players. Several well-known figures in both MLB and the NFL came from Damien. Somehow, I don't think any of that weighed too heavily on my mother's mind. However, there was another NFL that caught her attention right away. The National Forensic League is actually much older than that other NFL. It is the oldest and largest debate and public speaking honor society in America, famous for honing the oratory skills of lawyers, politicians, used car dealers, and many others who make their living through persuasive oral presentation. Damien has always had a good debate team and has been a top contender in this NFL; not long ago it even won the prestigious National Tournament, which is no mean feat.

So here it was—an all-boys school (i.e., none of the usual distractions that can divert a young man's attention away from his studies during those critical but confused teenage years) run by strict, no-nonsense Catholic priests, with a very strong debate team and an enviable track record for putting their graduates into top-ranked universities. Where do we sign our boy up? If there had been some kind of tie-up with Johns Hopkins, my parents would probably have killed someone to get me in there. As it turned out, they didn't have to. I had to take a tough entrance exam, write an essay, and submit teacher recommendations; all of that plus my junior high grades were apparently good enough to get me into Damien.

And there, just as the Fates and my parents had foretold, I was soon studying to prepare for medical school and learning debating and strategic communications skills. In fact, I discovered that the two coolest things to be involved with at Damien were the football team and the debate team; the jocks went one way, and the geeks went the other. I went the other. I doubt that learning to debate well was such a prestigious activity at most other high schools, probably just the opposite. But at Damien, it was important, and the school was duly proud of the high percentage of Damien grads who went on to become successful attorneys, as well as the very high percentage who found seats waiting for them at top-notch colleges.

Of course, I had no great interest in debate or anything else on the curriculum when I entered the school. I'd done all the math they were preparing to teach me, I wasn't sure if they had anything interesting in science, and the rest of the subjects were completely irrelevant. One subject in particular I felt was a total waste of my time: English. Not because I couldn't speak it well; in fact, by high school I was a lot more confident of my speaking skills and could even think seriously about going out for the debate team. However, the course called English, which is inevitably filled with boring readings from dusty classics, struck me as a monumental waste of time. Don't get me wrong, I like to read. When I was very young I read all the How To books I could get my hands on. My parents got me the kids' version of the *Encyclopedia Britannica*, and I read every volume cover to cover in about a month. Then they bought me the junior set, which took me a little over a year to digest. Then, as I got older, they got the full, zillion-volume Britannica set (does anyone still buy printed encyclopedias? do they still make them?), and I chewed my way through half of that before becoming too distracted with computer-related pursuits. So reading was not the problem. I'd devour anything I could find on science topics, especially computer-related articles. But *Moby Dick? Tom Sawyer? Great Expectations?* How could those possibly be of any practical use? In other words, I read nonfiction voraciously but abhorred fiction. "Where are the facts?" I'd think, "Where's the data? Where's the information?" In short, I saw fiction as a colossal waste of time, and so I had somehow managed to slide through junior high without actually reading any of the things I was supposed to.

All that came to an abrupt end at Damien. My English teacher told us to read Shakespeare; I balked; we discussed the matter—me explaining why I thought Shakespeare was a waste of time, the teacher explaining why it was good for me. I refused to budge. Then out came the heavy artillery: "If you don't read some of this material, you won't complete Freshman English, which means you'll be taking it again next year. Is that how you want to play it?" I'd just entered Damien, and it was already starting to look as if the Bard could single-handedly keep me from graduating. By the way, if anyone out there thinks it's ironic that my name is a tribute to this 400-year-old specter whose works I absolutely refused to read, you'd be absolutely right.

Ultimately and under considerable duress from a good teacher who, I must admit, genuinely wanted me to develop an appreciation for fiction, I began to read Shakespeare. It was the first bit of verse fiction that ever entered my brain, and so I typically read the whole thing: all the comedies, all the tragedies, all the histories, the sonnets, and other poems. One of the interesting things about Shakespeare's plays in particular is that so much is left open to interpretation. Shakespeare's meanings are not set in stone. This allowed me to find my own interpretations and argue (debate) my own views in class, and that more than anything made the experience bearable. At first, I read each piece with that attitude: I don't care about this story, I'm not interested in this in any way, but if we're going to have to discuss this or write an essay on some part of it, I will definitely argue something contrarian. It was the debate quality of the text that got me, using the material as the basis for some future argument. That really engaged me and held my attention for quite awhile, so I kept reading Shakespeare and only Shakespeare for quite awhile. I think the teacher was smart enough to see that I was aiming for the debate team and that this contrarian aspect of my personality would latch on to the multiple meanings in Shakespeare, and that would hold my attention. Teachers are insidious people, aren't they? In any case, the strategy worked, and to this day I still enjoy Shakespeare, and when I encounter young, self-driven geeks who remind me of myself decades ago, I urge them to read fiction, including the Bard, to broaden their minds. Learning to imagine, to think creatively, is one of the most important skills in any kind of endeavor, and I am eternally grateful that I acquired it when I did. It is interesting to note that my namesake, my grandfather, and my English ability all converged at this point.

Yes, I did make it onto the Damien debate team—something my elementary school teachers would have found miraculous—and for once I was doing something that I thought was really cool, my peers thought was really cool, and my mom thought was wonderful. In fact, what I learned on the debate team turned out to be much more important than I thought at the time. First, it really helped to build confidence in my own speaking ability, helping my mouth catch up with my brain, an awkward gap that had been closing gradually for years, but which debate really helped to close for good (okay, maybe not). Second, it gave me the ability to explain, or make a case for, difficult subject matter. I often say that I can bridge the gap between the Chief Technology Officer (CTO) and the Chief Financial Officer (CFO), for example.

Debate also trains you to see both sides of an argument. At a tournament, you have to argue one side, and then the other, and explain why in both cases. I would eventually put those verbal skills to good use in making countless business presentations and speeches, and in negotiating deals with various companies in two countries.

Something much more important grew from my experience at Damien, and it has actually become a cornerstone in my personal philosophy. I don't know what the best name for it is, but I usually call it volunteerism, which means a fundamental attitude of helping other people and always looking for ways to give back to the society that gave you so much. At Damien, every student was required to perform 100 hours of meaningful community service every year. That's a lot of hours and a lot of hard work. Some of the other kids went to South America or some place for the summer to help poor people and clocked their 100 hours quickly, but many of us worked in our local community. We learned the value of helping others and the personal rewards of giving of yourself and your time.

Of course, one of the things I wanted to do was find a way to combine my computer skills with these mandatory volunteer activities. I decided to work in the Walnut public library. I knew that libraries were very labor-intensive, all the books and information being filed by hand, really nothing automated at all. I set up a program to greatly improve that filing system. I did the same kind of thing for the city hall and the reception desk of a nearby hospital. Just setting up a database of frequently used data made a big difference in these places, organizing a system so that anyone could quickly search for and access important information.

I learned a great deal by taking volunteerism seriously and making it a part of my life. For one thing, it helped me to look at both sides of a problem, at first social problems, but later on all sorts of issues that I encountered in business. Volunteerism taught me about the importance of relying on others; it's not just about helping other people, but also about being willing to ask for help yourself. That affected my understanding of working with teams, one of the cornerstones of my business philosophy. And perhaps most important, volunteerism taught me that sometimes you do things just because it's the right thing to do, without any thought of monetary compensation or any other kind. It's not about religion or Morality with a capital "M" or anything else I can put a name to; it's just about seeing that something needs to be done and stepping up to do it. This essential part of my character was probably there in the DNA from both my parents, but Damien really brought it out, and it has been an important part of my life ever since.

Part of the downside of going to Damien was that it was about two hours by bus from my home. Normally, I'd get home around 4:00, which was too early for me because my parents would have prepared all sorts of extra homework (usually Japanese math texts, etc.) above and beyond what the school was giving out. So my long bus ride was kind of relaxing; I felt free—not in school and not at home, which was often more stressful than school. As it happened, one of the transfer points on the bus route I took going home was in front of Mt. San Antonio Community College. I had to wait at that stop for 30 minutes anyway to change buses, so one day I decided to go check out the college library. I don't know why, but I liked the place, and pretty soon I decided to audit a couple of classes. Before long I was auditing college-level math, chemistry, astronomy, and other classes. Of course, I wasn't a registered student, so I got to sit in the back and actually enjoy those classes. I thought, *Hey, this is really cool.*

This had two benefits: (1) I got to study a number of interesting things; and (2) I also got to go home later than usual, which meant less time for the dreaded extra homework and, most importantly, piano drills. Not only that, but when I did arrive home late I had a great excuse: I've been taking extra classes outside of high school; I've been at the college library, studying, and so on. After a while, I started taking courses for credit, and then I discovered that I could apply them both to graduating from high school early (more on that in a moment) and also to eliminate some of the General Education courses when I got to college.

TAKEAWAY: Encourage a Culture of Empathy through Volunteering

At my high school in California, every student had to perform 100 hours of community service in order to advance to the next grade level. The focus was not on impersonal activities like cleaning up a park, but on providing meaningful service to the less privileged people in our community. Volunteering to help people instills the idea in young minds that giving back to society is a natural part of life. Young people discover that volunteering pays rich dividends in community appreciation, self-esteem, compassion, humility, and gratitude. Equally important, they learn that asking for help is nothing to be ashamed of.

First, it helps young people learn empathy for others, and thus grow into compassionate adults. Second, it leads people of all ages to reflect on their own strengths and weaknesses. And third, it teaches people to ask for help when they need it and both give and receive assistance from others as a matter of course.

A broader, deeper culture of empathy could also help to energize the business environment. Reaching out to help others is essential to helping a venture business succeed, just as employees being willing to help each other inside a start-up company is essential to its success. Venture businesses are handicapped by a lack of experienced management, lack of access to capital, and lack of appeal to attract talented employees. Ventures succeed when people in the business community see their potential and offer them different kinds of assistance to help them grow.

While the effects of a wide-scale volunteer program are impossible to estimate, one result would certainly be an increase in personal empathy, a greater feeling of kinship with, and responsibility to help others who need help. And that would include businesspeople feeling more inclined to help rather than hinder others, both within their companies and in the business community at large. In this sense, the growth of venture business—which I see as essential to invigorating the economy—will rely as much on individual and corporate assistance as on government support. So, as volunteerism promotes empathy, it not only humanizes society but indirectly helps to energize the economy.

Chapter 2

Finding a Business Partner (Opposites Attract)

Another thing, actually the most important thing, that happened during my years at Damien was not something I learned at the school. In fact, it was not a thing at all, but a person I met, a guy who would become my companion on the wild, unpredictable, white-water ride of a start-up business. I would sit in the back and try to steer while he would sit up front and point out the various rocks we were about to smash into. I'd invariably hit them all, but we didn't sink, and, thanks to the combination of our efforts, we made it down that river in one piece.

I met him—where else?—in math class. Thanks to my parents' incessant drilling from an early age, I had been excelling at math all my life, and my high school courses were no more challenging than my junior high math courses had been. So my attention was obviously miles removed from the blackboard or the textbook.

There was another guy who seemed to have the same problem as I did. He was a quiet kid, the son of Hungarian immigrants, and like me, he seemed to have no interest in what was being written on the board; instead, he routinely had his nose buried in one of the computer magazines that had appeared in recent years. Like me, he was getting in trouble for not paying attention in class. The two of us quickly realized we had something in common besides being first-generation Americans. His name was Tas (pronounced Tash), and I soon discovered that he was an electronics whiz, the kind of guy whose first response to any problem was to reach for a soldering iron. Tas also loved to take things apart, but unlike me, he had a weird habit of actually putting them back together. He even knew how to use a soldering gun correctly and actually seemed to enjoy it. Of course, he also had a PC, which he loved to play with, so the two of us connected instantly. There wasn't anything in high school math to interest either of us, but it provided a great opportunity to sit in the back of the room and pore over the latest issue of *Computer Shopper*, which back then was a 2-inch-thick catalog of computer parts. We didn't even pretend to be listening. Since we both had perfect attendance (we came to hang out with each other) and we were both acing all the tests, the teacher couldn't complain too much and she just left us to our magazines.

Tas is a very interesting guy. He's my polar opposite in many ways. He's quiet and shy by nature, whereas I love to meet interesting people and talk to them (well, actually, only if somebody else makes the introduction; I guess I'm pretty shy, too, but next to a recluse like Tas I look like a social butterfly). My brain naturally concocts big ideas one after another, but with only the vaguest clue as to how I could actually execute them (a trait that would haunt me for years to come), and when I try to explain something, I'm usually all over the map. What? You didn't understand that I started with Step 9, then went to Step 14, then back to Step 3, and then, almost as an afterthought, explained how and why this thing got started in the first place? C'mon, you've got to keep up. Tas was just the opposite: logical, methodical, clear-headed, and conservative. He would pour cold water on lots of my wild ideas, forcing me to rethink or abandon my approach and start over. Later on, when we worked together in business, he would be the first one to say let's weigh all the options before we decide to do anything; let's examine the practical aspects of William's crack-brained scheme; and then, if we're crazy enough to do the thing that he's just suggested, let's try to approach it rationally, step by step, and not jump in feet first. Tas doesn't believe in an ordered universe; he's living proof that this *is* a well-ordered universe. I am living proof that the universe was created without an instruction manual (something neither of us ever looked at).

For example, I like to cook, and I have ever since I was about six. But I approach it in my own way. I get creative; I like to experiment, and I almost never follow directions or measure anything, but I know that if I just follow my instincts everything will turn out all right, usually much better than all right, in the end. So yes, I'm the kind of guy who can spend eight hours making soup. Of course, I think it's really good soup, but you might say that spending the day making soup is not the most efficient use of anyone's time. I would probably agree—if I took the time to think about it, but that's just what I wouldn't do. I'd get into the kitchen and start experimenting, and I wouldn't stop until I was satisfied that I'd produced, through whatever odd series of trials and errors, the perfect recipe for some otherwise ordinary soup. Tas likes to cook, too, but if the instructions run longer than three steps (and opening the box counts as one step), he's already abandoned it and is looking for something faster, simpler, and cheaper. He says he has a bad sense of smell, and thus no interest in food. He is also frugal to the point of parsimony, so he likes to buy food based on calories-per-cents ratios, which pretty much eliminates haute cuisine from the menu. Ordering a coke was out of the question because it was more expensive than milk or gasoline. But in the end, I think his logic circuits are just telling him that eating is a distraction and the most efficient course is to minimize wasted time and get back to whatever he was doing before the interruption.

To other people, we probably looked like a slightly odd pair: a cool, rational guy teamed up with a ready-fire-aim independent thinker. But the truth is that Tas and I were natural partners right from the start. Our personalities complemented each other perfectly. What was really important was that we were both junkies: we shared the same addiction to all the fun things that happened in, around, and because of personal computers. In no time at all, we were both engaged in the business I had started up in junior high: building and reselling PCs. In addition, we were both programming software to make our products into fully functional packages.

Since my junior high school days, I had been writing programs for lots of local companies, building personal computers and selling them. This not only continued but increased after I met Tas. By that time I was already turning out a fair number of computers on my own, and with his help the output increased. To me, it was just a very profitable hobby, nothing more. I wasn't thinking of anything like incorporating. However, I was vaguely aware that I was paying double sales taxes to operate this little PC business. That is, I was paying tax when I bought the raw computer parts and then paying tax again when I sold them as finished machines. It took me a while to discover that there was something called a reseller permit that could eliminate this problem. The only hitch was that it's much easier to get a reseller permit if you have a registered company than if you're obviously just a high school kid working in his spare time. So one day I bought an off-the-shelf "incorporate yourself for $15" kit at a local bookstore, and I did all the paperwork, and the next thing I knew I was the owner of a real, legitimate corporation in the state of California. One of the key concepts in computing is called "input/output," abbreviated as I/O, and so I dubbed my little paper company I/O Software (this would later come back to haunt me, as lots of people didn't get the I/O reference and thought the company was called VO Software). It's important to remember that I was not trying to compete with Microsoft or Apple; I wasn't trying to become Michael Dell or anything like that. I just wanted to keep buying and selling PCs and lower the costs involved any way that I could. It's hard for an entrepreneurial evangelist to admit, but the real reason for incorporating I/O Software was not to change the world or even to become a millionaire, but just to get my hands on that reseller's permit.

Although I/O started out as my own company, with me as CEO and 100 percent shareholder, there was no question in my mind that it was a partnership. Tas and I both felt that the work we were doing together was a lot more fun and probably more important than anything they were teaching us in school. And we knew it was going to turn into a real business sooner or later. We just had to keep doing what we were doing and follow our instincts. The world would catch up in time.

Shrink-Wrapped Success

One of the science magazines back then had an article about something called autostereograms, a kind of 3D optical illusion created with printed 2D images. Stereograms were a big hit back in the nineteenth century when people used special viewers called stereoscopes to see these 3D images. The magazine article said that a PC could actually generate very impressive autostereograms. Tas thought this was cool, so he sat down and wrote a program that would do the kinds of things described in the magazine. We looked at the pictures that resulted and agreed that people might want to use that software to make their own. Which meant that we could actually sell the software to make stereograms. This was a new step for us, because up until then we'd only been selling hardware (PCs), although the computers usually came with some of our own software included, but basically people were buying the hardware. Now we could take a relatively simple program, package it, and sell it. Cool.

How did people market software back then? You couldn't go on the Internet and download it. You went to a computer store or some other place and bought a bunch of floppy disks in a shrink-wrapped box, maybe with an instruction manual. So Tas and I bought some 3.5″ floppies in bulk and started copying our stereogram program onto the floppies. We didn't have a machine to mass-produce copies; we copied each floppy one by one from a PC. Hundreds and hundreds and hundreds of floppy disks, all done by hand, and each one with a label that we printed and attached by hand. We also printed up manuals and spiral bound them (it takes longer than stapling but looks more professional), and we bought our first shrink-wrap machine to package the whole thing up like *real* software companies did. Then we sold our stereogram product to other software companies. We were written up in over a hundred computer and electronics magazines and some of them were giving us five-star ratings. Back then, many magazines included reader response cards printed with dozens of numbers corresponding to products that were featured or advertised in that issue. Readers who were interested in getting more information about certain products could circle the numbers and mail the card to the magazine, which would then pass the requests on to the manufacturers. We got tons of cards, and we thought it was great. I still remember when Oprah ordered from us. We were pretty excited.

Just as an interesting side note, we didn't put any kind of copy protection on our software. That may seem odd in light of my background and the kind of business we developed later on, but to us it was a point of pride. Back then something called a Bulletin Board System (BBS) was the rough equivalent of an Internet portal site, a place where like-minded PC users came in search of information, and one day we found our software pirated and posted on some prominent BBS. Instead of being angry, we were honored. Someone thought that what we had created was actually worth pirating. We were a success!

But we did a lot more than just run a mail-order service. There were all sorts of fairs up and down the West Coast every weekend, and many of them now had an area where people could sell computer stuff. So we would follow these fairground marketplaces on the weekends. We'd stay up all Friday night shrink-wrapping boxes of software, and then we'd head out on Saturday, set up our 10-ft. folding table, and open for business. Meet the customer face-to-face instead of just through the mail. It was a lot of fun. Of course, almost everyone in this space was selling some kind of hardware back then, so our table would be sandwiched in between a guy hawking motherboards and somebody showing some weird-looking disk drives or something. We were that strange little company that sold *software*. But at the end of a two-day show, we'd sold every single box. We were selling it for peanuts, so we were making some money, but we weren't getting rich. Still, it meant that we could buy new computers whenever we wanted to, and we had a little bit of cash on hand, which is always nice. The joke was that someone took our program and generated lots of stereograms and published them in book form. The book sold very, very well, and the profit margins were much better than our little software packages, so I think the people who put our technology to work in a different medium and figured out how to market it through a different channel were amply rewarded for their work. They created the book once, and the publishing company did all the rest, while we were still staying up all night burning floppies and shrink-wrapping boxes.

When I talk to people about my history as an entrepreneur, I usually refer to this episode as my first failure in business. Technically, it wasn't a failure at all, because we sold thousands and thousands of units (we sold everything as fast as we could make it), and we were turning a small profit, but over time it became less and less interesting. And when we saw how someone else leveraged our work to produce a much better income stream (the *Magic Eye* series of books, which became huge bestsellers, were based on our software), it was a little disheartening. However, the important point had nothing to do with profit and loss or how much effort went into making the product. What we learned from doing this was that we really didn't want to make our living selling entertainment software. So we stopped. We pulled the plug on this enterprise rather than go on and build other kinds of games and things that might have sold much better as the years went on. I call this a true failure because we did something and we gave up.

And yet, one of the things that I tell young entrepreneurs over and over again is that a failure is the best learning tool there is—if you're really willing to learn from it. In fact, I always tell my students that the opposite of success is not failure but actually not trying. The time we invested in the stereogram business was well spent. Most importantly, it proved to us both that what we could create on the computer could be commercialized—not like the programming I had done for Merrill Lynch, which was specific work for a specific client, but making software products that had enough value to generate independent sales. It also taught us a lot about the importance of PR, of getting good reviews of your products in the computer press, plus all the things you learn from selling your product over the counter to real people. In that sense, as I have described, failure was an excellent teacher. We learned that we could program something and sell it commercially, and we also discovered one more thing that we *didn't* want to do. That's important, too.

High School Daze

Looking back, high school seems like just a blip on the scope—it came and went. What else do I remember from those days?

One of my clearest memories may seem the most frivolous, but I will forever associate it with high school—the taste of hamburgers. No, not the school lunches. My parents were definitely not rich, and Damien was quite expensive, so I went to school with a pretty tasteless sandwich day after day. But every now and then my mom would give me a little money to splurge with, and I knew that once a week the In–N–Out Burger truck would come around. This was part of a hugely popular fast-food business started in nearby Irvine, California, long ago. To the best of my knowledge, it still hasn't spread across the country, which is too bad. I loved them. (Still do!) Back in Damien, I couldn't afford to eat those delicious burgers often, but when I could it was an experience you don't quickly forget. All the cool kids were getting the big Double-Double, while I had to settle for the regular Hamburger, but I didn't care. It was wonderful.

Some of the kids at Damien were from really rich families. Some of them were driven to school in the morning and picked up in the afternoon; a lot of them had their own Porsches. It was that kind of place. After a while, my mom got tired of driving me to school every morning (it was a long drive), so my parents bought me a car, too—a really beat-up 1978 Caddy Fleetwood (aka "the boat"), which they got with the idea that wrapping a couple of tons of solid Detroit sheet metal around their son was probably the best protection in case of an accident, and everyone knows high school kids got in a lot of accidents. Although I started to develop my impatient, lead foot driving style early on— probably because of the V8 engine—I managed not to crash-test the Caddy. That humongous trunk also proved very useful for lugging around assembled PCs, monitors, and so on. The car doubled as my delivery truck.

In case you're wondering if I had any academic inclinations while I was at Damien or if I ever thought about college, the answer is yes. I studied hard, and I took the SAT test early, either my freshman or sophomore year. I wasn't actually worried about getting into college, but I was curious to take this test that everyone seemed to pin their futures on. My friend Tas took it first; I think he scored in the 1500s on that initial try. He told me all about the test, and I took it, mostly for fun. Tas took it again, too, and we both hit 1600 (the maximum score). Then we took it again. We realized that we could rack up 1600s every time, so we started to experiment: What would happen if we answered (A) to all the multiple choice questions in the math section? We were having fun with the tests, looking to see how randomly the correct answers were distributed and things like that.

Shortly after finishing my first year at Damien, I realized that I wanted to finish high school early and get on to college. There were a lot of reasons for that (e.g., no more piano), but one of the biggest drivers for anything in my life has always been impatience: Once I can see the goal, I want to get moving toward it ASAP. I knew the theory said that I had to do well at Damien so I could get into a good college, where I would need to do well in a premed program so that I could get into a good medical school, where I would work my ass off and ultimately obtain that all-important M.D., which had been drilled into my head since I was a Cub Scout as the Über-Goal of All Goals. That meant I had a long road to follow, and the least important part of it seemed to be the years right in front of me. So I started asking teachers and staff how I could accelerate my high school graduation. Their first response was amusement, but when they saw that I was serious, their faces looked much less amused. I got a chorus of: "You can't graduate early.... No one has ever done that.... There's no precedent for it!" To which I kept replying, "Why not?" The only answer I ever received was that it had never been done before, which doesn't seem like an answer at all, just an observation of fact. So I went to the administration, and they were just as adamant, even telling me straight out that it could not be done. I'll tell you right now that few things get my goat, like being told that something can't be done. Even if I hadn't already set my mind on doing it, hearing that would have been enough to get me fired up, determined to prove everyone wrong. Phrases like "can't be done" or "it's the rule" have since become an ongoing challenge.

Sure enough, I didn't get what I wanted; I *created* what I wanted. Big difference. I set up an accelerated program, completed all the required courses (yes, including English) early, and thanks to my extra courses at the community college, I was able to skip my entire senior year at Damien and graduate at 16. Not only was I the first student ever to do so (they'll never be able to tell another kid, "It's never been done!"), but I believe I am still the only student who has ever done so.

By leveraging both my Damien record, my SAT scores, and all my college credits from Mt. San Antonio CC, I was accepted to the university of my choice later that same year. Was I ready to rush off to college? Not quite yet. There was still one important hobby that had nothing to do with computers that I wanted to devote some time to before I rushed off to university.

Interlude: Cooking in France

At the end of my abbreviated high school career, I followed the instincts implanted by two generations of chefs and the cooking DNA inherited from both sides of my family tree, and decided to go to cooking school. I know, this isn't part of the standard resume for someone who plans to become either a doctor or a computer geek, but both of those futures looked pretty fuzzy to me at the time, while the joy of cooking was real and immediate. I asked around, trying to find a good French cooking school that didn't have a lot of Japanese or tourists, and ultimately I found a first-rate school outside of Paris. I couldn't wait to go. Back at Damien, I'd had to choose a foreign language to study. I already had Japanese covered, German and Latin seemed too mechanical for my tastes, and if you lived in southern California, you heard and read so much Spanish every day that the idea of sitting in a classroom and doing homework in the language was a complete turn-off. But French sounded like something connected with recipes, so I studied French. No, I wasn't the world's best student, but I was confident enough that between my innate cooking skills and my rudimentary language skills, cooking school was going to be fun.

And it was. I was enrolled in a short course, a summer program that was filled with chefs and would-be chefs from all over the world. Fortunately, I was already an old hand at cutting, sautéing, and so on. Never one to start at the beginning when there's an option for a short-cut, I started learning how to make desserts. Over the next four summers, I worked my way through every aspect of French cuisine, and I got pretty good at it. Not only do I still enjoy a good French restaurant, but if you give me a well-stocked kitchen, a few hours, and someone to cook for, I can still whip up quite an impressive bit of haute cuisine.

One important lesson I learned is that cooking is actually a crash course in time management. For example, I used to have Thanksgiving parties for 80 or so people (in fact, I designed my first house around the kitchen to optimize the work flow for Turkey Day, because Thanksgiving in a kitchen really teaches you how to manage time). First, I'd go shopping for two days before the big event. Then I'd get up at 5 A.M. that day, and I'd just live in the kitchen. I did all the cooking—c'mon, who needs an assistant chef when I can manage all the tasks myself? Well, the truth is any assistant would go crazy watching the way I do things, but I do them my way, and it tastes great in the end, which is all that matters. When I make turkey, I often make pasta as well. And I didn't even have to tell you that I don't go out and buy pasta—I make my own. I choose the flour; I knead the dough; I cut it and dry it, and I get all this done while the turkey is cooking. And I make all the sauces, stuffing, side dishes, and everything else. It's a challenge—not just to prepare it all so that it tastes good, but to make sure the hot things are still hot and the cold things are suitably cold and everything is done just when it's supposed to be done, and it comes out of the kitchen right on time and reaches each table just when it should. That kind of cooking is a huge operation, and frankly, I love the challenge.

Cooking also provides a good chance to experiment, to try different things and learn by doing. It reminds me how important it is to stay open minded. In fact, I recall my dad's story about the day he knew he wanted to become a chemist. It was when he learned that sodium, a highly volatile reactive metal—when combined with the deadly gas chlorine, produces plain table salt, an edible additive that happens to be critical for cooking, too.

The best things sometimes come from experimentation, and different combinations taste very different from what you might expect. Things often don't come out the way you want, but part of the challenge is to improvise, to turn a failure (an overcooked entrée or missing ingredient, for example) into a rousing success (a soup or a stew perhaps), ideally without anyone catching on. Cooking also reflects my personality. I know lots of people who cook with a cookbook propped up on the counter, and they read every little detailed instruction and follow it to the letter. If it says one level teaspoon, they carefully measure out exactly one level teaspoon. Me, I just get the main ingredients (or some approximation thereof), combine them in what seems a good ratio, and don't worry about it. Type-A people who are watching me tend to freak out. They can't believe I'm so nonchalant and inexact about it all. But I always say, relax, it'll all work out fine. And I can say from experience that the meals that detail-obsessed chefs prepare do not taste anywhere near as good as food prepared by good cooks who relax and enjoy their work. People who get creative and feel free to make changes, adjust measurements, and take risks produce a better result. I'm the same way in business: I'm a chef. I take whatever ingredients are available and make something great out of it. In business, you don't always have all the ingredients you need, or you might not have the quality of ingredients you'd like, but you don't have time to wait. You have to cook with what you've got. Working with what you have on hand and making something much better than anyone would have imagined possible is a true sign of managerial and operational excellence.

So cooking school turned out to be even better than I'd thought, and I kept going back year after year. After that first session, though, I had some serious things waiting back home for my return. Little things like college and my future, which my parents were more interested in, or at least more worried about, than I was. So I hung up my apron at the end of the summer and headed back to California.

TAKEAWAY: Learn to Rely on Others

"Always play tennis with someone better than you are" is a good rule for any CEO to remember. No matter how smart you are (or how smart you think you are), your little brain can only hold so much. That means you need to surround yourself with lots of smart people and leverage their brainpower. Look at me. I'm not a genius; I need help with all sorts of things, especially to run a business. For each of the areas that I thought were critical to my business, I tried to get the smartest person I could find to handle that responsibility, starting with a really sharp business partner who was my opposite in many ways.

A CEO can never be a one-man show. Think of a CEO as a coordinator, a conductor leading an orchestra full of very talented people. No one person can play every instrument, but only one person can lead all the players to perform to their maximum potential, and that creates something really special.

I know people who feel threatened by anyone smarter than they are, so they avoid hiring smart people to help them, and they lose out big-time in the end. That's why I say that knowing your own weaknesses is vitally important, and being willing to complement your own knowledge or skill set by relying on others can be crucial to your success.

I cannot overemphasize the importance of teams in building your success. Nowadays, I remind all the venture companies I talk to that doing anything meaningful requires a team. Sure, you can probably run a good noodle stand by yourself, but if you dream of creating a world-shaking technology, you're going to need a lot of help. If you're going to look for outside financing, from a bank or a venture capitalist or a family friend, the first things you will be asked are, "Who's on your management team? Where do they come from, and what have they done?" Outsiders understand that no matter how brilliant you are, you need other skills, other information, and other perspectives in order to run a company successfully. The key equation for teams is that $1 + 1 = 3$.

Chapter 3

Learning to Juggle (Med School, Business, and More)

By leveraging my Damien record, my SAT scores, and my college credits from Mt. San Antonio College (Mt. SAC), I was able to get into my first-choice school, the University of California at Riverside (UCR). You might think I was on a fast track to the Ivy League, but that's not what I wanted. People have occasionally asked why I chose UCR over some place like Harvard or Stanford or MIT. There were two good reasons. First, it was close to home, which meant I could be close to my family, but maybe more important, close to Tas, whom I had sort of abandoned by bailing out of Damien a year early. Tas and I were just getting into the swing of our computer business, and we both knew that was more fun than anything that either high school or college was likely to offer. Yet we were not just having fun working together; we were both starting to get a strange sense that our collaboration could lead to something bigger, more interesting, and hopefully, more lucrative than anything we'd done so far.

Second, the California system of public higher education has a great system where anyone who wants an education is given the opportunity to go to college. Specifically, given that people have different life schedules, abilities, and needs, the California higher education system provides three options to allow anyone to get a college education and to have the credits accumulated transferable to any of the institutions in the system. For example, an adult who entered the workforce soon after graduating from high school could earn credits by taking evening classes at a community college. Once enough credits were accumulated, they could potentially be transferred to a University of California (UC)-level campus for a bachelor's degree, allowing flexibility at a much lower cost. Therefore, the credits that I accumulated at Mt. SAC were transferable one-for-one to either a California State or University of California campus. I know people who have gotten 90 percent of their credits from a community college (it takes longer, of course), then transferred to University of California at Berkeley (UCB) and finished the last 10 percent, thus obtaining their degree from UCB. Moreover, the equivalent units are several times cheaper than four years of study at UC. Besides, under the "Master Plan for Higher Education," the University of California (10 campuses) accepts only 12.5 percent of high school graduates, while California State University (23 campuses) accepts 29.6 percent, and community colleges (112 campuses) accept everyone.

Third, there was method in my madness. UCR was part of a special accelerated joint premed/medical program that linked up with the UCLA medical school, which meant I could do college plus medical school in one nonstop blitz and graduate with an M.D. in only seven years instead of the usual eight. Sound familiar? As I said, I'm all about short cuts, and I will often go to some extremes to find the shortest way to get what I want. Did I really want to be a doctor? Fair question. My parents had beaten the idea into my head from such an early age that it certainly wasn't my idea. On the other hand, I convinced myself that being a doctor sounded pretty cool, so why not? But damn if I was going to spend any more time in school getting the degree than I absolutely had to.

There were only two seven-year med programs that I knew of: one was on the East Coast and the other one was right there in my back yard. So I went to UCR and enrolled in the biomedical sciences program. The next year, Tas graduated from Damien and entered Harvey Mudd College in Claremont, just 20 miles away from UCR. Harvey Mudd has an excellent chemistry program, which suited him perfectly (he eventually went on to get a PhD in chemistry), but his ulterior motive was the same as mine—our physical proximity allowed us to stay in close contact and keep working on computer-related projects.

When I tell the story of my years at UC Riverside, people always ask, "Didn't you ever study?" That's because all the fun stuff, the things I enjoy talking about, were happening outside the classroom. But for the record, yes, I did study. That seven-year accelerated medical program was not a laid-back, do-what-you-want kind of course. It was tough, and there was lots of work. But my brain had long ago learned to compartmentalize school work, set aside the minimum amount of time needed to get it done properly, and then focus on other, more interesting things.

Like many other colleges, UC Riverside had dormitories and on-campus apartments. And like many other colleges, it had a lot of student couples who preferred to live together but couldn't do that anywhere on campus. They wanted to get off-campus apartments; that meant sneaking off campus together. If her dad or his mom happened to call the dorm and their dutiful son or church-going daughter were nowhere to be found, there could be serious repercussions. Coming from an all-boys Catholic high school and being a year younger than even the youngest freshman, this was a whole new world for me, but at least the college environment was exciting and stimulating. I heard guys complaining about how they wanted to move off campus with their girlfriends, but they were worried about how to deal with the dreaded calls from home (remember this was the early Jurassic Period when almost no one had a cell phone). To me, this looked like a relatively simple technical problem—someone just needed to do a bit of creative rewiring. I could handle that easily.

Of course, I had an ulterior motive. Tas and I were starting to do more and more work, still building PCs and still writing software, and trying to develop it all into something like a business. At UCR,

I quickly met people with a similar computer fetish, and it was easy to get these friends to come on board to help with both hardware- and software-related work. The problem was that we didn't have any open space where we could do that work. A college dorm room is not exactly Bell Labs; it was hard enough for me to work on my own PC in a dorm room crammed with all the usual collegiate junk, so the idea of getting a bunch of people together in my room for work sessions was out of the question. But what if there were a couple of *empty* dorm rooms available? What if some people actually wanted to move out of the dormitory and go live off campus, but for various reasons were reluctant to tell either their parents or the school administration that those paid-for accommodations were now vacant. A couple of empty dorm rooms would make very convenient and serviceable workshop space. So, both to help out classmates at school and to free up some good workspace for the computer business, I volunteered to set up a special answering service. I like to think of it as my first *social* business.

Basically, I rewired the dorm phone system so that calls coming into my wing could be rerouted. For example, if a parent were calling to talk to his daughter, we could intercept the call and say, "I'm terribly sorry. Susan isn't here right now; I think she's in class" or "I think I saw her on the way to the library." Then we would call the student's apartment off campus and warn her that Dad had just called and would be expecting a call-back from her in about an hour. It was a simple idea and a simple technical solution, and it was good for everyone. My friends were happy, their parents were happy (misinformed but happy), and my little PC business soon had more and more available rooms to expand into, so Tas and I were happy. Compared to all the other stuff that goes on in college, this seemed pretty tame, so I never gave it a second thought. After all, I didn't take drugs; I didn't party until dawn (who had time to party? I was programming until dawn!); I didn't try to determine the lethal dosage of alcohol through trial-and-error experimentation with a bunch of frat brothers or drag myself into morning classes with a massive hangover; I didn't get anyone pregnant or put the dean's car in the swimming pool. I was just using my skills to help out some people who needed help. No harm, no foul. Of course, from time to time, the love birds broke up and I had to juggle accommodations again. This ended up being good training in the field of "human resources."

My custom-built PC business continued to do well, mostly because so many name-brand PCs were pathetically bad back then. The hardware quality was inconsistent, and a lot of the software was undependable. PCs crashed so often that people made money selling PC-shaped pillows that you could punch when the stress level with your $5,000 investment got to be too much. Computer nerds who could select the best parts and wire them into a generic box, add a keyboard, a mouse, and a disk drive, and thus create a custom-built home PC for considerably less than the off-the-shelf units were not wanting for customers. In Texas, another premed student a few years ahead of me named Michael Dell had come to the same conclusion and was running a very successful, low-overhead, custom-built PC business that seemed to grow bigger by the week. I wasn't making his kind of money, but I was doing all right, and it was all off the books. Once I/O Software had been registered and received its reseller's permit years before, I'd basically ignored any of those pesky legal requirements of corporations, like paying taxes on earned income.

If I'd stuck with that PC sales business and taken it to the next level, perhaps I would have become another Michael Dell. Lots of people were asking me to build more and sell more, but I just didn't want to do it. To be honest, building computers from parts got boring pretty quickly, not to mention that your hands were always getting cut up on the edges of those old circuit boards. Electrical work always meant burns sooner or later, and when you were all done, the damn boxes were pretty heavy. You want to unload a dozen of those and drive around delivering them? Not me.

So at one level the idea of mass-producing a whole lot of hardware, even with some of my own custom software inside, seemed like more pain than gain. If I'd thought of it as simply a matter of hiring dozens of slave workers to do all the painful work so that I could swing in a hammock all day, counting my profits while I sipped on a cool drink, maybe I would have ramped up the business, but I doubt it. For one thing, I wanted to be integrally involved with the work, not just the profits. Managing a lot of people to do my job while I did nothing didn't feel right. Then again, the whole thing would become a lot more complicated. To take the business to the next level, all the parts needed to be quality-checked, the wiring assemblies needed to be checked, and each machine needed to be run for at least 24 hours before it was shipped to the client. I realized that I wasn't enough of a detail-oriented person to turn this spare-room/spare-time operation into a smooth industrial process, to manage the quality control, move up to real mass production, and expand the business. But the real deal-killer wasn't any of these rational arguments; it was a certain sense that guided me and Tas for the next decade: all this hard work was okay when we started, but now we'd done what we set out to do with hardware assembly, and it just wasn't *fun* anymore. Software was easier; it allowed for more creativity and expression, and it felt better.

However, one force was pulling us increasingly toward the software business, and that force had a lot to do with the country my parents came from.

The Japan Connection Begins

I wasn't one of those Japanese-American kids who discovered Japan as a teenager and wanted to learn something about the country and its culture so they wouldn't feel so cut off from their heritage. I had been going to Japan to visit my grandmother since I was too young to look out the airplane window. I still remember making my first *solo* flight to Okinawa at the ripe old age of five. The planes back then stopped in Hawaii to refuel, and there I was, five years old and all alone, wandering around Honolulu Airport. Independent as always. I got confused (I never use the word *lost*) and almost missed the connecting flight, but somehow I found my way back to the Pan American gate and finished the trip. From then on, I would travel across the Pacific by myself every year. Basically, every summer and winter I spent the long school vacations with my grandmother in Okinawa. I was one of the older grandchildren, and I really liked her. She doted on me like a son, a really spoiled son, of course. Partly, it was because I reciprocated the affection more than some of the other grandkids, and I think part of it may have had to do with the timing of my birth—I came into the world three days after her husband passed on. And to her Catholic mind, this was a big deal. She seemed to transfer a fraction of her grief into joy at having a new grandson. Whatever the reason, she spoiled me. For one thing, she gave me a huge allowance, too much even by today's standards, which I immediately spent on sheets of colorful Ryukyu stamps. Not Japanese stamps, but Ryukyus (the 1,000 km–long island chain, the lower part of which is now Okinawa Prefecture, was controlled by the U.S. after World War II and only became part of Japan in 1972. The stamps I was looking at in those early transition years were written in Japanese but were still denominated in U.S. cents). You might say I was a nerd back then, but the stamps looked pretty cool (especially since everything was written in Japanese but denominated in dollars and cents), and I happily brought them all back to California after each trip. I still have boxes and boxes of neatly preserved old stamps from Okinawa that must be worth a small fortune. But I digress.

I mentioned that my grandmother used to run an elite cooking school. As a young kid, I loved hanging around that school. There was an elementary school on the upper floors, and the cooking school was on the first floor, so the food that was prepared by cooking students was used to feed elementary school students upstairs, which I thought was a neat idea. I got to go to the Japanese school while I was there, and also work in the kitchens downstairs. Of course, I already knew my way around a kitchen. My father's whole family liked to cook and was good at it, and some of them worked as cooks in hotels and restaurants. My mother also loved to cook, so my parents used to fight over who would get to cook that day. I enjoyed cooking from an early age. I used to cook all sorts of strange stuff in Okinawa, things no Japanese had ever seen. Of course, my grandmother would always eat whatever I made and compliment me, but I could see that the other Japanese were not exactly bowled over by my early efforts at international cuisine (e.g., I tried to convince the other students of the merits of toasting bread or the miracle of gravy as a versatile condiment—something not popular in Japan at the time).

Still, it was a good experience, every year traveling overseas and spending time in Japan, talking to elementary school kids upstairs and cooks in the kitchen, my own version of an *Upstairs/Downstairs* education. Of course, my parents spoke Japanese at home, and as I grew up I was still shuttling back and forth between the West Coast and Okinawa every year, so I was pretty comfortable with my Japanese roots. But my influences were still largely family members. Then some new "teachers" came to my house.

My mom, always restless, quickly grew bored with being just a housewife. She had been a vet in her early years in Japan, and as her kids started to grow, she wanted to get a real job. Luckily, she found a teaching position at Cal Poly Pomona (California State Polytechnic University, Pomona if you're from out of town), one of only two Cal Poly schools that taught agriculture. This was important because it gave Mom another way to channel her abundant energy and put her brain to use somewhere outside the kitchen. It also put her in contact with a whole new range of people.

Around this time, a Japanese government scholarship program was created to assist graduate students to go abroad to study agriculture techniques in the States. Mom met a lot of these kids at school, and so over the years we served as a host family for many students from Japan. More than that, we became hosts in a much more practical sense. Most of these students (there were about a dozen at a time) were in their early twenties and living in the United States on minuscule stipends. Mom took pity on them, and since both she and Dad loved to cook and throw parties, they threw a big Bar-B-Q bash every few weeks. Dad would cook up a whole side of beef; Mom would whip up all sorts of special dishes. We'd buy lots of beer, and they'd create weekend poolside parties, southern California–style. Sometime before this, we had moved again, still within Walnut, to a bigger house with a swimming pool, so we had a great location to help Japanese exchange students relax. You can imagine the scene of a dozen starving Japanese college students coming to our place, stuffing themselves with more food than they would see for the next couple of weeks, tossing down cold beers, and lounging around our pool on a sunny day.

Since I could speak the language (though with some heavy Okinawan accent thrown in here and there), I was happy to join in the fun, and these exchange students became my new elder brothers and Japanese teachers. I not only picked up a lot of new words, phrases and slang, and even different dialects, but they also played hours and hours of mahjong with me, honing skills that would serve me well later on.

Rain Bird

Mom enjoyed teaching, and through the college she met all sorts of people. One of the corporations involved with Cal Poly Pomona was Rain Bird Corporation, a major supplier of irrigation equipment to institutions and golf courses all over the world. In 1984 Rain Bird had developed a PC-based central control system to manage golf course irrigation. This product, which they called MAXI, was quite advanced for its time, and it claimed a big piece of the American market, but the problem was that all its menus were in English. Around the mid-1980s the Japanese started to build golf courses like there was no tomorrow, and Rain Bird knew they wanted to be a big player in the Japanese market as well. But how do you get a strong foothold among Japanese golf courses when all your software only displays in English? Japanese groundskeepers don't want to use a dictionary in order to water their fairways, which meant that very lucrative market would automatically go to some local firm. Rain Bird was adamant that its products could take on the fast-growing Japanese market. All they needed was to port their English-language MAXI software into Japanese. How hard could that be?

The vice-president of Rain Bird happened to run into my mom at the university, and since she was Japanese, he mentioned the problem. Of course, Mom didn't hesitate for a second to volunteer her eldest son; you know, he speaks Japanese fluently, and he can program a computer to roll over and play dead if you ask him to. I'm sure he can create whatever you need in no time at all. One thing led to another, and before I knew it I was sitting across a table from the VP, discussing the scope of this translation project. To be honest, I had never even tried what he was talking about and hadn't a clue how I would or could do it. So, when he said, "Do you think you can handle that?" I thought for a second, Gates style, and said, "Sure. When do we start?"

It goes without saying that this very positive, let's-try-anything attitude was inherited; my basic "What've-we-got-to-lose, let's-try-it!" gene probably came from my grandmother's DNA, and some of it passed down through my mother. Whatever the pedigree, I thought it was kind of cool. Tas and other people I worked with over the years had other views.

What I had just agreed to do was to figure out a way to display Japanese characters on English software. Not knowing that this was impossible, I just charged ahead. For one thing, simply displaying English in some standard format on a computer was a matter that had only recently been laid to rest at that time. Computers gobble up data in chunks called bytes. Early computers used what is known as a 7-bit byte, which allowed the machine to handle information in chunks consisting of 128 characters, what came to be known as the basic American Standard Code for Information Interchange (ASCII) character set. (Don't worry, I'm going to keep this real simple.) How important was that development? Well, back in 1968, the president of the United States decreed that all computers purchased by the U.S. government must support ASCII text. That's what I call an endorsement.

Now, you may wonder why we needed 128 characters to display a 26-letter alphabet, but let's not get bogged down in detail here (there's much more tedious stuff to get bogged down in later on). Suffice it to say that you need separate characters for the lower case and upper case letters, plus the numerals 0–9, plus a couple of dozen characters to represent punctuation marks, parentheses, and so on. In addition, there were a lot of "invisible" characters that were used to tell printers and other devices connected to those early computers to do things like advance the printing tape by one line, backspace, delete, and so on. By the time I was learning to program software, most computers had switched from a 7-bit to an 8-bit byte. Anyway, the key point here is that this change allowed computers to "read" 256 characters per chunk (byte) of information. IBM computers like mine (and all IBM-compatible computers) used a Microsoft operating system that was already becoming the de facto global standard, and this, too, was based on the revised ASCII 8-bit/256-character architecture.

All's well and good. If you could display the entire English alphabet and throw in all the punctuation and everything else with 128 characters, you could really go to town with the 256 layout. You could display anything you wanted to with 256 characters.

Anything, that is, except ideogram-based languages like Japanese and Chinese, which had *thousands* of characters, most of them far more complex than the English alphabet. Probably over a thousand Asian characters consist of more than 10 separate brush strokes, and hundreds of them have more than 20 strokes. Compare that with English letters that are almost all simple 2- and 3-stroke forms. So what I had just promised to do was to magically shoehorn 15,000 to 25,000 very fat characters into 256 skinny telephone booths. Moreover, this process would have to be carried out inside the computer very quickly and efficiently in order for the characters to appear on screen smoothly, and there would have to be no errors at all. That would have been a tall order if I'd had a room-sized mainframe to play with; trying to do all that with a PC back in the late 1980s was . . . a challenge.

At first glance, it really did look impossible. And yet, if crazy teenagers like me didn't come along and volunteer to do these things, we'd never know what is or isn't truly possible. So I worked on that problem for quite a while. It was a kind of puzzle, and all my life I've liked puzzles. Give me a new software program with some "unbreakable" copy protection at age 11 and you wouldn't see me again until I'd broken it. I loved a challenge, especially if it involved programming, and this was a whopper.

Ultimately, I devised an elegant, efficient, and thoroughly practical solution to the problem using two bytes to represent each character. I could explain it all in minute detail, but that would take up the next chapter of this book, and, aside from me, no one would think it's very interesting. Today, all double-byte character sets and the old ASCII code have been replaced with something called Unicode, in which all characters are represented flexibly by either 8, 16, or 24 bits, which is how modern computers and web browsers understand text. That powerful but flexible system can handle Chinese and Korean and Japanese characters just as easily as English. In fact, Unicode can use up to four bytes to represent a single character, and has codings for hundreds of thousands of characters in a huge variety of languages. But back then, in the dark ages of computer code, this was all a pipe dream, and what I needed to do was to solve an immediate problem.

Eventually, through a huge amount of work, we figured out how to use double-byte characters to display Japanese menus, we successfully ported Rain Bird's American software into Japanese, and got it to run on non-Japanese computers. That was a very, very difficult task, but it was good experience for me and Tas, and it was very good knowledge for us to have. At that time, we didn't know it but the PC market in Japan was ruled by NEC. They had a famous model, the 9801, which really dominated that market. It was nominally PC-compatible, and it was the only PC-compatible (i.e., Intel chip/MS-DOS-based) machine of its kind that could display Japanese characters. What we had just done, NEC would have said was impossible. Ironically, that clever bit of programming for a golf course sprinkler business opened the door to doing much bigger business with the 9801's maker.

The story we heard later was that someone from NEC was playing golf with someone from Rain Bird and asked about their MAXI software, which was running in Japanese but not on an NEC machine. How was that possible, was the natural question for any NEC manager. The answer must have blown him away: some small, independent outfit in California had actually programmed 8-bit IBM computers to run in Japanese. That was a little like telling Honda that some no-name Nigerian company had figured out how to stuff a Ferrari V-12 engine into a Civic body and go tearing around the racetracks. Not only did it mean that someone had done an incredible piece of engineering, but it also suggested that this someone might be called on to manage similar kinds of cross-platform engineering on demand.

TAKEAWAY: Make the Most of Diverse Experiences

Even though I never practiced as a physician, I'm fortunate to have taken the medical route because of the way it makes you think. For example, doctors need to work together with patients to determine the cause of their illnesses. But even patients may not know exactly what is wrong with them, and finding a solution or cure on their own is even more difficult. Children can be particularly hard to diagnose. My mom told me that veterinarians have an even more difficult time, since the animals cannot tell you where it hurts. The ability to figure out the root cause of a problem and to develop an optimal solution is something doctors are continually trained for. The solution may be based on something you can't see (below the skin), and the patient's assessment is not always right. Similarly, in business, a customer may think they know what they need or how to solve a problem a certain way, but later find they had not understood the situation correctly. That is why being trained to look for clues, to get to the essence of a problem in order to develop the best solution with limited information is a useful skill in business, especially in projects like software development. Physicists are also in this same category because they are attuned to think abstractly, creatively, and imaginatively to solve their problems as well.

Interestingly, not all of our computer programmers had backgrounds in computer science. In fact, people from different backgrounds, such as English majors, medical students, and so on, bring a different perspective to programming, whereas a computer science major will make certain "book" assumptions about what is or is not possible and thereby limit the options. People without preconceived notions (ignorance is bliss) will tend to just do it, and many times it works out elegantly. Steve Jobs' Stanford commencement speech is very inspirational and a good example of how a calligraphy course he took led to the beautiful fonts on the Macintosh computer.

Chapter 4

Building a Real Company

W hen I first started using computers, one of the cool things people did was to set up individual PC-to-PC connections over a telephone line using a coding device called a modem. Today we have fast, reliable e-mail, but in the 1980s that wasn't even a pipe dream. Simply being able to connect to another individual with the same digital addiction as yourself and type messages back and forth ("chat") until 4:00 A.M. was a thrill. It was incredibly slow by today's standards; it couldn't come close to handling a low-grade video signal, and even the plain text capabilities were only a little faster than an old-fashioned telex, which is the slowest form of digital communication known to man. This kind of PC-to-PC communication was done with special software that gave you access to a bulletin-board system (hence the once-common name BBS) where you could dial in and—if you were lucky enough to get connected—contact friends, strangers, and beings from other planets. In fact, I ran my own BBS at one point (yes, I was one of those mysterious, unseen, all-powerful forces in the telecom world known as a SysOp), and it was fairly popular. Of course, "popular" back then was a little different from having a website with several thousand hits per day. Because my BBS ran on a single telephone line, when one user would call in, that would tie up the system for however long that user would stay online. Everyone else who tried to access the network would get a busy signal and have to call back later. Maybe it wasn't the most sophisticated system in the universe, but back in the 1980s (shortly after the invention of electricity, as most kids will tell you today) it was all we had, and compared to sitting alone in front of your PC night after night with no one to talk to, it felt pretty cool. You could dial up a BBS and get all sorts of information, have a real-time chat and basically reach out beyond the confines of your own machine to talk to other users, not just in the neighborhood but all over the world. Of course, the whole thing ran on a real telephone line, so you had to be careful not to get *too* addicted or your long-distance phone charges for the month would cost more than your father's car.

One of the hottest products in this space was a shareware program called ProComm. It was coded to run on IBM PCs and compatibles, which is to say it worked with Microsoft's ubiquitous operating system. Just to give you an idea of how popular it was, in 1992 ProComm won the first Dvorak Award (a reasonably big deal at the time) and the following year the advanced version, ProComm Plus for Windows, hit number one on *PC Magazine*'s list of best-selling software.

The company behind this hit product was Datastorm Technologies, Inc., a little firm that grew rapidly thanks to their success with ProComm. Sometime after we cut our teeth on the Rain Bird software development, we were contacted by NEC. They had heard about our work for Rain Bird, and they asked if we could do the same kind of thing for ProComm Plus—translate the menus and commands and port the software over to the 9801. NEC wanted to show off its wide range of U.S. software for their flagship PC series so they could constantly reinforce their already strong market share.

Of course, we already had some experience localizing software into Japanese, and we'd learned a lot from that experience, but we were not a software translation company. We didn't really know the 9801 well, and we were as usual, understaffed, short on dorm room space to work in, and not exactly flush with cash to support new projects. However, like many small businesses before us, our motto was "Take whatever you can get." We took the ProComm job. Our faxes started humming, and I/O Software became a de facto subcontractor for NEC.

At the time, NEC had several thousand companies in its domestic subcontracting pyramid, and it was expanding its operations all over the world, so it was easy to start sending programming work out to an American software company that had proved it knew what it was doing. Fortunately, by handling all business communications by fax, I could make I/O Software, Inc., look like a much bigger, more well-established company than it really was. Like the famous cartoon that says, "No one knows you're a dog on the Internet," facsimiles were a wonderful way to allow little companies such as ours to cook up an impressive-looking logo, dummy up a corporate letterhead, and do business without ever having to actually meet a client or let him discover that you had not yet begun to shave. And as one of the first customers of the recently released Motorola cellular phone (the size of a shoe box at the time), our company could appear to have a dedicated business number even while we were working out of our dorm rooms.

In fact, there were so many things we didn't know; we often had to wing it. Because we were dealing with the crown jewels, or intellectual property of these companies, we were once asked for an NDA, or Non-disclosure Agreement. We had no idea what that was, so we said, "Ours isn't so good, so send us your copy."

In Japan, the 9801 was billed as an "IBM compatible," which was a big deal, partly because, in theory at least, it gave the NEC machine access to a large universe of software written for IBM compatibles. The problem was that the 9801 was only fully "IBM compatible" in NEC's marketing literature. In practice, it was a bastardized variation of the standard architecture. NEC didn't want to use the original Intel chip that ran the machine, so they created their own look-alike version of the chip. This created all sorts of interesting intellectual property issues back then, which we won't go into here, but the relevant point is that NEC's microprocessor was a lot like the standard Intel chip but also significantly different. That caused us endless headaches; trying first to figure out how they had changed the chip, and then to hammer U.S. software into a shape that would run smoothly on that machine. Although, the upside of all that pain and effort was that we got to know the NEC 9801, the king of PCs in Japan, inside-out, and we got more experience looking at hardware instead of only software, we suffered with the ProComm job. We hired Japanese exchange students and others to be our translation department, and we stayed up a lot of late nights wrestling with the 9801 architecture, the ProComm commands, the modem connections, and the Japanese translations.

Just to give you a tiny example of the kinds of issues we ran up against, issues that had nothing even to do with the 9801, telecom modems were used the world over, so you would expect they would all be standardized. Think again. To connect reliably with another modem involved a data hook-up known as a handshake. U.S. modems used software to confirm that handshake, but Japanese modems had a hardware-based handshake. We didn't know that, and it didn't make any sense, but we had to figure out how to deal with this hardware problem in order to continue working on our software development. Needless to say, no one was paying us to learn about the hardware (or use an oscilloscope)—they assumed we were experts at dealing with U.S.-Japan software issues and could handle anything. Ultimately, we proved them right. We went way over budget and spent way too much time, but we did it. The results weren't exactly pretty, but anything that ran all right and didn't outright crash the system was considered a success back then. (Sometime after all this, Datastorm was acquired by Quarterdeck and then by Symantec.)

By doing all of this work, we were steadily building credibility with NEC, who was increasingly impressed that a company in the States could successfully port non-Japanese software to run on their flagship machine. There was a whole world of popular software outside of Japan. If someone could just translate it and port it over to the 9801, it would make their machine unbeatable in the local market. So, doing the ProComm job was a little like opening a spigot. Work started to pour in from NEC's offices in Tokyo.

One of the biggest, nastiest jobs we undertook involved a piece of software that every computer user is familiar with, even today—Norton Utilities. Peter Norton released the original version of his multi-floppy disk package around 1982, and it almost instantly became a must-have, Swiss-Army knife utility program for the PC. Later, that company, too, was acquired by Symantec Corporation, which still makes Norton Utilities, and the current version is still very popular. NEC was satisfied with our ProComm work (don't ask me why) and came back to ask us to create a Japanese version of Norton Utilities to run on the 9801. I guess a smarter CEO than myself would have said, "No thanks. We've ported enough American software to the 9801, and frankly, it's a pain in the butt. What else have you got that we could work on?" But a client in the hand is hard to resist, and one thing we didn't want to do was go to a bank or a vulture capitalist for operating funds. So we did what we always did. We said, "Sure, no problem. When do we start?" In no time at all we were back under the hood of the 9801.

All the problems with the NEC architecture aside, we discovered that Norton Utilities back then was a *monster* to work with. It went very deep inside the system, and it had system-specific commands that were not like what you'd find in other utility products. Norton reached its tentacles throughout the system all the way down to the hardware. That's serious. We learned—the hard way—that we had taken on an even tougher job than the ones we'd already finished. In addition to the simple translation work, which is really not simple at all, there was a ton of work rewriting bits of the engine software to make it run on the 9801. It was a huge, massively complicated project, but in the end it ran (sort of) on the NEC machine. It wasn't our finest hour, and I would never stand up in a crowd of software engineers and proudly proclaim, "I created the Japanese version of Norton Utilities," because it was really kind of half-baked. Then again, almost all the software back then was half-baked. Everything only sort-of worked. The only question was did it run or not? If it ran in any shape or form and the machine didn't crash, you were okay, and you probably weren't going to get sued by your client. Or so you hoped. We sure struggled with that one, and we really did wonder if somebody was going to sue us, but in the end it was reasonably good, and everyone was satisfied. All the same, I think I aged 10 years working on that one.

NEC Comes Calling

Of course, all of the work we were starting to take on for Japanese companies was done under the name I/O Software, Inc. To the outside world, we looked like a respectable, downtown kind of company, the kind of enterprise you'd expect to find occupying a couple of floors of an office building in an industrial park somewhere. Obviously, anyone who could do the kind of heavy lifting we were doing on these translation jobs must be a solid company with a few dozen highly skilled programmers on their payroll. No one, certainly not NEC, imagined that this was a hole-in-the-wall operation run out of a bunch of empty rooms in college dormitories. Thanks to the magic of the facsimile and the new cellular phone technology, I was able to keep in touch with people in Japan on my (I hoped) corporate-looking fax stationery, and no one was the wiser. We figured we could probably get away with this for years.

We figured wrong.

One sunny Thursday afternoon I got a call, not a fax, from NEC. They told me matter-of-factly that some of their people were heading to the States to attend COMDEX, the big electronics industry trade show in Las Vegas, the following week. "We'll be arriving in LA on Monday," he said, "And, as long as we're stopping over in California anyway, we'd like to take this opportunity to come by and visit your offices. . . ."

I knew this is perfectly standard Japanese company protocol—sooner or later, someone from the head office visits the subcontractor and checks out his factory, his equipment, his staff, and so on. If they haven't met in person before, this is the time to meet the smaller company's CEO and size up the quality of the management. Of course, it's a friendly visit, but it's friendly in the way that a bank coming around to visit your offices before approving a business loan is just a social call.

What could I say? We'd just been hit by a tornado, and our office had disappeared? They might not fall for that. So I said sure, we'd love to meet them face to face, talk about business, and stop relying simply on faxes for communication. By the time I hung up the phone I was starting to sweat a little.

It was Thursday; representatives from NEC, our biggest client, would be here in four days, expecting to see a real, professional-looking I/O Software. What they would see was a bunch of college students operating out of empty dorm rooms in their spare time. They would quickly discover that the two managers were likewise still college students and not even at the same college. When NEC discovered that they were relying on this sham of a company to handle critical software engineering, that contract would evaporate in a split second, and we'd be lucky if our next phone call was not from their U.S. attorneys.

So we did what any normal, well-run, international corporation based on time-tested Peter Drucker management principles would do—we went into panic mode. We had to set up something that looked like an office, and we had to do it fast. First question: Where? Tas and I pulled out a map of southern California and measured with a ruler to find the exact halfway point between Harvey Mudd College and UCR. It turned out to be a little town called Rancho Cucamonga, which neither of us knew much about. The "management" of I/O Software quickly decided that the new "corporate headquarters" would be in Rancho Cucamonga. The next day, Friday, we headed over there to scout some decent-looking space in a typical office park. We found a place that looked about right and rented it on the spot.

Saturday we hit the local office supply store. Desks, chairs, filing cabinets, lights, a couple of bulletin boards, stacks of paper—whatever would make this empty space look like a real office. And we needed it delivered ASAP. Quick, somebody get some phones on the desks! They don't have to be connected to anything, just make them look like business phones! We needed computers, complete with keyboards, printers, and other peripherals. There was no budget left to go out and buy that stuff, so on Sunday we liberated a couple of carloads of equipment from the UCR computer lab. All for a good cause. What about staff? I think maybe we had about 20 "programmers" altogether back then, really just friends from school who worked for us on and off. We convinced them to show up at the new "office" on Monday morning, bring a few girlfriends to fill out the office staff, and look busy when the curtain went up.

And it went up right on schedule. Before we were even finished setting up our charade, the NEC representatives arrived. We gave them a tour of our fairly substantial-looking offices, me guiding them around and explaining our sophisticated operation in my best business Japanese. They were impressed to see rows of people hard at work at computer terminals, people talking on phones, programmers conferring with each other in little ad hoc meetings, and so on. I had to admit, given just a quick walk-through, if you didn't look too closely at anything, it could pass for a software company.

It passed. The NEC people were satisfied. We were obviously a real company, not some fly-by-night bunch of pizza-fueled collegiate hackers. NEC had found a good, responsible firm to partner with on these important software translation projects. Off they went to COMDEX.

After breathing a huge sigh of relief once they were gone, we suddenly realized that we had taken a significant step in making our business look and feel more like a real business. We had just rented a good working space equidistant from our two campuses, and we might as well put it to good use. So Rancho Cucamonga actually did become the company headquarters. This is probably the point at which Tas and I decided to take the whole thing seriously, to make it our business. Although I'd actually incorporated back in the 1980s, I had never paid taxes or done those other little things that real companies do, but now the time had come to shift gears. If our clients were going to accept us as a real business, we should start acting like a real business. Beginning that year, I/O Software magically appeared on the local tax rolls, and if you check the company histories or any of our bios, it says, "I/O Software founded in 1991." In that sense, NEC really caused us to found I/O Software, taking it off campus and making it something more than a shared hobby.

Just as a final note to this episode, after the NEC reps returned home and talked about their very successful visit to COMDEX and the interesting little company they had met in the LA area whose young CEO spoke Japanese, a new door swung open. We were contacted by *Business Computer News* (BCN), an important trade newspaper that is still well known in the electronics industry even today. They had heard about NEC's visit and wanted to know if I/O Software would help to organize COMDEX tours for other Japanese firms. All my volunteerism training at Damien came to the fore, and I agreed instantly. No, I didn't have time to do it, and, no, it might not bring in any new business, but it seemed like the right thing to do. So in addition to everything else I was doing, I became the organizer, a tour conductor, and translator. Groups of anywhere from a dozen to 20 Japanese mid-level managers would fly into town, I would pick them up at LAX, rent a bus to Las Vegas, set up late-night activities for them, guide them around the floor at COMDEX, then take them back to LA, where I would arrange meetings for them with some of the leading companies in the area. All along the way I had to act as a very bad simultaneous interpreter, which allowed them to see one of America's premier electronics shows up close, meet with lots of interesting companies, and feel they were communicating at least reasonably well wherever they went.

Although I expected nothing concrete to come from all this activity, it actually paid off in many ways. For one thing, my very simplistic, conversational Japanese language skills improved tremendously, giving me the beginnings of proper business Japanese, which would become essential to furthering our business down the road. Second, I became friends with hundreds of mid-level managers, introducing them to the United States, showing them COMDEX, eating and drinking with them, and so on. At the time I didn't realize what a big deal this was. In Japan, someone my age would be carrying the manager's briefcase for him and walking a few steps behind. Here, I was the guy who was giving them linguistic access to a whole new world they desperately wanted to see more of, and so they treated me more or less as an equal despite the difference in our ages. We only spent about a week together, but in that short time we became fairly close. Over the years, many of these managers rose through the ranks, and some of them eventually became presidents of Japan's biggest electronics firms, giving me direct personal access to people I would otherwise never meet. My Rolodex of Japanese executives whom I could call on confidently began to expand rapidly. Even the managers who did not become CEOs all got promoted, they all had good contacts of their own, and they were happy to introduce me to influential people on my trips to Japan, which were just starting to become a regular part of doing business.

Just an Ordinary College Student

In most respects, I felt like an average American kid growing up. Of course, I knew I was a little different from other kids, but I didn't go around thinking I was really smart or anything. Sure, I could nail high marks on my SATs, I carried a big, bulky cell phone (it looked like a brick with an antenna) back when *no*body had a cell phone. But I had a cell phone even back in high school—it wasn't to look cool or impress girls, just a necessary tool to help me create a virtual office, originally for my private programming and computer sales work, and later on to maintain the fiction of I/O Software's corporate office. I took calls in the car and when I was out on lunch breaks. Again, I never thought this was particularly cool, but rather embarrassing, so I remained discrete about it. I'd got myself into this situation where I had to make people think I was a legitimate business, and part of that was having a real phone number that a real person would answer. Unlike many countries, cell phone numbers in the United States don't look any different from landline numbers, and the built-in voice mail was great for taking messages from clients in different time zones. If I had more income, I might have thought about getting a real office and hiring a secretary, but in the early years the cost difference between paying for a mobile phone and hiring a full-time, bilingual secretary to answer occasional calls was a no-brainer. The cell phone, however clunky, was the most efficient solution.

Yes, I was the CEO of my own corporation, and maybe somebody else thought that was cool. It didn't do anything for my ego—I did not talk much about my other job to my university peers. What I was proud of was doing the things that I wanted to do, like playing around with computers because I really enjoyed that, and taking advantage of opportunities that came along. That didn't make me especially smart, just motivated and creative, two things I will happily admit to. I stood out more than other kids because of those achievements, not because of my IQ. I graduated from high school a year early because I was in a hurry to get to college. The thing that made it possible (attending a community college when I was 15) was pure luck. I wandered into the college library to read some books because I'm naturally curious, and then wandered into some classes, pretending to be a student, so I could study things they didn't even teach at Damien. I discovered that no one at the community college cared how old I was (the adults even asked *me* questions), so I became a real student. I studied things I wanted to and got college credits for it. Then, because I'm always looking for shortcuts to get where I'm going, it made sense to skip a year of high school. To me it was no big deal. It seemed obvious. The last thing I was trying to do was to look cool or look smart. I just wanted to get on with my life and couldn't see how spending another year at Damien would help with that. One thing just led to another.

Of course, I was aware that I was getting ahead farther and faster than most people my age, both in high school and in college (sometimes not the wisest thing to do, I realized later), but that wasn't because I had some overriding fear of poverty or deep-set need to overachieve or anything like that. I just liked to do stuff, and the stuff I got to play with became more and more interesting as I went along. Other people may say that they became who they are because they made smart choices in life, had a clear goal in mind, and drove toward it come hell or high water, or maybe just persevered in some task until they achieved great success. I respect whatever route brought those people to their version of success, but I can't say I studied them or learned from them. I just followed my nose, first in one direction, then in another, and another, always trying to do something different and challenging, usually discovering that I'd bitten off more than I could chew, and eventually overcame most obstacles by a combination of brainpower, hard work, and luck. Don't ever discount the value of luck.

Newspaper Publisher

The University of California at Riverside was, and still is, a great place to go to school. The bell tower in the center of the campus looks out over acres of lush green foliage and modern architecture, all of it benefiting from the warmth of a typical Southern California climate. UCR is known as an outstanding research university, and the science emphasis of my undergraduate biomedical program certainly attested to that.

I was also told that the surrounding city was boring, which was probably a good thing so I could focus more on my studies. In many ways my life there was a lot like that of other college students. Well, more or less. I didn't carry my original cellphone around with me most of the time, because it was huge, and I did feel self-conscious about it. A little later, when the Motorola MicroTAC came out, a phone I really could slip into my pocket, I was happy to carry it all the time, but I sure didn't flash it around. The last thing I wanted to do was to attract attention to the fact that I had lots of other things on my mind beside my studies.

Because I had entered college at least a year earlier than other freshman, I was uncool in a number of ways, principally with the women on campus. Most of them wanted older boyfriends to begin with, and many wanted a boyfriend who was at least 21 so he could buy alcohol legally, and here I was—a nerdy-looking, underage computer geek. On the rare occasions when I went to dances or parties, it became obvious that I had "UNCOOL" printed on my forehead, and girls would stay clear. I was frustrated and, of course, wanted to have a girlfriend like anyone else, but in the long run being single at college freed up my time, my savings, and my attention for other things.

Although I thought of myself as just another college student, there were a few things in my environment that said otherwise. For example, my dorm room was outfitted with a state-of-the-art PC, a fax, a desktop scanner, a laser printer, and lots more. That may sound pretty ordinary today, but back then it was very extraordinary. Especially the laser printer—most people didn't even own a printer, and the ones who did had a little dot-matrix machine that produced text and images that can only be described as rough. No one had a laser printer in his room; they were big, bulky, and quite expensive. People who didn't know me probably thought I had a rich uncle who bought me expensive toys, but the reality was much better. I didn't need a rich uncle because I'd been building and selling computers since high school, and I was making enough money even in the lean times to buy whatever new toys—I mean tools—I needed whenever I needed them. And the electricity was free.

And I put them to good use. For example, I used that scanner and laser printer for all sorts of practical projects, like making up discount food coupons for local restaurants. It is a well-known fact that even the most epicurean meal served on campus never tastes as good as the lowliest off-campus diner food, and even the most ordinary off-campus food tastes twice as good when acquired with a little creativity. No, I didn't do it often, but every now and then, when we realized we'd missed the sale at some local fast food joint, I could extend the "good until" date printed on the newspaper coupons and take a few friends out for a good hot meal. Even the local Denny's gave away free Grand Slam breakfasts on your birthday. You can probably imagine what happened there. On a more serious note, I used my computer equipment and skills not only for the work that Tas and I were constantly engaged in, but also for one of the most creative and labor-intensive projects of my college years—I published a popular underground newspaper. The *Tammany Times* was my first venture as author, editor, and publisher, and it did quite well, attracting a strong readership across campus. I like to think it was part Twitter, part WikiLeaks, and part Facebook for its day, telling people what was really going on around the school every week, posting information from the editor-in-chief (me) as well as letters and articles from people who wanted to communicate via that unofficial medium. I edited the paper, laid it out on my PC, and printed the master copy of each page on my laser printer. The final product didn't look like a cheap underground paper at all; it looked as good and the content was considerably better than the official school paper.

Of course, the major cost item for any publication of this sort, when there is no Facebook, is printing. We knew that the best way to get those master pages printed nicely was to use the high-end copy machines in the school library. Of course, to access those machines and run off hundreds of good-quality copies required an ID card with a magnetic stripe that computed the remaining stored value in the card (essentially a debit card for copy machines). Once I figured out how the monetary value was encoded on the card, in no time at all we were using the school copy machines as if they were our own. Well, we were paying tuition, so in a sense all the facilities of the university could be seen as shared assets. Besides, I was providing a valuable community service just by editing, writing, and publishing this newspaper. It took a lot of time each week, which for a kid in an advanced premed program who was also running a company on the side, was not a commodity I had in abundance. Still, the paper was fun, and I have a way of sticking with things regardless of the hardships involved so long as they hold my attention. When the fun in the top of the hourglass runs out, my focus shifts elsewhere.

Interlude: Japan in the Bubble Years

As I've mentioned, I started visiting Japan before I was old enough to remember it, and I went to see my grandmother quite often from then on. We had Japanese exchange students living in our home, and my parents used to throw parties for other Japanese students in the community, which is where I learned to speak more fluently and hone my mahjong skills. I never thought all that much about my Japanese cultural identity. There were lots of Japanese-American families in California, and Japanese food, language, and culture was just part of my upbringing. Not the only part by a long shot, but it was always present, and there was no special reason to think about it as something special or unusual.

That changed a little when I was in high school. Sometime in 1986, the value of the yen began to rise against the dollar, and Japanese companies suddenly discovered that they could not only buy American goods but also buy the companies that produced them. Over the next few years, the U.S. trade surplus with Japan shot up and Japanese merger and acquisition (M&A) activity in the States went through the roof. Both trends became causes of major concern (or at least great sound bites) for several U.S. politicians. A wave of Japan-bashing followed. Loyal employees of Detroit car manufacturers were in big trouble if they drove to work in the family Toyota or Honda. Signs on the parking lots said NO JAPANESE CARS ALLOWED! After a scandal involving a subsidiary of Toshiba, some congressmen gathered on the steps of the U.S. Capitol, sledgehammers in hand, and smashed a big Toshiba boom box cassette player in front of eager TV cameras.

Watching all of this insanity play out on TV and in the papers, I became more conscious of my Japanese heritage. Now I actually felt proud to be Japanese. A lot of what was going on in Japan, especially in technical fields, was really cool. I decided I wanted to visit Japan, not simply hang out in Okinawa with my relatives, but go to Tokyo for a summer and see what it was like, find out what makes Japan tick. My mother mentioned this to a well-connected friend of hers, and he asked me what kinds of things I was interested in. Of course, I said computers and software, and he said he had a friend with some connections in that area. One thing led to another, and soon I was invited to work as a summer intern at a small, owner-run software company in Ueno, a big, drab, older section of Tokyo.

The company was nothing to write home about. It had about 200 employees and was not exactly a start-up, but in true Japanese fashion it existed to supply goods to a larger firm way up the food chain. In this case, the big company doing the ordering was electronics giant NEC.

This little firm's main job was to change signal switching equipment from analog to the new digital standard called Integrated Services Digital Network (ISDN). Japan's national telephone service, NTT, was pushing ISDN service as the Next Big Thing, even installing ISDN ports in phone booths all over the country (for the millions of people who would undoubtedly want to carry a laptop computer into a phone booth, of course), and NEC was one of the biggest parts suppliers to the phone company—and not just computers.

So part of NEC was, in effect, a subcontractor for NTT, and the company I worked for was a subcontractor for NEC. We were pretty far down the food chain, but because the work we were doing was related to ISDN, this little company had a steady stream of orders. I got a chance to do a lot of programming there, which was exactly what I wanted. I also got a chance to show my stuff. For example, because the company was a supplier to NEC, we had mostly NEC computers to work with. There was a big Fujitsu machine in the office, which was hardly ever used. Having some experience with the NEC system already, I decided to take a look at the Fujitsu, which turned out to be considerably faster. With some effort, I managed to port the slow C compiler on the NEC machine over to the Fujitsu, where it ran much, much faster. No one had ever thought of that—after all, it would be wrong to do NEC work on a Fujitsu machine, right? That was one of my first lessons in how the American approach to a simple problem, what would later be called out-of-the-box thinking, could easily trump the rigid groupthink of Japanese corporations. In any case, my programming resulted in speeding up some of the very important but time-consuming work. At small subcontracting companies, where time really is money, a big boost in efficiency does not go unnoticed.

The owner of the company knew I was not just another dumb intern, and he treated me well. He invited me to sit in on some of his business meetings. Of course I didn't say anything, just kept my mouth shut and eyes and ears open, and in the process I learned a lot about day-to-day business in Japan.

Actually, the thing I remember most about that summer was not my brilliant programming but my stupid planning. As I said, the dollar was dropping steadily against the yen, and prior to my trip I had estimated my living expenses based on what I knew, which was dollars. On top of the depreciating currency, I had never lived on my own in Japan (or anywhere else for that matter), so I had very little idea of what living costs in Tokyo were like. The period that I chose to do my intern visit happened to be right in the middle of what is known as the bubble era, the short-lived asset bubble that drove stock, land, and other prices through the roof (this is the period when the land under the Imperial Palace was estimated to be worth more than the entire state of California, and Ginza real estate was selling for the equivalent of $100,000 per square foot). At that moment, Tokyo was ranked as the world's most expensive city to live in.

The result was that young William Saito, who was accustomed to delicious, home-cooked food, a house full of people, and a swimming pool, was suddenly occupying a lonely garret in Oi-machi, an unattractive area in Tokyo's Shinagawa Ward several train stops from the software company up in Ueno, with no home cooking and no one to talk to. I had hardly unpacked my suitcase when I realized that I was broke and alone and had no relatives nearby to help me out. I was eating *onigiri* rice balls from the local convenience store and hanging out at the cheapest fast food joints I could find.

Fortunately, during my early teenage years I had mastered the only form of combat that could help to keep me alive in this vast, impersonal concrete jungle. Yes, I'm talking about mahjong. The Japanese exchange students we'd entertained at home loved to play the game, and over the years I grew to enjoy it. I have said many times since that mahjong actually helped improve my negotiating skills, my ability to read people's faces, even my pattern recognition skills. But here, on the streets of Tokyo, my mahjong ability had a much more practical use. One night, someone at the office took me out to a mahjong parlor in Ueno just for fun, and I quickly realized that some people played the game for money. Actually, the seedy areas around the big train stations in Tokyo are full of third-floor, walk-up mahjong parlors and smoky basement mahjong parlors, and *lots* of people are playing for money. It wasn't like getting paid for programming, but as an intern I had no salary, and a guy's got to eat. So I started going up to Uguisudani, an even shabbier part of town than Ueno, to hit the mahjong halls after work. I discovered they have *chahan* (fried rice) and all sorts of other cheap food you can eat right there, so the mahjong parlor became a good place to hang out. Also, as I'd managed to pick up some real countrified Japanese dialects from the exchange students back home, I found that I could communicate easily with the various strata of society that I met after dark in those gaming parlors.

By counting the cards (actually plastic or ivory tiles) and doing the probability calculations in my head, in short order I was winning a lot more than I lost. Sometimes I felt as though I was robbing people, but I never let it get out of hand. Mahjong halls are basically a fun place where people go to have a good time, not to fight or cause trouble. Also, it's important to remember that these parlors are not Las Vegas casinos; we weren't playing for thousands of dollars or anything like that. Even when I was winning, I wasn't making any big money. Far from it. All it meant was that I had a couple of bills in my pocket instead of nothing, and that in itself was a big deal. I didn't go to play every night, and I didn't bet all the time, but even so, mahjong probably saved my life during that period.

To stretch my meager budget, I used to visit the *tachigui* (stand-up eatery) *soba* stands, one of the cheapest meals in town, on a regular basis, and I still remember hanging out at the local Yoshinoya, a fast food chain specializing in cheap but stomach-filling cuisine. What they call beef bowl in English is shredded beef of dubious origins, covered with some tasty sauce and spread over a bowl of warm rice. When I had some mahjong winnings in my pocket, I'd really splurge—that is, I'd order the egg topping, which must have cost an extra 50 cents at the time, and that's how I knew it was a really special day. Even now, decades later, I still enjoy the "beef bowl with egg option" from time to time, and every now and then I astonish luncheon companions by suggesting we pop in to the local Yoshinoya for a bite. It never fails to bring back memories of my first experience of living on my own in Tokyo.

In sum, work was okay, and the occasional after-work card games were fun, too, but my solo lifestyle was anything but enjoyable. I caught a couple of bad colds during my short internship, which meant I had to stay at home by myself for a few days each time. No one to talk to and nothing to do in an empty one-room apartment. It was like being sick in a solitary confinement. Not my happiest hour by any means. When I was feeling a little better I'd go down to the nearby *konbini* (convenience store) for sustenance. There was a girl working there who took one look at me and knew I was a thousand calories short of the minimum daily requirement of anything. Fortunately, Japanese law requires all the convenience stores to throw out every bit of food that has passed its sell-by date, which means a truckload of sandwiches, *bento* boxes, and *onigiri* rice balls go into the garbage every night. The girl who worked the night shift would always give me a wink and a small bag full of food to keep me going. Between my gambling at mahjong and the angel behind the counter, I managed to keep body and soul together.

Translating Success into Failure

It took me seven years to finish the Biomedical Sciences program at UCR and the companion program at UCLA. To me, the exciting part wasn't that I was going to get to be a doctor in only seven years, or that I got to take all my premed courses and then transition directly into a top-class medical program and intern at a major hospital (Harbor UCLA Medical Center). In fact, all of that seemed relatively unimportant. Since I always finish what I start, I did complete the program and got my M.D., but that was the end of my medical career. All that studying, training, and interning was ultimately background noise while Tas and I worked on the thing that mattered most to us—turning I/O Software into a real business.

In many ways, it already was a real business, just not the kind of business either of us dreamed of. Our success in porting American software to Japanese computers had put us on the radar for companies interested in that kind of work. We started getting more and more orders to port software so that it would run on the NEC 9801 series machines and to localize it, which means translate the software so that all of its on-screen text appears in correct Japanese, and in addition we were expected to translate the software manuals and all the other documentation. That's a lot of work—both heavy programming work and tons of labor-intensive translation work for our English-to-Japanese translation team. The work kept coming. Everything was great.

For a while, that is. But I thrive on a steady diet of challenges. When things start to get too routine, I go back to the refrigerator to see what else is available. Our obvious success in supplying NEC and other firms with localized software was okay, but something about it was starting to rub me the wrong way. First, the programming still held some challenges, but nothing compared to the mountains we had scaled with Norton Utilities or some of our first attempts to write code for the 9801. Most of the problems that came up were things we could solve easily, or they were problems that our programming staff (still just friends from our respective colleges who were helping us out) could handle on their own. That's *Alarm number one for me:* the work coming in was not terribly challenging. Imagine if every Rubik's cube you picked up was only three steps away from being solved, or every crossword you looked at had only one or two easy words left to fill in. You'd get pretty tired of that in no time flat and start looking for something else.

Alarm number two was internal: Our company was growing, but not the way we wanted it to. Instead of rooms full of programmers seated at state-of-the-art computer terminals, we had a room full of translators juggling dictionaries and software manuals. Even then, they were not working all the time. There was lots of down time. Imagine the culture gap between the gang of nerdy software guys and the growing army of chatty Japanese women thrown together for a project that doesn't occupy all of their time. This was not a good combination. I will be the first to admit that I am not good at managing people who were obviously more interested in talking with colleagues than in doing some boring translations, which didn't leverage their other skills. The HR side of a company is not my strong suit, and even with the relatively manageable number of staff we had to deal with, I could already tell that this was not going to work for me. As a business model, I began to realize that a system that didn't geometrically scale was not sustainable.

To make matters worse, I/O Software was getting a reputation as a translation company. Need that floppy disk and those two thick manuals converted into Japanese? You should ring up this little outfit in LA I've heard about. . . . Tas and I didn't have any clear vision of where we were going; we had no specific dream to achieve and no roadmap for how we would move forward, but we definitely knew what we did *not* want, and that included being known as a translation company. We both knew we weren't really creating anything, just converting programs that someone else had written. Of course, we learned a lot in the process, and it provided a steady income stream, which we needed, but the one thing it was missing was the one thing we needed most—a real, meaningful challenge.

To be fair, this business that I was growing impatient with and yearning to break away from could have turned into a very successful operation. Had we stayed with it and grown the company strategically, digitized every aspect of the translation process, farmed out work over the Internet when that became possible, managed our expanding translation staff and mined both our Japanese and U.S. connections for a steady stream of clients, we might have built the leading localization firm in the industry. The problem was that we didn't want to be the number one localization company; we didn't even want to be the number one firm porting American software to Japanese computers. We wanted something of our own, something creative and challenging, which this no longer was.

When I talk to people today about this major episode in my business history, I always refer to it as my second failure. As you will see, I think failure is a badge of honor for an entrepreneur. The old saying, "learn to fail or fail to learn" is very true when you're trying to start up a business. You learn from your mistakes—and many failures aren't even your mistakes; the market shifts overnight, or banks pull out of your financing or any of a thousand things that are out of your control can go wrong, but in the end, if you're the CEO, it goes on your resume as a failure. So I did not hesitate to refer to our years of porting and localizing software as a failure in the best sense—because we learned a lot, about markets, about clients, about dealing with Japanese business, and about ourselves as managers. If failing can teach us something valuable about our own strengths and weaknesses, then we should all welcome failures. It's only a milestone on the way toward something better.

TAKEAWAY: Use Language to Broaden Your Perspective

This always puzzles young CEOs whenever I talk about it, because it seems so unrelated to either technology or management. However, I am convinced that learning another language is important to help you open up your mind. Not just different words, because language is not about words. Language is a different way of looking at the world; language is perspective, and language is culture. If you want to run a business entirely within the state lines of Idaho, you may not need to learn a different language. But if you think you're going to export your ideas and products to other nations, you will come up against the problems of culture sooner than you think. I'm not saying you should learn one new language so that you can do business in that language; that would be almost as limiting as speaking only English. Instead, I believe that learning a foreign language (and the more foreign the better) is a way of opening up your mind to different ideas, and it helps you see things from another perspective.

As you begin to understand different cultures from the inside, you gain a new viewpoint on your own culture, and you start to grasp the problems of operating in a global environment. Nobody can teach you that in the abstract. When you first discover that there are words that don't exist in your language, it's a surprise. When you discover there are ideas that don't exist in your language, it's a shock. When you realize that some of those ideas are just as valid as the ones you were brought up with, it opens your eyes. That is what people mean when they talk about a CEO with a global perspective, not just somebody who reads the news from around the world and feels well informed.

In spite of our ethnic melting pot and our so-called international perspective, the U.S. suffers because we don't see any need to speak another language. We miss out on those multiple perspectives that many Europeans, Asians, and others take for granted. Even some of our best companies, limited by the local perspective of their management, are constantly trying to impose their ways of thinking onto other cultures and then wondering why they don't succeed. We all know that business is becoming more global every day, but it is the companies that learn how to operate smoothly on the local level that grow the most.

Chapter 5

Learning from Failure

There was one really important thing that came out of our localization business. Somewhere along the line we had the brilliant idea that we should be able to print this stuff out. We wanted to output documents, such as the source code and the report output from our software, and other files that contained Japanese. There was only one little problem; we didn't have a Japanese language printer. So we hauled some big, bulky, and very expensive printers over from Japan. Two problems arose: first, there were no consumables available in the States, so every time we needed to change toner we had to order something from Japan, and second, the output quality wasn't very good to begin with. These were not cheap printers.

However, we were on a roll with this porting and localization business, and when I got in that mood I look at as-yet-untried technological challenges like an overconfident young sailor looking out at the Pacific, thinking, "It can't go on very far; I could sail across this in no time." This is an attitude that would come back to haunt me well into the future. So, loaded with confidence and a healthy dose of hubris, we decided that we would not only design a Japanese-capable printer in-house, but make it a PostScript-compatible printer. Of course, there were no PostScript printers capable of doing Japanese characters at that time, even in Japan, but we weren't going to let a minor detail like that stand in our way.

This was stupid on at least three fronts: (1) We were going into hardware without knowing anything about it. Most software programmers look at hardware as something like stable or solidified software (no, I'm not kidding), so there's a blissful ignorance about hardware stuff, usually summed up as, "Yeah, but how hard can *that* be?" (2) We didn't realize that Adobe PostScript didn't fully support Japanese at the time, so we were trying to do the truly impossible. (3) We didn't realize that if you wanted to use Japanese with PostScript, you had to purchase very specific Japanese fonts for it. With English, there are zillions of fonts, some expensive and a lot free, and if you don't like what's out there, you can "draw" your own. But for Japanese, it would be a massive effort for a skilled team to "draw" over 20,000 complex characters and then develop the scaling equations for each one. The result is that PostScript controlled a very tight market, and people who wanted to use that system had to buy a set of good, but very expensive fonts.

One of the biggest obstacles, but in retrospect the most valuable lesson in the whole thing for us, was working on the device driver (DD), a small but crucial part of any hardware/software system, and something that would become our bread-and-butter very soon. In general, a device driver is an interesting bit of software that sits between the computer's operating system (OS) and whatever hardware the machine is connected to, including printers, scanners, CD-ROM drives, and so on. Think of the disk you install when you buy a printer, camera, or iPod. The device driver essentially takes high-level commands from the OS or from applications running on the OS, and relays them in a series of low-level, machine-specific instructions that the peripheral hardware can understand. Think of a device driver as a specialized translator that lets the "management" inside the computer talk to the various "staff" who have specific jobs to do. In that sense it is a key component in the smooth communication between a computer and its external hardware.

Since on-board memory in the printer was expensive to include, and we needed to manage large Kanji font files, we had to attach an external hard disk to the printer to hold the megabytes of fonts. That meant learning how to tell the printer to retrieve and scale fonts on the fly from the hard disk. We needed the PC to be able to talk to the printer and the printer to be able to talk to the hard disk. For a couple of software engineers, it seemed like hardware hell, but we sure learned device drivers inside-out.

As I've said, learning to design and build a printer is a challenge; learning to build a nonexistent printer that handles a non-Roman alphabet, "speaks" PostScript, and will function as well or better than commercial products designed by gigantic Japanese electronics companies was an enormous task. Still, after much hard work (and a lot of cursing and sleepless nights), we built the damn thing. And it was pretty good, if I do say so myself. It included an external 20 MB hard drive to store the Japanese fonts, which, by the way, cost more than the rest of the printer components combined, and it ran quite well. It was reasonably fast for the day, and the output was clean. Of course, it didn't take too long for us to come to the painful realization that we'd just created a white elephant—it was great for printing out translated user manuals and such for I/O Software, but as a commercial product it was going nowhere. We couldn't sell our printers to NEC, or to Fujitsu or Toshiba or anyone else, because every big company in the Japanese computer field already had a whole line of their own equipment, so there really was no market for our new no-name product.

Worse yet, we had used one of the best laser engines on the market for our prototype. It was made by a big Japanese company that produced engines for many, if not most, of the big printers on the market (including some American manufacturers). When we inquired about buying a few more engines to get this printer business started, they informed us that the minimum order was 1,000 units. Since we didn't know how to sell even 10 printers and had no outside financing, that was out of the question. However, in accomplishing another impossible feat of engineering we had surprised even ourselves, and while we were patting ourselves on the back we had to admit this was Failure Number Three.

Drivers of Success

One advantage we had was our ongoing relationship with Microsoft, which went back to our early NEC days. Back then, Microsoft was still in the process of becoming the big corporate behemoth it is today. I was going in and out of Microsoft's offices all the time, talking to their engineers and exchanging information. I explained that one of our problems in dealing with NEC was the much-advertised but poorly executed Windows compatibility of the 9801. To do our job porting U.S. software to the NEC machine, we needed to see the source code to Windows. Even back then, asking to see the source code for Windows was a bit like asking the Queen of England if you could just borrow the crown jewels for a weekend. And yet, despite its reputation in some quarters as a ruthless competitor, Microsoft gave us free access to the code, which was pretty much unheard of.

So as we looked around for a viable growth path to get the company out of the localization business and into something meaty, challenging, and hopefully profitable, we came to see our experience with hardware device drivers and our almost unique inside knowledge of the Windows operating system as a good business opportunity. We made contact with several Japanese companies, makers of CD-ROM drives, printers, scanners, disk drives, mice, trackballs, anything you can think of, and we offered to do Windows-compatible device drivers. That became our bread and butter for a while. We got to see just about every new peripheral that came out, because we had to write that critical piece of software that connected it to the computer. This was very cool. We're a small American company but getting almost all our orders from Japanese firms with cutting-edge products that we got to play with early on. At one point I said that if you saw a product from any major Japanese electronics maker that connected to a computer, we probably designed the device driver for it.

The problem with this critical piece of software is that it's invisible. Users don't see glossy magazine ads for "Sexy Device Driver ver. 4.1" and neither OS developers nor hardware makers pay much attention to them. In fact, software (OS) people think of the device driver as the family butler, a not-very-bright functionary who deals with outside guests and hired help, while hardware (peripheral) people aren't sure the butler can be trusted to properly convey simple instructions in a consistent and understandable way. In short, the device driver is an orphan, and working in that particular niche is a totally thankless job. When everything is running smoothly, no one even knows the DD team exists. You are a tiny, insignificant part of some other, much bigger and more important development team. But when something goes wrong, and something *always* went wrong back then, the spotlight shines on you from both sides, and suddenly everyone is shouting at the device driver team: *How come you guys screwed up?*

Even at this stage—the early 1990s—PCs were not very stable or reliable. They would spontaneously reboot or crash all the time, and the blue screen of death was more familiar to many users than the Microsoft start-up logo. Nor was the hardware all that much more reliable, which meant the device driver people were caught between a rock and a hardware place. For example, let's say we were writing the device driver for some famous maker's disk drive. They might set up a big demo presentation featuring this new drive only to have the system crash right in front of a room full of journalists or, worse yet, stock analysts. What happens? The head of their group is screaming mad, and he wants somebody's scalp. Of course, nobody is going to get on the phone to Microsoft and claim that their people screwed up. And no engineer at a big Japanese electronics company is going to suggest that his own colleagues might have screwed up. So who's left? Obviously, those half-wits doing the device drivers. "Tell them to rewrite the thing pronto, top to bottom, make sure they get it *right* this time, and have it delivered here yesterday. And while you're at it, tell our legal department to notify them we're ready to take them to court for this kind of incompetence."

The result was that we had clients screaming at us constantly, and a few did threaten to sue us. Come to think of it, a lot of them threatened to sue us, and they did it (threaten, not sue—we were never sued) pretty often. We felt like a punching bag, a little company caught between much bigger players in the computer arena. We did good work, and of course sometimes we made mistakes, but on more than one occasion we located the real source of the problem either in the OS source code or in the command structure of the hardware. Unfortunately, the device drivers ended up being the bubble gum and bailiwick part of the peripherals attached to the computer. All the same, saying, "It's not our fault," and pointing the finger one way or another doesn't win you any friends. We could stand working on invisible products, but could not live with a bottle of antacids in the desk drawer, always hoping that the next client wouldn't take us to court whenever some product did not perform as advertised.

We learned a great deal from making device drivers, but we also knew that it wasn't what we ultimately wanted to do any more than being a localization company. In both cases, we knew that if we persevered and learned our craft better and better, and if we strategically expanded the scale of our business and our client base, we could build a much bigger, more successful company. And in both cases we knew it wasn't what we wanted.

Let's call that Failure Number Four.

Interlude: The CEO Is a Cop

One night late in November of 1993 a couple of burglars broke into our office. The crooks knew that no one would be around our building over Thanksgiving weekend, and even though our office was up on the third floor, they didn't seem to have any trouble breaking in or lugging some heavy computer equipment down to a van parked outside. They stole mostly PCs, as many as they could carry (thank God they didn't take our servers—that would really have caused problems). When I found out, I was in shock. Not only had the company never had any kind of criminal problem, but I had grown up in an environment that now seemed a little like Disneyland. The worst thing that had ever happened to me was getting my wallet stolen in elementary school. This was a whole new world, and I didn't like it. I think I surprised myself, because instead of being frightened by the break-in, I got really angry. I was angry that some jerks had broken into our office, which in a real sense was more like a home than a workplace—this was where I spent way too much of my time and did my work and had fun, and this whole thing was something cool and exciting that I had created from scratch. It was a violation for some money-hungry creeps to break in here and just take whatever they wanted.

I called the Riverside Police Department (RPD) right away, and they came over, looked at everything, took lots of notes, and shook their heads. "Sorry to tell you this, Mr. Saito," one of them said, "But the chances of getting your PCs back are pretty slim. Once they're gone, the people who took 'em will sell 'em fast, collect the cash, and move on. I hope you're insured against theft."

I wasn't. In any case, it wasn't the dollar value of the equipment that mattered, but the data inside. Some of it was backed up elsewhere; some of it wasn't. Lost data means lost time and lots of work that has to be redone. Of course, it's not the end of the world, but it's a big pain in the butt. I was getting even angrier.

Then a few days later the police called us back. "We just caught a pair breaking into another office and stealing PCs. We arrested them and impounded all their stolen merchandise. Maybe your computers are in there with the rest. Why don't you come down and have a look?" That sounded good. I imagined a big table or two in a brightly lit room down at the police station with maybe a dozen or so PCs lined up, just the way you see evidence lined up on tables for press conferences on TV about captured drugs or guns. When we got to the police impound warehouse we were in for a real surprise—there were *lots* of PCs there. I could have opened a retail store with all that stuff and not needed new inventory for a while. Even so, it didn't take too long digging through all that equipment to find our machines. Of course, we hadn't labeled them "Property of I/O Software" or anything like that, because we never even thought about the possibility of them getting stolen. Still, we knew our machines when we saw them, and we pointed them out to the cops. "These here are ours, and that one over there, and that one on top of that other pile."

"How do you know?" came the reply.

"Well, because we've worked with the machines about 20 hours of every day for the past year or two. We know every smudge and coffee stain on the boxes. They're ours."

"I'm sure you're right," the senior officer said, "But we can't just hand them over to you because you say so. If we do that, then anybody can come in here and pick out any equipment he likes and say, 'Hey, that's mine,' and maybe he's no more honest than the crooks who stole this stuff in the first place. You see my point?"

I saw his point. We needed to find some way to prove that our machines really were our machines.

So I decided to do a little investigative work.

It turned out that this couple (it was a boyfriend and girlfriend team, obviously working on the premise that larceny makes the heart grow fonder) were not entirely stupid. In fact, they were pretty smart. They ripped off good PCs and then immediately wiped the hard disks clean. They knew that the only thing that could positively identify those machines and connect them to specific owners was the data stored on the disk drives. So they reformatted every hard disk within 24 hours of liberating it from its original owner. If they were ever caught with the goods, they could simply say, "Hey, these are all our personal machines. We bought 'em at an auction. There's no data on any of the machines, so how can you say they belong to somebody else?" Which is exactly what they were doing. Remember, this was in the early 1990s, and neither cops nor crooks nor many other people were as savvy about computers as they are today. All of this looked pretty high tech to the Riverside Police Department.

Of course, I was not happy. Because of these two-bit burglars, we were wasting valuable time, we couldn't get our computers back and get them running again, and clearly a lot of people in the community were in the same situation. Worse yet, the cops didn't know what to do about it. So I convinced them to let me have access to one of our machines. It only took a minute to boot the thing up and run a utility program (ironically, it was Norton Utilities) that told me when the drive had last been formatted. Guess what? The drive on this machine—and all the other machines I told them were ours—were reformatted the day after we were robbed. It wasn't a smoking gun, but it was enough to convince the RPD that we had, in fact, identified our own machines. Then my natural instinct for community service kicked in, and I said, "You know, I could start up each one of these machines and do the same thing, tell you what day the computer was reformatted and from that information determine what day it was stolen. Then you could identify the stolen goods from each individual crime and get all this stuff back to its rightful owners."

The police were impressed. They said they'd be grateful if I could help them out, and so I did just what I'd promised. Within a short time they had located the owner of every single stolen computer. But that was just the beginning. The police asked me to testify in court about how I determined the dates of the thefts. I was still angry at the two thieves for breaking into my company, and as a result, I was only too happy to help out the police. I showed up in court and explained to the jury exactly what I'd found and how I'd done it. They understood, they were convinced, and they awarded the enterprising couple a matching set of His & Hers holiday suites in a nearby penitentiary. I was satisfied. Justice had been served, and I got my machines back. When the police called me some time later and asked if I would help out with a similar problem, I was glad to be of service. Pretty soon I became their go-to guy for IT-related crimes. That began my relationship with the RPD.

People have occasionally asked why I went out of my way to help the local police. After all, computer people have their own world, and cops have their own world, and the two seldom intersect. Moreover, I had a company to run and was not overburdened with too much free time. In other words, I needed to budget every minute of my time pretty well, and running down to the local police department to help out on cases that had nothing to do with me or I/O Software, and going to court to testify as an IT expert were probably not the best use of my time. But I enjoyed it, and I felt it was my duty to help out. Undoubtedly, all that training in socially meaningful activity and the spirit of volunteering that Damien High School had instilled in me had left its mark. To this day, I often overcommit my time and agree to help out all sorts of organizations simply because I have a hard time saying no. If people need me and ask me to do something I know I can do reasonably well and fairly quickly (like give a keynote speech or advise on some new project), I usually say yes. And I also preach what I practice, telling other individuals and groups how important the spirit of volunteering is, and how much better societies like Japan would be if they adopted it and inculcated it at an early age. So, the fathers at Damien did their job well.

The other thing that got me involved with the police in the first place and kept me involved with them long after was that, as I noted previously, I tend to get angry at people who knowingly break the law, especially if it causes other people to get hurt. What I didn't realize at the time I started helping out the local police department on a regular basis was that I would eventually move up the ladder of law enforcement and get a chance to go after a better (or worse) class of bad guys. In some ways, that break-in at I/O Software started me down a long road that would occupy a small but significant part of my time and energy each year, qualify a geek like me to use firearms, and work with various types of law enforcement agencies around the world. All of that would take several years, of course, but that first close encounter with neighborhood crime was a life-changing event for me.

There's a New Sheriff in Town. . . .

I continued working on and off with the Riverside police. I discovered that the charming little area where I'd set up my company was even then vying for the title of Methamphetamine Capital of America. There were meth dealers and meth labs all over the place. And the dealers were getting wise to the advantages of using PCs to create databases of their connections and customers and even record ongoing money transactions, some of which was thought to be used to fund terrorism. After the police arrested some guy, they'd get a warrant to examine his PC, and that's when I would get called in to help open and decode any encrypted files, or even a password-protected Excel file. If I could unlock a list of dealers, for example, it could not only help put the guy away for a long time, but also contribute to busting a whole ring of dealers.

So one day, after I'd helped RPD extract some crucial data from some drug boss's laptop, I had to go to court to testify. This time the defense pointed out that the computer and the data it held were evidence in the case. I had not only handled the evidence but had performed certain operations on it, and I was not a law enforcement officer, just a civilian advisor. Because of that technicality, my testimony and the evidence I had produced were judged inadmissible. The defendant (a real nasty piece of work) got 2 years behind bars when he should have received at least 10. I thought this was a shame; a serious threat to the welfare of our community would be back on the street again all too soon because my expert testimony was now ruled invalid. The cops said we're sorry, but that's how it goes. Other defense attorneys will use the same argument, and your testimony will be ruled inadmissible. I asked if the police didn't have some of their own IT people who could handle this job. They said sure, they hired people, but by the time they could get somebody well trained and up to speed on fairly sophisticated software stuff like the decryption of encrypted files, the guy would take his services to some big IT company who would pay him a lot more than what the RPD could afford. And the regular cops knew nothing about IT stuff. I was told that sometimes cops would find PCs at a crime scene and they would confiscate the monitors instead of the CPUs as evidence because they didn't know any better and that thing that looked like a little TV must be important. "Okay," I said, "this is a problem. You don't have people who can do this job, and you can't train them and hope to keep them (not back then anyway), so you need someone like me. But I'm off limits because I'm not a law enforcement officer, right?"

"Right."

"Okay," I said, "so what if I became a cop?"

That threw them. Do you know what you're suggesting? I did, and I said let's get on with it, because damn if I was going to let hardcore drug dealers walk away from prosecution because the police lacked the legal resources to put them behind bars.

In California, Peace Officer Standards Training (POST) is a 10-month basic program on weekends and some evenings, which at that time was required for every level of officer (I'm told there is now a special training program for reserve officers, but when I had to do it, there was only one big program for every sworn law enforcement officer in the State of California). The program was divided into three levels, running from the A course, which was the whole nine yards, the course that all the regular cops took, down to the C course, which was essentially for shopping mall guards and rent-a-cops. When you saw some of the guys who signed up for the C course, you couldn't help but think, "Half of these characters should be in jail, not in uniform," but I tell myself that appearances are often deceiving. Look at me—any ordinary person who saw me in training would swear that I was some kind of computer nerd, not a red-blooded, he-man all-American cop. So I did the full A-level course, which included doing the B and C courses. It meant putting in a lot of tough hours every weekend, and, believe me, it was grueling. I did lots of physical training, hand-to-hand combat, the whole thing. In addition, I had to take the PC 832 Arrest and Firearms Course, which meant I spent a lot of hours learning how to operate a Glock handgun (turns out I'm a pretty good shot, including with my less-dominant hand). When I finished the course, I passed the test, got myself sworn in, and became a licensed Peace Officer in the State of California.

Not long after I got my credentials, the cops busted some big-time meth producer and confiscated his PC. Inside was a database chock full of information on his main dealers and other customers, the cuts they're using, the ingredients, shipments, inventory in different locations—the kind of treasure trove of information that can wrap up a very big case and put a few scumbags away for 10 to 15 years. The dealers went to trial without breaking a sweat, secure in their knowledge that all of their data was encrypted and *nobody* was ever going to know what's in there. They calmly denied any knowledge of a database full of drug-related information. Then I got on the stand and read excerpts from the version I had just decoded and handed over to the prosecution. Believe me, the shock on the defendants' faces was worth all the pains of the whole 10-month course. Now that I was a LEO (law enforcement officer), and the chain of evidence was intact, my testimony was completely admissible.

This kind of activity continued for quite a while. I was still busy with the company, but when the Riverside PD needed me, I was happy to make time to help them out. I went on ride-alongs on the weekends, which opened my eyes to a whole new world that had been all around me but which I had never seen before. I got to see up close how the less fortunate (the bottom of the pyramid, or BoP) in our own society live, and it gave me a good perspective on work. Designing a new iPad or something is cool, I can't argue with that. But creating stuff only for the most affluent 5 percent of society is something you want to think about. There has to be some way, either through the technology itself or through your activities later on, that allows you to pay back something to society.

I enjoyed my work with the police—I mean, how often do you get to drive through your town at 100 mph with lights flashing and sirens wailing? Also, I had to requalify with firearms on a regular basis, but instead of picking on me because I was some weird computer geek, the regular cops and SWAT guys became my friends. They'd take me out into a field and let me shoot all sorts of special weapons, do live fire drills, armed role-playing scenarios, and more. Nine times out of ten, of course, my work was more mundane, usually cracking whatever kind of encryption (from primitive to fairly sophisticated) drug dealers were using to protect their data. Still, there's nothing I like better than solving a puzzle, especially when it's for a good cause. My work helping out the local police (and the lengths I was willing to go to in order to be sure my work met the chain of evidence rules) undoubtedly got talked about here and there in law enforcement circles. One cop tells another who mentions it to somebody in another town, and sooner or later someone other than local cops is listening to the story with interest.

I assume this is how the FBI learned about me and my company, and knew that they had a pretty good chance of getting full cooperation when they came knocking at our door that day. Although I fairly quickly connected their visit with the work I was doing for local law enforcement, not everyone in the company was aware of my extra-curricular activities, and I'm sure some people were shocked when those two big FBI agents showed up in our reception area.

Essentially, they wanted to know if I would be available to help them deal with IT-related issues (including breaking file encryption) for cases that might come up in the future. It was the same thing I was doing for the RPD, but at the federal level. The request came from Quantico, and it meant that I would be working not only on cases for the LA field office, but on all sorts of projects. You already know what my answer was.

It might seem strange that the FBI would need or even want to solicit the opinion of someone in the private sector like me, but at the time it was necessary. In the mid-1990s there were new IT firms popping up like crabgrass, so many start-ups and venture companies and firms no one had ever heard of, there was no way any government agency, including the IRS, could keep track of them. Plus, the World Wide Web had just been created, which meant the Internet was just about to explode into a wild, untested global phenomenon with lots of potential for abuse, and the FBI was grossly understaffed in the whole IT area back then. Just as the local police department, in the 1990s the feds couldn't hire, train, and hold onto enough good technical staff. People must have discovered that having "Federal Bureau of Investigation" on their resumes helped them to get hired elsewhere, and those who jumped to the private sector were probably well rewarded. So right at that time—the mid- to late 1990s—there was a growing tidal wave of both new companies and new technologies, and the FBI found itself a little behind the curve and in a perpetual Whack-a-Mole. There just weren't enough people to focus on all the real issues and possible problems that needed to be examined. Thus, it made sense to turn to private industry for help, which is why they came to people like me.

Just to set the record straight, that was a long time ago. The FBI is a whole lot more sophisticated these days, and so are the people they're trying to catch. The Internet has given birth to a whole new range of criminal activity, making it more difficult to track down and arrest the perpetrators. Fortunately, there are lots of good people both inside and outside the Bureau working to put the bad guys where they belong and looking for ways to make it more difficult to commit certain kinds of crimes.

TAKEAWAY: Failure Is the Key to Success!

Einstein famously said, "Anyone who's never made a mistake has never tried anything new," and I couldn't agree more. I tell all the young venture people I meet (and that's a lot of people) that it's important to make mistakes. This is a mantra with me. I say, if you're not making mistakes, you're not trying hard enough. Making mistakes is an educational process and as such, it should not be penalized. In fact, when I am interviewing some young CEO who wants funding from my personal venture fund, one of the things I always ask is, "Tell me about one of your major failures. Tell me why it happened and what you learned from it."

Why is failure so important to success? Because failing at something you care about helps you to know what your boundaries are as a person. It allows you to be comfortable with mistakes and failures, and to learn from them. When you're very young, how do you learn to walk? By making lots of mistakes, failing all the time, and getting back up. As we get older, we become self-conscious, we worry too much about how things look, and in some ways we become conservative even when we are still quite young.

Learning should be a continual process. Learning what it means to fail is part of discovering what life is like outside of your comfort zone, and that's important. Always working inside your comfort zone is not learning, just repeating what you already know. There is a Japanese expression about trying to reach beyond your grasp, but the Japanese meaning is negative: don't aim too high. I say just the opposite: aim high, aim for a home run, and learn as you go along. What we call stretch goals in the West are critical. It is important to aspire to something big, something challenging, and maybe something that other people say is impossible. I remind people that if a goal is too simple, the path ahead of you is short and well marked. That doesn't leave you much room to be creative. With a big, far-off goal, the road is not so clear, which means you are free to come up with a new creative process to reach that goal. Going into the unknown forces you to be innovative, and that's essential.

Will you make mistakes along the way? Of course you will. Does that mean you give up? Does that mean you are not fit to reach that goal? Certainly not. Aiming high implies you will make mistakes, but entrepreneurs take that for granted. You don't even think about mistakes; you just do the best job you can, and when you bump into something, you back up and go around it.

Failure is what you call someone who quits, or someone who doesn't try at all. When you get back up and learn from your mistake, that's called education.

Chapter 6

Developing for Toshiba (Camera Obscura)

T hose of you who owned a VHS recorder way back when may remember seeing or even owning one of Toshiba's popular VHS machines. But those who remember the great Beta-VHS War of the 1980s may remember that Toshiba's first machines were all in Beta format. One reason was that Toshiba belonged to a powerful industrial *keiretsu* group, and one of the group's up-and-coming stars was Sony. So when Sony released its Beta decks in the 1970s, group partner Toshiba was almost duty-bound to get on board, a situation that became less and less tenable as the JVC-led (Victor Company of Japan) VHS camp gobbled up market share.

I'm bringing up this bit of corporate history because losing the video format wars hurt Sony financially, and Toshiba seemed to gain in strength once it decoupled from its fraternal obligations to Sony. At the time that we were deep into the device driver business, Toshiba was as much a powerhouse in the laptop PC market as NEC was in desktops. Like other giant electronics makers, Toshiba controlled the entire vertical market for parts and assembly of its key products. In other words, every part was either made by a Toshiba subsidiary or by a trusted subcontractor who produced it to Toshiba's specifications. One of those trusted suppliers for key components was Sony, which was trying to recover profitability by subcontracting hardware design and development for all its rivals. At that time, Sony was developing cameras, CD-ROM drives, and various other products for firms such as Toshiba, Fujitsu, NEC, and Hitachi. I think almost everyone's CD-ROMs were made by Sony and licensed to the brand name under which they would be sold (a process now known as OEM). Some greybeards out there may remember that one of the hot products of that era was Apple's new PowerBook line of laptop computers, and the very first model (the 100) was largely outsourced to . . . you guessed it, Sony.

At this point, Toshiba was developing a new, high-end line of laptops called the Tecra that they expected would make a very big splash in the PC market. They wanted every bell and whistle on this new model to wow critics and users alike. One of their ideas was truly eye-catching—to have a high-resolution video camera that you could clip on above the screen to capture images of the user. Of course, attaching a camera to a computer was nothing new. There were plenty of cameras that connected to a computer, but they all had to be connected through the parallel port, which was originally developed to connect printers. There were a couple of neat technical things that made a parallel port useful for cameras, but ultimately it was a clunky, low-performance solution, because the video data had to go through the main data bus on the CPU, which meant that the throughput was limited. Video signals produce lots of data, and you can't transfer that much data over the bus and still have the CPU available to do other things, like keep your operating system (OS running). Video-related system crashes were commonplace, and when you did get a steady video signal, the picture looked jerky (you all know what really bad Internet video looks like today; imagine something about half that good or worse).

Toshiba developed a whole new approach, something they called zoomed video, or ZV for short, which would completely bypass the old parallel port. They created a special ZV port, which connected to a unique ZV bus, and the combination allowed data from a real-time device (like a video camera) to feed at reasonably high speed directly to the video memory. No more parallel port, no more slow internal connections, no more unwatchable, jerky video. At least that was the theory.

I/O Software was one of the companies working on that project for Toshiba, and we were involved in the design of the ZV system. Toshiba desperately wanted to make a big bang with the Tecra at a COMDEX show in 1996, so they hired us, the device driver experts, to act as the interface between their own hardware people developing the ZV bus, the Sony team that was developing the miniaturized charge-coupled device (CCD) camera, and Microsoft, because if the OS died while all of this heavy-duty processing was going on, the user would experience a system crash every time he tried to turn on the video. Once again, we were stuck in the middle. How do we get a Sony camera to work with the Windows OS running on a Toshiba laptop, and get the whole package ready to demo smoothly at COMDEX, which was right around the corner? Aside from the lack of time, the difficulties of being in one country while our client was in another, and the obvious enormity of the programming task before us, this was a totally novel experience.

As you can imagine, I was flying to Japan all the time, and my once-rudimentary business language skills were now honed in hundreds of endless, smoke-filled meetings. The place where I spent the most time was Sony, because they had the key component that was going to impress the audience—if it worked. And true to form, Sony's engineers had developed a really great little camera to use with the Toshiba laptops. It was sleek, elegant, and, in my opinion at least, very cool. Nobody else had such a small, easy-to-use clip-on back then, and it connected to that new, high-speed ZV port. It was exactly what Toshiba had in mind.

Unfortunately, it was performing terribly. To make the video look smooth, Sony wanted at least 24 frames per second (fps), which was standard for film and TV, and ideally, 30 fps, which was about to become the new digital video (DV) standard that Sony would help to promote. Yet for some reason this hot little camera was only delivering a lousy 4 fps on the prototypes of the laptop they were testing. Now, 4 fps is truly awful, unwatchable video. Everyone was puzzled. How could the throughput be so bad when the camera was connecting through this new, high-speed ZV port, bypassing the main bus, and writing directly to video memory? In theory, the video data throughput (speed) should have been the same as the speed of the camera's CCD chip, which was a blistering 60 fps. They only needed half that (30) or less, which should be simple to do. So why were they getting 4? Something was very wrong. Sony thought the problem lay on Toshiba's side; Toshiba thought differently, and Toshiba was paying the bills.

This is where I stuck my nose in, as I usually do, and in some ways that decision started me and I/O Software down a long and challenging road that changed our fates and fortunes.

I knew that the ZV hardware was working, and I trusted that Sony's camera was top-notch, so the problem had to be somewhere else. Based on our experience of the past few years, I asked the Sony people if they had developed the device driver for the camera in-house or if it was being done by some other firm. Just as I'd suspected, they had sub-contracted the device driver to a little company in another part of Tokyo. Tas and I went to check on that firm, and then we reported back to Sony that this one crucial element in the process might be the problem. If the device driver wasn't performing as it should, the camera couldn't communicate efficiently with the computer. Sony was getting desperate at this point, and their engineers' response was essentially, "If you think you can do better, go do it. But do it fast."

We flew back to the States and immediately went to work. Within about two weeks we had completely rewritten the device driver, and it worked beautifully. I took it back to Japan and showed it to the guys at Sony. They couldn't believe it. Just two weeks ago their little pride-and-joy video camera produced images on the Toshiba laptop that would make a normal person seasick. Now it was running smoothly at 30 fps, the picture looked great, and the OS wasn't crashing. Everyone was blown away. We had, in effect, come out of nowhere and saved the project. The Japanese equivalent of, "Who *are* those guys?" echoed through the halls of Sony's Shinagawa campus for weeks afterward. We became legends inside the company, and every other department wanted us to write their device drivers.

Were we the geniuses they thought we were? Of course not. We had the advantage of coming in fresh, with no preconceived ideas about the product or the right way to design something for Sony. We weren't even thinking outside the box because we didn't have a clue about where the box was in the first place, so we just did what we thought needed to be done, and in the process we hit a home run.

Although Toshiba was technically paying the bills back then, this episode brought us much, much closer to Sony. Not only did I/O Software develop an inside channel for Sony-related work, but I became more involved, both personally and professionally with the company. As time went on, there were more than a few people who viewed me, the boy wonder who had helped to save their reputation, as a future executive of the company (I was offered CxO level jobs on several occasions). Tas was not one of those people. He knew that, just like himself, I was born to be an independent operator, for better or worse. We had experienced our share of tough times, but we'd never once thought to throw in the towel and go get regular paychecks from some big, stable company. We told ourselves that if we'd wanted to be employees of Microsoft, we'd already be working for Microsoft, and if we'd wanted to be employees of NEC or Toshiba or Sony, we could have made that happen. But that's not what we wanted. Our personal goals always revolved around creating something cool, attention-grabbing, and ultimately meaningful with our skills, and developing and marketing it ourselves, not wearing suits every day and working nine to five in some giant corporation that could tell us what to do and how long to do it and ultimately would take ownership of whatever we'd developed. I'm not saying that's a bad life or that people shouldn't work for big companies, but it's not the life I wanted, no matter how big or famous the firm or how impressive the title they might offer me. My geeky I/O Software business card was the only one I planned to carry.

In short, I was delighted that we had—through brainpower, hard work, and luck—earned a place as one of Sony's most trusted partner companies. There would certainly be ways to maximize the benefits of that relationship in the future, and they did not require me to wear a Sony lapel pin.

Could You Please Turn the Camera Off?

We had been doing device drivers for some time. We had become so good at it that we were impressing firms like Sony and Toshiba, and we had orders coming in left and right. We'd been down this road before, and we knew exactly where it would lead. After surviving the bumps and the potholes and the twists and turns, the little dirt track of our business was finally turning into a big, smooth highway. That meant it was time to look for an exit ramp, because it just wasn't all that interesting any more. We didn't set out to become a device driver company any more than we'd set out to become a Japan localization company or a stereogram software company; it was just the best option that was available at the time. In this case, we'd seen an opportunity to do device drivers, we knew that we had experience and skills in that area, and so we did them. Now, as we approached the summit of that niche business, a point at which we really *could* set up a dedicated device driver business, I was anxious to move on. As always, the big question was, "What's next?"

Tas and I spent a lot of time kicking that one around. We had a lot of experience under our collective belts now. Although we were Americans, we'd worked with several of the largest, most influential companies in the world's leading consumer electronics industry in Tokyo. We knew device drivers inside out, which meant we had a lot of experience with hardware as well as software. We were also on excellent terms with Microsoft and had gained privileged access to the Windows code. All of these and other skill sets put together should lead us to the next logical step in our corporate growth. We kicked ideas back and forth, and we brainstormed all kinds of possible paths and technologies that we could pursue. Finally, being the kind of guys we are, we came back to the fun question: What is the most interesting technology we've been involved in recently? What's been fun to work on and might actually hold our interest for the next year or two?

One of the answers that popped up was a little surprising to both of us: the work we'd done with Sony based on their cool little CCD camera was interesting; the camera was a great piece of technology, the kind of hardware that we would never create on our own, and it was just waiting to be applied to something new. Moreover, we had a stack of good credit with Sony a mile high, so why not use it for something? The next logical step was for us to devise a killer app that could make good use of Sony's state-of-the-art camera tech and the fabulous interface we would write for it.

There, too, we kicked around a few ideas. What would be the best application to make good use of this camera? There were all sorts of possibilities. Somebody came up with the crazy suggestion of putting a tiny camera in a cellphone, but I vetoed that idea. I hated having my picture taken, so my first reaction was, "What a dumb idea. It'd never work." I don't even want to think what would have happened if we had actually created that product. (Of course, I was dead wrong in this area, and my personal bias got in the way of something that has become a required feature in cell phones.) Instead, with my infallible instinct for picking the most difficult road to follow and the path with the least chance of serious commercial success, I announced decisively: "Video-conferencing!" Tas rolled his eyes. "What the hell do we know about videoconferencing?" Well, nothing. But what do we need to know? Half the problem is having good hardware, and we've already got that covered thanks to Sony. The other half is just writing some compression algorithms so you can transmit video signals over a telephone line. How hard could that be?

Tas should have learned back in high school to keep a baseball bat handy and apply it forcibly to my skull whenever I made pronounce-ments like that, but I guess he was either too good a friend or too caught up in the Saito Reality Distortion Field. So, before we knew exactly what we were doing, we'd already bought tickets to sit in the front car of the next big development roller coaster.

The first thing we discovered is that videoconferencing had been around for a very long time, as long as television, in fact. A pair of closed-circuit TV signals had been used for this purpose way back in the 1930s, and NASA had used a similar system in the 1960s. There were several problems with these systems, but the biggest one was not even the limitations of the technology; it was the enormous cost. To do any kind of videoconferencing essentially required having a TV studio in both locations, which not even the largest corporations were eager to shell out for.

In the 1980s, companies like PictureTel Corp. released serious commercial products that attempted to compress the moving images into a more compact data stream and transmit that in a real-time, two-way signal that looked more like what we think of now as videocon-ferencing. These products were more affordable than building an entire

CBS TV Studio in your office, but they were still not cheap. The answer was to develop a PC-based system that looked and sounded good and delivered true two-way communication in real time—and remember, the Internet was not an option, so all the video signals had to go over standard, copper telephone lines.

I won't bore you with all the various standards of the International Telecommunications Union (ITU), but two of them ruled the tele-conference business. The Common Intermediate Format, or CIF (sometimes called Full CIF), was a hefty standard that worked for things like TV-based systems. (For you die-hard video techies out there, CIF is a data rate of 30 frames per second, with each frame containing 288 lines and 352 pixels per line.) The second format was called Quarter CIF, or QCIF, because it transmitted only one-quarter as much data (30 fps, 144 lines, 176 pixels/line). That doesn't sound like much today, but back then PC displays were pretty low-resolution, which meant that QCIF was suitable for what we wanted to achieve: videoconferencing bet-ween compatible PCs operating over standard telephone lines. In the mid-1990s when we were trying to develop this system, QCIF was about the same resolution as a normal PC monitor, so there was no need to aim for anything better. And, as we soon found out, just trying to deliver a QCIF signal over a crappy copper telephone line was like trying to get Niagara Falls to flow through a drinking straw.

Of course, we were not going to take any of the previous attempts at PC-based videoconferencing and build upon them. No, that would be way too easy and not much fun at all. Instead, we would start with nothing and design our own system from scratch, write every line of code, and create any new specs that we needed as we went along. Now *that's* programming, I thought. It's also a little like hitting yourself in the head with a pipe wrench day after day.

My biggest skill set has always been math. I had been doing advanced math problems from a very young age, and I've always had (and still do) a natural ability to see all sorts of technical problems in their most basic mathematical aspects, and to be able to crunch through the multiple levels of calculations needed to solve them. To me, video compression was fundamentally just a simple math problem. Well, maybe not so simple, but if it were too simple it wouldn't be interesting, so that was good. I had been fascinated by the mathematics of compression from way back when, and I'd spent a lot of time figuring out why one compression algorithm was better than another, studying frequency analysis and so on, so none of this was new to me. I was sure that whatever we were going to achieve would depend largely on our ability to cook up some incredibly efficient approach to video compression, so all of my earlier study was going to come in handy.

What I discovered, of course, was that the various aspects of video compression were not like other problems I had encountered, and the work was on a scale I could not have imagined at the time. Then again, I've never liked the easy road when there's a more challenging option ahead of me.

One of the big problems was that PC-to-PC communication over regular telephone lines (as opposed to the new, digital ISDN lines) required the use of a once-ubiquitous piece of equipment called a modem (you may remember we talked about modems and PC-to-PC telecom a little earlier). Although Ethernet ports have replaced them on most modern PCs, until recently lots of computers still included a modem port (essentially a telephone jack) just in case some poor soul wanted to try connecting to the Internet over a telephone line.

What is a modem exactly? Well, to put it simply, computers speak Digital and telephones speak Analog, two totally different languages that neither understands. If they're going to talk to each other, they need an interpreter. In order to get any kind of data, even a simple "Are you there?" text message, to travel from my PC over a phone line and appear on your PC is to "modulate" (translate) the computer's digital signal into an analog signal in the range of a human voice (i.e., something a telephone line can understand), then demodulate (retranslate) it on the other side of the connection, coding the analog data back into digital data that the PC can understand. Hence, devices that *modu*late/*demo*dulate the signals came to be called "modems."

For many years, the speed constraints of commercially available modems had been the biggest limiting factor on what kinds of signals could go through them. Instead of acting like a fully bilingual simultaneous translator, older modems seemed more like a high school French student with a dog-eared dictionary. Instead of facilitating PC-to-PC communication as they were intended, the modem became the bottleneck in the system. Lots of early modems transferred data at a paltry

0.3 kilobits/second (called 300 baud back when I bought my first Hayes modem, which was probably during the Lincoln administration). With a 300 baud modem, you could just barely support a decent text chat, and you needed a fair amount of patience to wait for each sentence to come and go. Think about it: Modems were sending only *text*, not video, and even that had to be compressed because the signal speed was so slow that it couldn't even handle uncompressed data. However, dial-up modems gradually moved up the speed ladder to 1200 baud (or 1.2 kbit/s), then 2400, 4800, 9600, 14.4k, and then to a robust 28.8 kbit/sec, and *finally* things started to become more interesting. At 28.8, file transfers were a no-brainer, and the dream of sending a two-way video signal over a telephone line was no longer inconceivable, just practically speaking, impossible. Now we were cooking.

I could easily spend a whole chapter describing the mental gymnastics I went through over the next few months, but just remembering it would be painful for me and might push nonprogrammers in the audience right over the edge into deep sleep. Suffice it to say that every day was a challenge, and writing the code that would allow a moderately fast (10 fps) video signal delivering QCIF resolution in two directions over a standard, twisted-pair copper telephone line, with a 28.8k modem as gatekeeper on both ends, was like nothing I'd ever done. An incredible team of highly skilled people, Tas, and I created something that was truly hard to believe. For us, it felt like the Apollo program— one small, continuous headache for the programmers, one giant leap for the technology as a whole. And there were days when I thought it involved as much coding as putting a man on the moon.

The final result was a stand-alone videoconferencing system like nothing that had come before. By the time the 56K modems hit the market, we could deliver up to 24 fps (on a perfect telephone connection), which was superb video back then. It was a technically superior product in every way. If we all had to spend the rest of our lives in some quiet sanitarium trying to recover from the process of building it, that was a small price to pay. We knew the product was good. Lots of people had been talking about "teleconferencing," and the high-tech media were all saying that the age of "TV telephones" was right around the corner, so we knew that latent demand was out there. Not just from corporations, but from ordinary individuals who could now make video calls almost as easily as picking up their phone. It was a runaway hit just waiting to happen.

Of course, it still had limitations, but they were the limitations of the age—principally, the need to use regular telephone lines instead of high-speed dedicated data lines such as we are accustomed to with the Internet. I still remember going to Japan to do a demo of our new product. Sony, among others, was very interested in what we'd done with their camera and had an eye on ramping up their own video-conferencing business. I booked a room at my usual hotel, the Pacific in Shinagawa, and set up my equipment in the room so that I could do a demo right there for a group of prospective customers. What I had forgotten was that the only terminal fully compatible with this system was back in the States. So I dialed in, established a good connection, and did the demo, all in just a few minutes. The video looked okay, but when I checked out of my hotel I was horrified to learn that my phone bill came to $3,500!

As part of our pre–roll-out marketing strategy, we began running demonstrations for various groups of people and asking for their impressions of the product (what professional market communications people call focus groups). We weren't any kind of marketing pros, but we wanted to find the best strategy to market this product so as to maximize sales right out of the gate. No sense in wasting effort with off-target promotions when there was such a massive, pent-up demand for the technology. Besides, sometimes in designing a system that is so complex, the builders get too close to the technology and underestimate the value of certain features. Focus groups packed with average users are quick to point this out, suggesting ways to improve the user interface or requesting extra features that will make the product more attractive. That's why we were eager to hear the candid reactions of several groups.

In a nutshell, what they said to us was: "Wow, it's almost like TV. Can you turn it off?"

What? What do you mean turn it off?

That's exactly what they meant. "The camera; turn the camera off."

You see, the system not only worked well, it worked *too* well. Many users, women in particular, felt very uncomfortable sitting in front of that high-resolution lens and realizing that someone on the other end of the videochat was seeing them up close, in clear detail—their hair, their clothes, their make-up, everything. Hence, the "feature" most requested by our focus groups was: "How do you turn off the camera?"

We had killed ourselves to make this system look *so* good, and now people were telling us that maybe videoconferencing was an idea whose time had not yet come. All the unseen benefits of that clunky, century-old technology called the telephone suddenly seemed conspicuous by their absence. When you're on camera, you can't fidget while the other person talks, or read the newspaper or watch TV while pretending to listen. You have to look good, dress right, sit up straight, and pay attention, especially in business calls, because you don't want executives in the office across town or across the country to see you yawning or trying to wipe that coffee stain off your shirt

For decades the telephone had protected people's shortcomings by providing a virtual blindfold for both sides. Yes, the technology was limited, but it was also wonderful. Now, this new technology stripped off the blindfold, left you naked (hopefully in the figurative sense) in front of your friends, colleagues, superiors, the local police department, or anyone else. Although the product hadn't even been rolled out yet, and we had no delusions that the world was about to have TV phones in their homes overnight, our demos obviously got people thinking. And what they thought made them very uncomfortable. Not everyone, of course, but enough people had the same reaction that we were knocked speechless. Several people asked us to turn off the camera!

Okay, now we had a great videoconferencing system that could be a big hit if we just got rid of the cameras and the mind-blowing codec (a portmanteau of compressor-decompressor) we'd written to deliver that steady 24 fps video signal. It took a while for the reality of this situation to sink in. We didn't want to believe it, and we had every reason to hope that our test subjects were not representative of the real potential market—hadn't they read all the articles on the coming wave of videoconferencing? Apparently not. Or more likely, they just didn't care. What we finally came to realize was that video phones looked great on *Star Trek*, but nobody wanted one in their living room.

It was a bitter pill to swallow. If our technology had been lame, if we'd miscalculated something in the system design, or even if a rival firm had beaten us to the punch with a faster, cooler product, we could have lived with that. We know all about those kinds of risks, and we were not so impressed with ourselves that we didn't think such things were possible. But this wasn't a technical problem. There wasn't anything wrong with our system; it was terrific. It was better than terrific; it was a near miracle at the time. And no other company was stepping up with something that could compete with it. Tas and I knew we should be standing on a podium somewhere, accepting congratulations from our peers and reading about our achievement in all the PC magazines. But it wasn't going to happen. The problem wasn't with the product but with the customer; it was psychological or maybe cultural rather than technical, but the end result was the same: We (gulp) can't sell this product.

Fortunately, we knew there were other companies who did care about technical excellence and had forgotten more about high-power marketing than we would ever learn. When we showed off the finished product, they expressed a serious interest in adding it to their line-up of business tools. I didn't ask if these guys had done focus group research or if maybe they were reading those same magazine articles about the imminent coming of the videoconferencing era, but when they offered to buy the technology, I was only too happy to sell it, lock, stock, and codec. Call it an exit strategy from heaven, but it saved us having to toss away a massive amount of development work.

So, in a relatively short time, I'd gone from, "Hey, let's do something with videoconferencing!" to what I would soon be calling Failure Number Five.

TAKEAWAY: Keep Your Passion Burning

Passion is essential to becoming a successful entrepreneur. When I speak to rooms full of eager young start-up CEOs, I sometimes ask how many of them want to be rich? Some hands always go up. I ask how many are hoping to IPO some day. More hands go up. These are not impossible goals, but even thinking about those goals early in your company's growth means you've fallen for the media hype about what being an entrepreneur is all about. Most of these people think they're about to launch the next

Google or the next Facebook, and the world will beat a path to their door. It isn't like that. For every Mark Zuckerberg, there are a zillion starving Zuckerberg wannabes out there, and make no mistake about it, most of them are very smart and their companies are full of good ideas or good technologies or both. Still, almost all of these companies will fail within a few years. Why that is so is another whole discussion, but the statistics tell us that most ventures simply do not last. Understanding what you're up against is part of the essential mental toolkit of any entrepreneur.

I would love to tell people how great it is to be a winner, how exciting it is to be the CEO of a company that rockets straight to the top, but that's what the media do all the time. In all good conscience, I don't want to add to that. Success comes from a lot of things, number one is sweat, and number two is sweat, and number three is more sweat. I'm not kidding, 99 percent of an entrepreneur's life really sucks. That's the truth. Sure the 1 percent feels good, but it still isn't going to get your picture on any magazine covers or put your phone number on Goldman Sachs' speed dial. The reality is that while the media constantly focus on the tiny, tiny number of companies that become big success stories, thousands more go belly-up. That's why I say, if you don't love what you do and if you don't have the passion to stay with it no matter what, your business is going to lose ground from Day One. You need to have the passion to continue, to sustain it, to keep doing the job, day after day and not get tired of it. Getting things done in a company requires lots of discipline. How can you convert that discipline into passion so that it doesn't all seem like drudgery? That's an important question for any CEO to consider. How can you sustain the passion long-term? For those in it for the money, as soon as things get hot under the collar, it's easy to quit. It takes passion to power through the tough days.

I sometimes tell people, "If you're doing something that doesn't really excite you, that doesn't inspire you, or ignite your passion, then stop now and go do something else." I don't want to be Mr. Negative, but there is so much ridiculous, ego-inflating hype surrounding high–tech start–ups that somebody has to tell the truth. You don't start out wanting to IPO; you start out wanting to do something because you love to do it, and you keep doing it and doing it, and you never give up. And if you can acquire some decent management skills along the way and lead other people to share your passion and your vision, you just might survive when other firms do not. Even then you'll be way too busy to think about how cool it would be to do an IPO or whether *Time* magazine wants to come interview you next week. You'll be thinking about meeting your payroll, keeping your main teams on task, and looking for ways to ratchet your business up to the next level. Believe me, it's a lot of work, and passion is one of the essential ingredients if you want to go the distance. Finally, for those who say going IPO is their goal, these people aren't meant to be entrepreneurs. They forget that the "I" in IPO stands for initial and all your work prior to the IPO is just in preparation for the real, even tougher work ahead.

Chapter 7

Developing for Sony—Fingerprint ID

Thanks to the success of the original Sony-Toshiba camera project, as far as Sony was concerned, we were family.

All of that was fine, but it didn't put food on the table. For me, food on the table didn't mean new job orders or new clients, but a new project. Something big. Something challenging. Something that a few months down the road might make me wish I'd never thought of it, but in the end I would triumph and know the satisfaction of a job well done. The video project was all of that, but I was robbed of the satisfaction at the finish line due to the unpredictable nature of the market itself. I wanted it all: good work, hard work, a big challenge, and a big payoff, both in terms of revenue and acclaim.

Sony had its own corporate version of the same dream. The camera development for Toshiba was great, but now it was time to follow up with something new. They were asking the same questions I was: What's next? We've got this great camera; now tell us what else we can do with it. I had many brainstorming sessions with Sony engineers, often over beers in Shinagawa area bars. I don't remember exactly how it happened or how many beers had come and gone that night, when I suddenly blurted out, "What about fingerprinting?"

Puzzled looks all around the table.

Try to imagine the Japanese versions of: *Fingerprinting? What do you mean? What the hell are you talking about? I think he's had enough for one night.* And more.

I thought for a few seconds. "You know, like fingerprint recognition. We have this small-format, high-resolution camera—" The Sony guys all nodded. "Why couldn't we modify the lens, you know, give it a short fixed focal point, light up a transparent surface at that fixed distance from the lens, and take a picture of someone's fingerprint? Then all we'd have to do is tie in some pattern-matching software, and we'd have portable fingerprint-recognition-in-a-box."

I told you he's had enough.

No, wait. I knew I was onto something. The more I thought about it, the more interesting it sounded. Then somebody asked the obvious question.

"Have you ever done anything like fingerprint recognition algorithms before?"

Well, no, not exactly.

"How would you go about doing that?"

Hmmm. Not really sure, but I think we could do it. I'm sure we could do it. Why not? It's got to be just a kind of pattern recognition, which is basically all math. How hard could it be . . . ?

Somewhere in the heavens above, the gods were laughing themselves silly. Here he goes again.

Puppy Chow

Sony basically liked the idea of doing some kind of fingerprint recognition, but their idea was to use it principally for office door locks and such. High-security entrance controls, all very hardware-oriented, which is how the Sony mind works. I saw it right from the beginning as the kind of thing that could be applied to PCs, eliminating all the tiresome passwords and access keys, replacing it all with a simple, unique biometric lock that could secure your whole computer or individual hard drives or specific folders, or whatever you wanted. Sony was not strong in the PC space back then (this is way, way before VAIO), and the Sony guys always got a funny reaction when you start talking about software—their faces looked as though they'd just discovered some slimy insect crawling up their legs. Ugh! Software-based? What for?

I tried to convince them that there were a *lot* more PCs in the world that needed easy, foolproof password substitutes than there were offices that needed really sophisticated high-tech locks. They saw my point, but only in an abstract sense. Sort of, "Sure, that may be true, but where does the cool, elegant hardware come in?" Sony people were trained from birth to eat, sleep, and breathe hardware. They literally scoffed at the whole PC industry; at least as far as the software side was concerned. And yet, through persistence and determination, I began to convince them that there was a future in this PC-based fingerprint stuff, and it would certainly have a very visible hardware component. I think once they started to envision something physical, something that came in a box with SONY printed on the front, a something-or-other unit, a thing they could develop and mass produce and sell, it all began to look slightly more attractive to them. I felt we just might be onto something.

Back at the office in California I got my usual reception. I'd just told Sony that we would do *what*? Don't worry, I kept saying, it can't be *that* hard . . . And I wasn't lying; my gut told me that we weren't so very far away from the kinds of things we had to deal with in designing the videoconferencing software. Sure, it would take some major effort, but in the end everything boils down to math, and math is my comfort zone. It's my home country, and I speak the language fluently. Video algorithms require all sorts of visual pattern matching, which is all math, and signal compression requires more math. This fingerprint recognition stuff was going to be the same basic idea: take an image, identify key components of that image which were unique, analyze and compare them at very high speed against a known data set. The new hurdle was going to be putting pattern recognition to work with a PC. Challenging? Absolutely. I wouldn't want it any other way. But no, it wasn't rocket science. We could do this; I knew it.

As usual, I grossly underestimated the difficulty level and the amount of work involved, but that, too, was getting to be so common that even it felt normal.

So we dug into this new project. I was the broad-brush guy, explaining my vision of how the thing should work and what pieces needed to be developed to make it operate as I wanted it to. Tas was, as usual, the detail guy. He organized everything, from the specifications to the work allocation and scheduling, and our cost management. Our Chief Technology Officer (CTO), a guy named Patrick Masse, handled even more detailed technical work, and under him were about two dozen excellent programmers. With this team, I knew we could make whatever we set our minds to.

Sony helped out a lot with the firmware portion of the embedded software, and their team did some heavy lifting there, but we still had the bulk of the development work to do. Part of the strain of developing what was being called the fingerprint identification unit (FIU) was just the back-and-forth with Sony, trying to explain what we wanted, how we wanted the device to work, and what details we needed to build in. But the big problem always came down to the same basic mind-set mismatch: they were Hardware people, and we were Software people. Hardware was what made Sony famous, and the hardware guys ran the show. Of course, hardware guys don't have a lot of respect for software people, especially those who work in another company or, worse yet, in another country. So even though we had done some very impressive work to make their hardware look good on the Toshiba laptop, and we'd received all sorts of kudos inside Sony, when we started work on this project we were ultimately talking to very proud, very single-minded hardware people. To a hardware guy, all software looks pretty easy. They usually have an air of, "Look, if I really had to, I could sit down and figure out all that software stuff myself. What's the big deal?" We knew there would be a few intercorporate communication issues to deal with, and they didn't disappoint us.

But our biggest challenge was entirely of our own making—literally. It's what we call the nothing-to-steal problem. We couldn't borrow ideas, structures, a user interface, or anything else from existing technologies, because there weren't any. Of course, there was fingerprint recognition long before we started building our FIU, but the old technology was based on a different concept. What we were talking about now would break new ground, and that meant we couldn't start by cobbling together bits and pieces of code from other products, not even the basic look and feel of some other device, because there wasn't any other device. We were going to make the whole thing from scratch.

Until that time, fingerprint recognition was essentially driven by law enforcement needs: you captured someone's fingerprint and sent it to a big computer in Washington or somewhere for analysis. The goal was to find out who this print belongs to, in other words, *identification*. You start with a print of an unknown person and you ask the computer, "Who is this John Doe?" Unlike portrayals on TV or in movies, this can sometimes take hours. What we planned to create was a simple, reliable way to confirm whether a specific fingerprint being input through our device matched a known user ("Is this John Doe's fingerprint or not?" in less than a second). That's *authentication*, which means the "FIU" was not properly named, but who cared? The question was: Could we make it?

The normal architecture for that authentication process involved a sensing device that would read the fingerprint and convert that image to digital data, then send that data to a computer, which would do the heavy number crunching necessary to produce a result. But that meant the sexy part of the business was going on in the CPU of whatever computer was managing the FIU. Sony didn't like that approach one bit. They insisted that the whole job should be done *inside* the FIU. Maybe this was just typical hardware geek thinking: "It's more impressive to make our device the centerpiece of the whole show; then it can be used with anyone else's computer but do all the work itself, no need to borrow processing power from somebody else's CPU. It also allowed the FIU to be integrated with legacy systems that lacked pro-cessing power such as time-and-attendance systems, safes, and, of course, doors. All we need to do is make it really small (no sweat, we're Sony) and cool-looking (ditto) and make sure the software can handle the job—hell, that's just software, what's hard about that? Probably take 'em two weeks at the most."

Despite the challenges this design presented, it had certain big advantages. Most importantly, the fingerprint scan would not be sent to some host computer either a few feet or a few hundred miles away; it would be matched against other data inside the FIU device and produce a simple Yes or No answer, or possibly a value indicating how close the sample print came to matching the stored user data. That meant that there was no stream of vital data going out from the device, just the Yes/No signal. Moreover, no authentication data would be stored on the PC to which it was attached, nothing would go out over the Internet or to any other device. The FIU would be entirely self-contained, which gave it a much higher degree of security against would-be hackers.

The only thing that needed to be secured, then, was the device itself. If hackers wanted to hack into the authentication codes, they had to break into the FIU data. In fact, some of the software developers that we asked for feedback early on in our development process complained about exactly that point—the vulnerability of the FIU. What's to protect a hacker from breaking into that unencrypted Yes/No signal? This opened up a whole new landscape for us, because we realized that not only our device, but actually all biometric data, needs to be extremely secure. Think about it—if I steal your password, you can just change your password, but if I steal your fingerprint, you're in a jam. Anything you're authorized to access becomes an open door to me, and anything sensitive enough to require fingerprint access in the first place is probably something you didn't want me looking at. In other words, authentication without security is worthless. We quickly realized that we had opened a different can of worms and that whatever we designed was going to need world-class encryption to protect it.

Interestingly, that led I/O Software into a new field, becoming a very high-class IT security company in addition to our other roles. We bought every piece of top-rated security software we could find and set about analyzing it. Our first level of interest was their interface design and their basic feature sets, things we needed to understand (borrow) in order to build our own product. Then we got serious. We started analyzing each product's strengths and weaknesses. What constitutes strong encryption? Just how strong is strong? How good do you have to be to break it, or is it unbreakable? We didn't actually *need* to break any of these security packages in order to make our own, but that didn't stop us. It's fun to try to open locks that other people have spent a lot of time and effort designing. This took me back to my youth, spending many days and nights from about sixth grade onward trying to break increasingly sophisticated levels of copy protection on commercial software. I'm willing to bet that most if not all programmers have gone through this phase at some point. The difference was that now we were able to do it as a team and do it as a necessary part of our business. If I said it was all work and that we weren't actually having fun pitting our skills against those of the security software firms that had designed this stuff, well, I'd be lying.

As I've mentioned before, when I was a kid, I broke every piece of copy protection I got my hands on. There wasn't anything I couldn't get into sooner or later, usually sooner. To my great satisfaction, I discovered that not much had changed: given a little time and some decent equipment, I could still crack any piece of security software on the market. While some of it was pretty ingenious, in a relatively short period of time, I/O Software developed a skeleton key for every lock in the commercial universe, and a few that were not commercially available. In the process, we discovered what it took to encrypt information so that people as good as ourselves could not get their hands on it. That was not central to our job when we started, but as the project developed, it became an essential part of our work.

You probably think that police or FBI computers scan fingerprints and compare every detail of each print against a huge database containing every detail of hundreds of millions of prints. That would be interesting, but as of right now, that just isn't practical. Each fingerprint contains tons of data and the kind of brute force computing power necessary to compare 100 percent of a single image against 100 percent of zillions of other images just is not available. So fingerprint analysis is largely based on a technique similar to video compression (you see, there was a method to my madness). So what we had to do in this case was to develop a program that could examine the scanned image of a single print and extract the essence, the key features that make it unique. If you think about it, this is a kind of compression technology, basically looking only at the outstanding differences between two sets of data, not examining every detail of every ridge, whorl, and crevice between them.

By the way, for those of you who have been brainwashed by *CSI* and Hollywood films, no computer ID system produces a single, unique answer with 100 percent accuracy and flashes "POSITIVE MATCH" on the screen. If you run a fingerprint check on someone, what usually happens is that you'll get several hits, sometimes even several dozen, which then have to be checked by old-fashioned means—cops hitting the street. At the time we were developing the FIU for Sony, the normal police procedure was to run fingerprint checks at night so that by the time detectives came back in the morning the data (a list of suspects) was waiting for them. In other words, fingerprint identification took a fair amount of time. But our authentication device had to produce answers immediately. The benchmark we were working against was how long it took someone to type in a password. By our own measurements, we had a maximum of 1.0 second to produce a match. If we could beat that, it would make sense to secure your computer and/or files with a fingerprint instead of a password. Just to add another layer of challenge—as if this wasn't difficult enough already—we had to display the output in Japanese Kanji, not just English, so the device had to do a phenomenal amount of data crunching inside of two seconds, which meant we had to amp up the compression and give the FIU a way to recognize fingerprints instantly and report back instantly. That kept us busy for a while.

Sony wanted the device to be intelligent, meaning it would have its own CPU and not operate as a slave to the processor of its host computer. So they put some serious horsepower under the hood—a 16-bit CPU, which was pretty sophisticated for what they saw as a little, plug-in peripheral, and 512K of onboard memory. That power pushed up the cost of the unit considerably, but it also allowed the FIU to process, encrypt, and store the fingerprint data internally. By keeping all the data internal and using a common serial connector (later a USB cable) to link up with a PC, the device became totally independent. A user could enroll himself by creating a single fingerprint template on the FIU, then unplug the device and connect it to any number of computers that he could be granted access to, and use just a fingerprint to identify himself to access the PC and encrypted folders on the PC.

When we finally began to get the software running, the system looked remarkably close to what we had envisioned. Our initial demo unit was good—it was bigger than a breadbox, but not by much, and it performed just the way we wanted it to. It was fast and simple to use. You could put your finger on a small, flat surface and the internal camera would read your fingerprint and send that data to the CPU to be processed, compare it to a stored value (i.e., a fingerprint previously recorded by the device), and instantly decide if the two prints matched. If authentication was achieved, the unit would immediately grant access to a Windows-enabled PC. It was new, it was different, and best of all, it worked just the way we promised it would. As we had expected, even the Sony hardware guys were impressed. Being able to control access to a PC was pretty cool, and they could already envision the market response to such a product—but not if the box took up most of your desk.

This is where the Sony guys got to show their stuff. We gave them a big, clunky box and showed them that it works. Then they took it over to Sony's famous "Honey, I Shrunk the Solar System" lab, and the result was downright amazing. The unit they ultimately produced was a little bigger than the size of a playing card and a little thicker than a couple of credit cards, with a cable trailing out the back end. All of that stuff that we'd worked on got miniaturized, and thus rendered commercially viable, thanks to Sony. The first version was dubbed the FIU-001, but that's not how they wanted to market it. To the Japanese mind, it was small and it was cute, and so it needed a cute, easy-to-remember name. The VP in charge of the project loved dogs, so overnight the Puppy was born. Having spent a lot of time in Japan, I knew only too well about the vast cultural gap in marketing psychology between the United States and Tokyo. There are so many examples that it's pointless to count them all, but just for reference, consider the famous Z line of testosterone-injected sports cars that built Nissan's reputation in the States. In Japan they're called the Fair Lady, because many years ago a senior Nissan exec had a thing about Audrey Hepburn, and the car has been stuck with that moniker ever since. Nissan was smart enough not to try to market a macho sports car overseas with the name Fair Lady, and so the Z cars were born. But other companies have different ideas about cute marketing. Also, by this time the Hello Kitty phenomenon had branched out to enslave the rest of the world, so it was not a huge shock, to me at least, when Sony told us that this new, ultra-high-tech biometric authentication device that would change computer security forever would be sold worldwide as the Puppy.

In the fall of 1996, we took a sample to COMDEX—then the biggest venue for electronics products of all kinds and a make-it-or-break-it showcase for new technologies that are hoping to become The Next Big Thing. The problem is that COMDEX is a great place to show off new stuff, but it's also a big gamble. If your technology isn't quite as good as you think it is, or if another company shows up with something better that you didn't know about, you can get laughed off the floor, which means terrible reviews, which translates into terrible sales. So a really bad showing at COMDEX can practically put you out of business before you get started. On the other hand, if you've got something so hot that everyone wants to get their hands on it on Day One, then you know you've got a hit on your hands and it's time to crank up your PR machine. We'd never had anything like a hit. Of course, we were very confident of the superiority of our work, but we were *always* confident of the superiority of our work; we'd been really confident about our ultracool videoconferencing product, too. That was also guaranteed to be a hit and pave the way for I/O Software's sure-fire success story until it crashed and burned. Still, we told ourselves, this time was going to be different. We had the whole Sony package, and we knew the technology was cutting-edge, so COMDEX was definitely worth the gamble.

Was it ever. The response to the Puppy was tremendous. There was nothing even remotely like it on the floor, and people were amazed. It was unbelievably small, portable, accurate, reliable, easy to use . . . we didn't have to do any promotion because everyone who saw it was wowed by the technology and the tiny form factor, and they kept giving us new adjectives to describe it. Who needs a PR team when technology writers, mainstream journalists, industry pros, even rival security firms were trying out our device and forming a loud chorus of ooohs and aaahs? People weren't even turned off by the cute name. It was different; it was original; it was easy to remember. We won a Best of COMDEX award just to make sure we understood that this dream wasn't happening to someone else. For the first time ever, we knew we had a real, unmistakable hit on our hands.

Puppy Love

Even looking back from this vantage point (and remember, just a couple of years in this industry is like a geological age, so 1996 was the Jurassic period in biometrics), I still think the Puppy was a cool device. You could just plug in a small, thin plastic accessory, put your finger on an exposed flat surface, and in a second or less, log into your computer without typing a password—and much more securely. It was elegant in the sense that software designers use that term, and it was also cool-looking, not a big, clunky device that you wished you could hide under your desk. It was small, thin, quiet and . . . wow, I almost said, "sexy." Yes, I guess as hardware goes, it was pretty sexy. And one of the best parts of the deal was that we actually got to sell this little device that we had worked so hard to create. Now, *that's* sexy.

Setting aside our crazy little experiment with stereograms, the Puppy was the first product for which we became the primary reseller. At that time, Sony was extremely particular about who sold its products outside of Japan. Aside from Sony Corporation of America, very few companies won the right to represent Sony goods in North America, and those that did were big, well-established firms. Sony would never consider doing a reseller agreement with a small, unknown company. However, our special relationship with Sony and our special relationship with this product in particular guaranteed that we would not be treated like other small companies. I/O Software not only obtained a reseller agreement, but we landed *exclusive* distribution rights for all of North America at the outset. That meant we completely controlled the market for the device that we had developed. After years of being the invisible device driver programmers, always having our work buried inside someone else's product and receiving only a flat fee for all the sweat expended in making the thing work, this was a huge step. Of course, the product said "Sony" on the case, not "I/O Software," but that was okay. We knew that consumers would flock to the Sony name, but inside that little case was our baby. The fact that they let us sell it into our own home market was like a license to print money: If you wanted to buy the Puppy, you had to buy it from I/O Software, which meant you came to recognize our company name and perceive our close relationship with Sony (a connection that would ultimately begin to trouble us, but which at this stage made us look pretty damn respectable).

So we imported products from the factories in Japan and shipped them all over the United States and Canada from our California-based operation. I say "products" because we had different flavors of the FIU device (different stock keeping units, or SKUs, for those of you in retail). We sold the device as a stand-alone, which was useful for embedding in doors and other things. As a matter of fact, we installed similar devices in our own office doors, and the technology proved to be a simple, effective means of access authorization. The stand-alone product sold quite well. Then we had a full software developer kit (SDK) so programmers could write their own variations for it, and that also sold well because a lot of people wanted to integrate the Puppy with their own products. Then there was a log-on-only product, which was also a big hit. If memory serves, there were at least four initial products to sell, maybe more, and we quickly got ramped up to become vendors. A new experience, for sure.

At one point, we had rooms full of shipping pallets of these expensive units in some rented storage space. We must have had a million or two million dollars' worth of inventory on hand, and that, too, was a first for us. But what really caused those pinch-me moments was the idea that we could get these boxes directly from Sony, mark up the retail prices any way we wanted, and keep the profit for ourselves. It was a dream come true.

The product received rave reviews around the world. One of the biggest of many big accolades was the much sought-after Editor's Choice award from *PC Magazine*, an industry standard bearer. Their review (of a slightly later model) said in part:

> Sleek and slim, the Sony FIU-710 (affectionately known as the "Puppy") is 1.4 ounces and about the size of a few business cards. The right mix of features and power sets it apart from the others we tested and makes it our Editors' Choice.... Installation, setup, enrollment, and verification were trouble free. The Puppy was the only model we evaluated that performed flawlessly on all of our tests.

That alone would almost guarantee good sales. We got dozens of five-star reviews, and not only in the consumer sector. *Government Computer News* named it a Reviewer's Choice and gave it their top A rating, beating out five other fingerprint ID products. We were on a roll that would last for years. We upgraded the Puppy, combined it with other software tools, and it just went on collecting more great reviews (another from *PC Magazine*, plus *Reseller News*, *SC Magazine*, etc.) and awards (*PC Week*'s Labs Analyst's Choice Award, *Network Computing*'s Flying Colors Award, Frost & Sullivan's "Technology Innovation Award 2000," etc.). The product really put us on the map. Suddenly I/O Software was being included among *Computerworld's* Top 100 Emerging Companies to Watch and Deloitte and Touche's Technology Fast 50. This was everything we had hoped for with our videoconferencing product and much more. The difference was that this time we had judged the market zeitgeist perfectly—if computer security was gradually becoming a hot topic in the mid-1990s, it gained a lot of steam in the late 1990s, and became *the* red-hot topic in the industry after 9/11. Our technology arrived just early enough to gain attention, win awards, and make people aware of its potential, and then was perfectly positioned as the number one product when the whole country suddenly became security-conscious.

We probably could have made a nice, successful business just with the Puppy, but there were bigger and better things just around the corner.

Interlude: Entrepreneur of the Year

I want to interrupt the Puppy narrative for a moment, because the success it brought I/O Software put me in the media spotlight as CEO. Both the company and I started getting more attention than ever in the past, and that was great. I didn't crave personal glory; in fact, anyone who knows me at all will tell you that I'm overly shy and usually need to be led by the hand into a roomful of strangers. And yet, something happened after the release of the Puppy that changed my life forever.

It must have been sometime toward the end of 1997 that people from Ernst & Young first came to visit our offices. They explained that there was a very prestigious award sponsored by E & Y (and supported at that time by *USA Today* and NASDAQ) that, "honors the most out-standing entrepreneurs who inspire others with their vision, leadership and achievement." I'm ashamed to admit it, but I was busy, I had a lot of other things on my mind, and I thought the whole thing sounded irrelevant. No one was offering to name I/O Software as Company of the Year or anything like that. What were they talking about? I'm a shy guy; I don't like going to events where you have hundreds of strangers in formal clothes walking around some big room. Take me to a big

Chamber of Commerce–type affair, and I just melt into the wall. Yes, you could say I don't mingle well. And that's if I'm a guest. What these people were talking about involved putting me in a tux, standing me in a spotlight, and having me give an acceptance speech in front of hundreds of people I didn't know. For what? If Kleiner, Perkins wanted to invest in us or Goldman Sachs wanted to manage our IPO, maybe. But honoring me personally as Entrepreneur of the Year just didn't seem very important at the time, and no matter how prestigious they said the award was, I knew in my gut that it would be the kind of event I would probably pay money to avoid. Plus, who says I would win it anyway? These people were coming around to ask if I would fill out the *nomination* form, which looked like an extra pain when I was already busy with important stuff. And besides, I probably wouldn't win. I showed them to the door, and I'm sorry to say I was pretty rude about it.

Fortunately, the Ernst & Young people were a lot more professional about their job than I was, because they came back. They explained the award in detail and said straight out, "We really think you should be nominated." I listened to them, said over and over again, "No, it's just not me. I'm busy right now. I don't want to do it," and I ushered them out once again. They came back a third time, and I had to be even more blunt. They obviously weren't getting the message. By this time the nature of their visit was well known inside the company, and my natural antisocial tendencies were equally well known. Piecing things together later, I figured out that my secretary spoke to the E&Y people after the third go-round and offered to fill out the form secretly on my behalf. They accepted her offer, and the rest is history. I became a regional finalist for the award, and then at the national voting I was named the 1998 Entrepreneur of the Year for people under 30 years old, and the first Asian to win that title.

Needless to say, the focus of the award was the fingerprint recognition technology we'd developed. To me, improved user authentication was just a natural outgrowth of the whole computer boom and the increasing need for security measures. There was nothing glitzy about it at all; authentication was just moving up from childishly simple password protection to a credible, businesslike technology that made sense in a risk-laden corporate environment. Obviously, other people saw it in a slightly different light. When I went up to get my award, they played the

James Bond theme music—the whole fingerprint recognition thing was seen as some kind of sexy, cool technology with 007 overtones. *Gimme a break*, I thought. I mean, I was sweating enough already without this. And yet, the whole thing was an exhilarating experience. My elementary school teachers would probably have fainted at the thought of William Saito, the kid who couldn't get his tongue around the English language properly, standing in front of hundreds of people in evening wear and giving a formal speech. But I did it, and later on people told me it was okay—I actually don't remember too much after I heard my name called.

And yet, that one award changed my life—and my company's fortunes—forever. If I'd known what a big impact it would have, I would have hugged those guys from Ernst & Young the first time they knocked on our door, and I wouldn't have let them leave my office until I'd filled out their form. The nuisance of being named an outstanding entrepreneur quickly turned into a gigantic door opening in front of me, and once I stepped through, I found a very different world on the other side.

USA Today, one of the sponsors of the award, did a nice article about I/O Software. In a sense, the award and the publicity that followed became our national coming-out party. Overnight we went from being a little company that people in certain corners of the computer and software industries knew about to being a company that most everyone had heard of. We were suddenly on a national stage. The media started calling, and before I knew it, I had to become the company's PR agent. Of course, we had been written up in newspapers before, and I had done interviews and been photographed as an up-and-coming CEO and so on, but mostly for local media. This was different. As I've already mentioned, I'm basically a quiet person, willing to debate with a roomful of software engineers, but almost pathologically unable to walk up to strangers at parties and introduce myself. And yet, if I call myself shy, Tas made me look like an old Southern politician back-slapping his way around a roomful of voters. Tas was definitely not a guy who wanted to stand up at a podium with a spotlight on him and make a speech. So I couldn't turn to my COO and say, "I'm busy; you handle this media stuff." The sun would burn out before that happened. Consequently, the CEO of I/O Software became a media personality, talked publicly about what we were doing and how we were not merely interested in fingerprint recognition, but in the whole area of bio-metrics, and how the company would continue to move in that direction. All of that media management experience would come in very handy just a couple of years down the road when I/O Software delivered a major, headline-grabbing announcement. But let's not get ahead of ourselves.

There was also a group of Japanese people from Ernst & Young's Tokyo office present at the ceremony. Afterward, they came up to talk to me. "Your name is Saito ... are you Japanese?" they asked. I told them yes, my parents were Japanese who had come to the United States and that I visited Japan a lot. They explained that they wanted to start up a local version of the Entrepreneur of the Year program in Japan but needed qualified people to advise them and help with the judging. They asked if I would be willing to help and I said of course, I would be happy to. That opened another big door for me: I started flying to Tokyo not just to meet with Sony and other clients, but also to help set up the Japan version of Entrepreneur of the Year, and once it was up and running, I'd go to judge the national competition there. That meant I eventually got to meet hundreds of Japanese entrepreneurs and gain access to a whole world of Japanese companies that even the business establishment over there is largely unaware of. That began a new segment of my life that would grow stronger as the years passed, but we'll save that story for later, too. Ironically, I found that many Japanese companies didn't want to bother with the application. Because of my similar experience, I began to make sure the promising ones applied.

If the Puppy helped me win Entrepreneur of the Year, the thing called BAPI (Biometrics Application Platform Interface) helped me and my company become even more famous, and ultimately led us all to the next stage in our lives.

To Clone or Not to Clone?

The massive success and industry acclaim for the Puppy produced several results. One was that all of our old clients, the dozens of companies that had contracted us to do device drivers for them, suddenly began calling up, asking us to adapt this fingerprint recognition technology for them. They were all creating their own FIUs now, and they didn't want to simply rebrand the devices from the original equipment manufacturer (OEM) or Sony; they wanted their own-brand fingerprint authentication products. That seemed like a logical next step. We could create a Toshiba-specific fingerprint authentication system and an NEC-specific fingerprint authentication system and a Fujitsu-specific fingerprint authentication system, and so on and so on. Each one would use roughly 80 or 85 percent of the code we'd already written for Sony, and the rest would be unique to that company. That would mean I/O Software would get paid a nice fee for customizing each product. Right off the bat we were thinking there must be 50, maybe 100 companies that would sign up for that kind of work. Our order books would be full for a couple of years, and the company would have a huge positive cash stream to use for developing other projects. It was a golden opportunity just waiting for us to say yes.

I said no.

Don't get me wrong—of course I wanted the giant payoff. We all deserved it for doing such a good job creating this software in the first place. We wanted to see I/O Software really hit it big, and now, at last, we had a business proposition that repaid us for being smart, creative programmers. No more shrink-wrapped software, no more invisible work where everybody was yelling at us and threatening to sue us, no more brilliant technology where users say, "Can you please turn off the camera?" This was real. We were selling the Puppy like crazy, and now we had a chance to do custom orders for dozens of follow-on products where, unlike the Puppy, we'd have plenty of existing material to steal from—the code we'd already written. What could be easier? At least that's the way many people inside I/O Software saw it.

But when I looked at the situation I saw things a little differently. First, the idea of having multiple versions of this software was problematic. We could see right away that the 100 different flavors approach was confusing, even for us. Just as one example, each version would need a slightly different user interface. So the Registration box for Company A would have to be different from the Registration box we used for Companies C and D and so on. Multiply that by dozens of minor changes times a hundred different products. That meant they would all need different user manuals and, the biggest problem, they would all require different technical support from our side. By building 100 different versions of the same thing, we were opening a huge can of worms on the support side. Were we planning to hire armies of new staff just to manage all the inquiries that would be coming once all these incompatible products hit the market? Were we going to sit each of them in front of a wall of 100 ring binders explaining the unique look and feel of each product? This was not only impractical; it just didn't feel right. It wasn't the smart way to do things, no matter how much income it might produce.

There was another, less tangible, problem. Doing 50 or 100 custom solutions for all those different companies went against my own internal programming. I've mentioned it before, and I'll be the first one to raise my hand when it's mea culpa time: I lose interest in things quickly. I'm not proud of that by any means, but I learned long ago to acknowledge it. I love challenges, and I love solving puzzles and all the more so when someone says, "Hey, you can't possibly do this." But when the challenge is met and I've done what I set out to do, I start looking around for the next mountain to climb. From that perspective, simply turning I/O Software into a Puppy-clone factory was like eating tofu burgers every day for the rest of my life. Sometimes what doesn't kill you makes you wish it had.

I knew there must be a better way.

TAKEAWAY: Don't Let Opportunities Pass You By: Lessons Learned

When I think about how close I came to turning my back on the Ernst & Young offer to help me apply for their Entrepreneur of the Year Award, or about how my life could have turned out differently, well, let's just say I am much more open and eager to discover opportunities wherever they appear. The benefits received from that one offer in 1998 are still paying dividends today.

I've heard it said that to be good at something you need to do it 10,000 times, and for over a decade I've had the opportunity to judge far more than 10,000 business plans. As a judge for local and national EoY awards programs in the United States, Japan, and even the annual world event held in Monte Carlo each year, I can honestly say that I've become good at identifying winning companies in a judging competition. Not only has this allowed me to travel to dozens of countries, meeting thousands of entrepreneurs around the world, but it has also led to some interesting discoveries. For example, I have found that age, background, or nationality doesn't matter, only passion and intelligence. Every entrepreneur shares similar concerns and similar problems. No matter the amount of revenue, the number of employees, or the total number of patents filed, the award-winning entrepreneurs all share a passion and the common desire to make a difference in the world with their product or service.

In the United States and particularly at the Monte Carlo events, I often wondered how I happened to be judging such awesome companies as Google, Home Depot, and Infosys. Many of the entrepreneurs and business leaders I met have become friends over the years, and we still stay in touch. Because everyone's knowledge base is limited, it is good business sense to leverage your skills and talents more effectively through a highly skilled network of like minds.

By participating in the judging process so many times, I've been able to discern intuitively just what makes a successful company and to observe the common traps people can fall into. If there is anything that differentiates my story from that of other business advisors, it would be the sheer number of entrepreneurs I have met around the globe and the vast repository of success and failure stories I have been privileged to hear. Rather than an academic overview of entrepreneurism, perhaps this book is really a distillation of all those stories from the point of view of someone who has also walked in the same shoes.

I will take every opportunity to continue learning from the hopes, dreams, successes, and failures of people who are passionately trying to make a difference in the world.

Chapter 8

Birth of BAPI

T he rationale for doing scores of Puppy knock-offs was that we had already done all the heavy lifting to create the device. In theory, it was just a matter of tweaking it a bit for each customer. When we were developing the Puppy, we wrote a software developer kit (SDK) so that other software companies could take advantage of the device. In writing that, we had to create what's called an application programming interface or API. Simply put, an API is a type of interface. For example, think of the user interface you see whenever you turn on your computer. Your desktop always looks fundamentally the same; you can open folders and applications in consistent ways, you can add and remove peripheral devices, and use the data or features they provide, and all of this look and feel of your computer remains the same. If it didn't, you wouldn't be able to do very much, no matter how sophisticated a machine you had or how smart you were, because you wouldn't know how to use the machine from one day to the next. Moreover, if I buy a word processor, I shouldn't have to worry about which printers it can work with, nor should my printer care which application is sending it a print request. This concept is called *abstraction*, and APIs help abstract the connection between hardware and software so neither has to worry about the other.

Another way to think of it is that the user interface provides a common, consistent set of rules, instructions, protocols, graphic designs, and so on that allows you (a highly illogical, visually oriented biological device running on pizza and caffeine) to interact smoothly with a computer (a highly logical, command-oriented computational device running on alternating current). The interface is the invisible interpreter that allows two radically different systems to communicate with each other, to interact, and for at least one of those systems to take advantage of the other's features. A software API makes it possible for a security application, for example, to use the authentication results of a Puppy-like device to unlock a folder on your desktop or unlock a door to your office. It allows different software to talk to the Puppy and put it to work doing specific tasks.

Writing an API is hard work, and we put a lot of effort into developing the API for the Puppy. When we wrote the first version of the SDK, which included the first draft of our API, we sent it out to several third-party software developers to get their reactions. This was an important step, because it provided plenty of outside feedback that we would otherwise not have access to (at least not until the product was on the market, and then feedback comes in the form of users, developers, and media critics trashing your product in public). The companies that tested our SDK gave us important feedback, which was very lucky for us. We discovered that people wanted all sorts of things that we had not imagined. That allowed us to fine-tune the API and add a variety of features to it.

It was partly because we'd done such a good job writing this API that I vetoed the Puppy-clone idea as the key to our future growth. It wasn't just that the idea of repeating the same job over and over provided no challenge to me (which it didn't); it wasn't just that supporting 100 or more different versions of the software would ultimately turn out to be a huge burden for the company (which it would). It really came down to my vision that there were bigger and better things we could do, and that this other road led not only to more satisfying work but, somehow, my gut told me, to greater business potential as well.

So I announced my crazy decision: We would *not* do all those individual versions, but instead would use the API we had already developed to create a single, generic authentication platform, what could serve as a global standard for biometric authentication. I compared it to the Microsoft operating system—one OS works with all different kinds of hardware and software. Your word processor doesn't care what kind of printer you have, and your printer doesn't care what kind of word processor you're using. Everything connects smoothly through the common interface of the OS (via the API). That's the kind of simple, elegant world I wanted to create for authentication software. Without it, I saw something like anarchy in the biometrics world, with everyone building proprietary models that didn't work with most of the other systems in the market. If that commercial chaos was the future, and if we were contributing to that future, there would never be anything like a biometrics industry.

Of course, everyone thought I was nuts, and they probably had more of a point than I wanted to admit. What I was proposing, in essence, was to build a full biometric operating system that controlled both applications and hardware. I was talking about doing more hard work just when we should be kicking back and enjoying the profits of all our earlier hard work. Tas and others said, just to put me on the defensive, "Who's going to write this 'elegant, one-size-fits-all' generic API?" Of course, my answer was that we would do it, however long it might take. "And who's going to pay for all this extra work?" I winced a little because that was a fair question and one I did not have a snappy comeback for. The truth was, nobody would pay for it, at least not up front. Sony had paid the bills to develop the Puppy, but if we wanted to go out on our own and develop some new API, that was our own nickel. A few people in the company pointed out the obvious: If we did customized versions of FIUs for scores of different clients, we could get paid by each company for relatively simple work and do very well business-wise. This other scenario of mine was all cash-out, no cash-in, and no guarantee of success. In addition, if we had worked with everyone, we could not be so closely affiliated with Sony and would eventually have to give up exclusivity for a perfectly good-selling product.

But my mind was made up. I knew that there was only one way for us to move forward, and that was not by cloning our own technology over and over again, but by making something generic that could become a common platform, like Windows, and if we went all the way, it could turn into a real global standard for biometric authentication. A global standard that we would own. The more I thought about it, the more obvious it seemed.

In the end, it only took me about a week to convince the whole company that this was the right road to take. Maybe they all saw the same vision I did, or maybe they all thought, *Once William gets an idea like this into his head, you're just wasting time and effort trying to argue with him.* I like to think it was the former.

We established a kind of skunk works inside I/O Software to begin development of our own biometric API, what we would soon call BAPI. We had teams of about five programmers each working on the hardware side, the software side, the API side, and so on, maybe about 20 people in total. And our CTO, Patrick Masse, pulled it all together, which was a major job in itself.

During this time, we were still developing new features for Sony's FIU. We worked on BAPI while we were developing Sony's applications, and we used a lot of the feedback we got from other software developers about how they wanted to work with a fingerprint identification unit to help us craft our own API. Thanks to that input, we got to see lots of different approaches to the idea of biometric authentication, and we came to realize the strengths and weaknesses of each. That was the school that taught us some of the key lessons we needed in order to make a robust generic product that would work flawlessly with all sorts of applications.

During this process, it became obvious to me that no matter how we wrote the software, the Sony Puppy was not going to be the perfect solution for every application. Sony didn't see it that way. Not surprisingly, they thought the Puppy could be used for anything. After all, their engineers were hardware geniuses, and they had us there to retool the software as needed, so anything was possible, at least in their view.

I agreed that the Puppy was great and the Puppy could be adapted to handle most anything on the market right now. But other types of sensor technologies were bound to come along, and there would eventually be other devices, devices not made by Sony, that we would want to support. That was tantamount to telling Sony—an immensely proud and close-knit group—that our relationship had really been great, but now we wanted to sleep with other people.

I won't say that this announcement was well received, but Sony certainly understood what we were thinking. It made sense. It was a smart move on our part, just not the kind of thing that any obedient subcontractor in the Sony Group (or any other manufacturer's group, for that matter) would ever think about. I also felt that this would "float all boats" and help Sony, in the long run, by allowing alternatives and competitors to grow and educate the market together. This is where being a non-Japanese company came in very handy. In one sense we were deeply indebted to Sony, and I was genuinely grateful for the opportunities they had given us. However, we were not a Japanese company and we were not captive members of a big *keiretsu* industrial group, unable or unwilling to go out on our own and do what was best for our company.

Sony at least understood where we were coming from with the we-need-some-space announcement. Then I went crazy again and said that we were not going to limit our new BAPI development to fingerprint units. After all, if we were going to do all this work to create a super-API for one type of biometrics, why not go all the way and create an architecture that was completely device-agnostic for *all* biometrics? Why limit it to fingerprints? Why not make it open to any type of device, any type of sensor or input? Let's assume that a decade or so down the road someone will develop a technology that can quickly and easily provide DNA-based biometric authentication. Our API should be able to work just as smoothly with that yet-to-be-developed hardware and yet-to-be-developed software as it does with the Puppy. It wasn't about fingerprints, I said. It was about biometrics.

That's when they knew I'd been drinking too much of my own Kool-Aid.

A Note on Biometrics

Biometrics doesn't sound much like something you'd find lying around your kitchen, but it isn't all that difficult to understand. Basically, every human being has distinctive physical traits, characteristics that are unique to that person—you already know about fingerprints and DNA (though the latter is shared among identical twins, it is otherwise unique to each individual), but what about your palm, your voice, the iris of your eye, or the shape of your face? They are all unique, unmistakable ways to pick you out of a crowd instantly, even if that crowd happens to be a few million people. The process of recognizing these physical, human (*bio*) markers and measuring them against known data (*metrics*) underpins the new science of biometrics. In fact, biometrics isn't really new—the Egyptians used a type of biometrics on documents, the Soviets used another form to secure their nuclear facilities, and several other applications of the science had been around for quite some time. But because computer-driven biometrics provides a fast, highly reliable way to authenticate someone's identity, it is of tremendous interest to any organization involved with security at any level—and that includes everyone from individual users (the guy in the local hardware store who keeps his accounts on a desktop PC) to enterprise users (global corporations like Microsoft and IBM) and government users like the FBI, CIA, and everyone else in any corner of the intelligence community. Everybody has a use for biometrics.

By the time we were developing the Puppy, biometrics was already gaining attention in the computer industry. Lots of people were developing their own products to deliver the same kind of user-authentication features; we just happened to be one of the first to do it successfully and attractively with a small, easy-to-use product. But we were by no means the only kid on the block. The problem was that biometric authentication was not like a bunch of different laptop makers vying to see who could get the biggest market share, but all functioning in basically the same way. Instead, each version of the technology involved proprietary software. There was biometric software that worked with this machine and that machine but not with any other machines. It was just like our dilemma about customizing our software for all our clients—the proprietary model guarantees that one's products are not compatible with anyone else's. Do you remember the chaos in the consumer videocassette market when there were just two different standards? Imagine that instead of Beta and VHS, every videocassette deck maker in the world used a different standard. No market that is so badly fragmented can survive. In a sense, the disorganized commercialization of the technology compromises all the benefits that the technology has to offer. If this was important for creating a single global standard for CDs back in the 1980s, you can imagine how important it was for creating a viable, worldwide biometric standard in the 1990s.

The problem was that there was no single standard to speak of; there were dozens of standards. Everyone was developing their own approach to biometrics, and most of them were incompatible with everyone else's approach. I was far from the only one who saw this as a huge potential problem that would permanently stunt the growth of this industry. A global standard was essential if we were all going to grow, and I was confident enough of our own development skills to know that whatever we created would be good enough to serve as the base, or at least a key component of this new global standard. Did it ever occur to me that we were a small, relatively insignificant company with a negligible track record in biometric authentication, or that we had less than zero clout in the international arena where heavy hitters like IBM, Intel, Compaq, Hewlett-Packard, Siemens, and all the giant electronics companies held sway? Probably not. Once I get it into my mind to do something, I generally put my foot to the floor and aim for the shortest possible route to get there. I've never paid a lot of attention to who else is on the road or how big their semitrailers look compared to my little Prius. When I know where I want to go, I just want to get there as quickly and efficiently as possible.

Standard Deviation

The American National Standards Institute (ANSI), headquartered in Washington, DC, is a private, nonprofit organization that deals with just what its name implies. For almost 100 years it has been establishing voluntary standards for products and services within the United States and coordinating those with global standards to make sure that U.S. products do not suffer from Galapagos syndrome (i.e., they work well at home, but are ignored by the rest of the world). ANSI also represents U.S. interests at the ISO (International Organization of Standardization). Just to bring things into perspective, ANSI provides specifications for everything from nanotechnology to nuclear energy (actually, they also have specifications for things like hot tubs, but let's not get into that right now). When a commercial industry such as computers or software wants to create a new specification, ANSI forms a panel comprised of leading members of that industry and other interested parties to discuss, debate, and resolve the question of what the new standard should look like. It isn't too hard to get onto one of the committees advising these panels, and I wanted to be involved in the standards discussion, so I unabashedly volunteered I/O Software as a member of the ANSI panel on biometrics, what was called the BioAPI Consortium.

One group, called the Human Authentication API (HA-API, and what we all called "happy") group, had published its own biometric API in 1997, the same year that we unveiled the Puppy. However, Happy's API was anything but a standard. ANSI created the BioAPI Consortium in the spring of 1998, and shortly thereafter I said that we wanted to be part of the team. The Happy guys were operating outside this structure for quite a while, but nearly a year after the Consortium was founded the National Institute of Standards and Technology (NIST) and the U.S. Biometric Consortium organized a major pow-wow to come to some kind of industry-wide consensus on developing a common fingerprint template. This led to an agreement to develop a technology-blind biometric file format, something along the lines we were working on, and the HA-API group agreed to bring their development work inside the BioAPI Consortium. That meant ANSI had as close as it would get to an industry-wide mandate to determine a single, universal standard for a biometric API. If you Google "BioAPI Consortium," you will find this impressive description:

> The BioAPI Consortium was founded to develop a biometric Application Programming Interface (API) that brings platform and device independence to application programmers and biometric service providers. The Consortium is a group of over 120 companies and organizations that have a common interest in promoting the growth of the biometrics market.

First of all, that gives you an idea of the size of this born-yesterday business: 120 companies and organizations already had some stake in developing a standard. One of the organizations sitting in was the National Security Agency (NSA), a group with more than a passing interest in the future of biometric security devices. Fortunately, the NSA was neutral—it wanted to see a first-rate standard, but it wasn't promoting the claims of any one company against those of another. Unfortunately, they were just about the only neutral player involved.

The Consortium was loaded with big-name firms: IBM, Intel, Compaq, Hewlett-Packard, Texas Instruments, Microsoft, Unisys, and lots more. We felt like mice in a field of dinosaurs, but we were also sure that we had something valuable to bring to the table—a clear vision of what was needed to help this industry grow, and we weren't going to sit this one out just because we were a tiny, privately owned company. There were some small, biometric-only players, but most of the attention was focused on the giant, international companies, because they generally decided what the new standards would be. Of course, while they all had something to gain by achieving a single bio API standard, they had even more to gain by making sure that the specifications in that standard favored one of their products. Okay, maybe I was a little naive at that point, but I really thought we were all getting together to do what was best for the biometrics industry. Then I discovered that everyone was actually trying to promote their own hardware, their own middleware, their own software, or something, and the quality of the standard was actually a secondary consideration. Even that was tolerable if one of them had a really kick-ass API that would make us all bow down and say, "That's it. That's the one. They nailed it." But that wasn't happening.

What was happening was a lot of infighting. Each company had some key to the puzzle; they were all playing their own variations on the biometric theme, and none of them was in any hurry to give ground to anyone else. It seemed that everyone had a self-serving motive that worked to sabotage consensus-building and slow down the decision-making process. Consequently, what should have been a rational process of comparison and analysis, leading to a streamlined progression toward the best of all possible standards turned into an endless series of pointless meetings that made a Congressional filibuster look fast-paced.

I had somehow managed to become the chairperson of the Device Level Working Group, which was a pretty important part of the consortium, and I saw a lot of this nonsense up close. Months went by, meetings dragged on, and we weren't getting anywhere. I'm not the world's most patient guy to begin with, and this was starting to push me toward the edge.

Fortunately, fate stepped in, and in a most unlikely way. My committee was chock full of big companies. Looking at the roster, I realized that all of them were big, publicly traded firms. They all seemed to fall into one of three categories: Big, Very Big, or Humongous. Except, of course, I/O Software. We were a small, independent, totally private company; a mouse running along with a herd of elephants. That fact didn't escape the notice of my fellow committee members and other people at the Consortium. As time dragged on, and we were making glacier-like progress, people started making comments like: "Who the hell is I/O Software? What are you doing here?" and "Why did you even bother to join? What do you expect to accomplish?" People said we would be damn lucky to contribute just a few lines to the final, official standard. They came right out and said that our little company was too small, too insignificant, and frankly, didn't belong on the same playing field with the big boys.

I'm a pretty easy-going guy. Only two things get my engines fired up. The first is if I see a big traffic jam ahead of me, I'm going to look for a shortcut that saves time, and if there isn't one, I'm going to make one. Like graduating from high school a year early—it was just a shortcut to get where I wanted to go. Basically, I have a gene buried in my DNA that tells me that first gear is no fun. I'm not trying to compete with anyone or get my ego involved with anything, I just hate to go slow.

The second thing that gets me fired up is personal: If someone tells me that something can't be done, there's no point in even trying; 9 times out of 10 I'm going to do it just to prove he's wrong. What? Nobody can display thousands of Asian ideograms in an 8-bit format? Okay, I'll do it. Nobody can compress a 30-frames-per-second (fps) Quarter Common Intermediate Format (QCIF) video signal and send it over a 28.8 modem? Just watch me. Industry experts say nobody can create software to run a stand-alone, credit-card-sized fingerprint authentication device? Give me a two-week head start, then start writing the press release. I love a challenge when it's interesting and good-natured, but even more when it isn't. This was nasty. People came right up to me and said we were a crappy little company that didn't belong there. We weren't good enough to be in the game. I'll skip all the personal insults; by that point they didn't matter much.

For me, this was the perfect storm of incentive—slow as molasses progress toward a known goal, a sea of selfish, pig-headed corporate infighting, plus outright insults toward me and my company. That's all the motivation I needed to go looking for an exit ramp and find a better way.

The 800-Pound Gorilla in the Room: Microsoft

With the twentieth century rapidly coming to a close, the media discovered two big stories that were sure to attract attention from readers, both high-brow and low-brow, and both involved Microsoft. For the masses, there was a big to-do about something called Y2K, the fear that Windows-based computers would all go haywire on the first day of the new millennium, shutting down the entire global infrastructure, crashing hundreds of jetliners, leaving the U.S. Navy stranded at sea, and on and on. Only a bit less dramatic was a series of lawsuits brought by the U.S. Department of Justice (DoJ) and 20 U.S. states against Microsoft. Essentially, the U.S. government was attacking one of the nation's biggest and most powerful companies (at this point in time Microsoft was an extremely powerful organization) for violating antitrust laws. Microsoft was no stranger to this kind of trouble. The company had been investigated by the Federal Trade Commission early in the 1990s and then, when that didn't produce results, by the DoJ itself. The antitrust trial started in 1998 and continued for two years, just about the same time that the ANSI meetings were going on. As a result, Microsoft was suddenly thrust into the public spotlight as the bad guy, the defendant in a case brought by the federal government. The papers were full of stories from rival companies about what an evil empire Microsoft had become. In many quarters, Microsoft bashing became a popular national pastime.

One by-product of this negative publicity was that during this time the company became extraordinarily nice to suppliers, business partners, and others with whom it was doing business. To everyone's amazement, this giant, powerful, and immensely influential company was an uncharacteristically quiet participant in the BioAPI Consortium. Instead of promoting a standard, Microsoft said they wanted to incorporate whatever standard emerged from ANSI into their new OS. However, it was easy to see that their representatives were no happier about the slow progress at ANSI than I was. This got me to thinking. If I was frustrated, and Microsoft was frustrated, and Microsoft was now under pressure to play nice with smaller companies, maybe this was a once-in-a-lifetime opportunity. At the very least, it was something that I had to investigate.

First, I needed to talk to somebody in charge, the key exec in Redmond who was responsible for biometrics—not the guys sitting in the ANSI meetings who had never heard of me. I had lots of personal contacts inside the company, and I could have called them and hoped for some kind of introduction—*if* they knew the right guy. But Microsoft is a huge company, and key managers change jobs fairly often, so the chances of getting hooked up with the person I needed to talk to were slim. As usual, I looked for a short cut. So I sent an e-mail to Bill Gates, and he responded.

Bill put me in touch with Microsoft's executives in charge of network security and said I should talk to them first. After some back-and-forth with those people, we were invited to come to Redmond to show our stuff. Tas and I took our BAPI and all the software that worked with it. We did the whole dog and pony show, explained how and why our approach was technically superior and why Microsoft should like it. The key point here was that our BAPI architecture was so close to the Windows architecture that somebody should have ordered a paternity test. We had been working very closely with Microsoft's hardware group for many years, and we knew the Windows OS inside out. In short, we had the best BioAPI in the market, we were an independent company with no other hardware or software to promote in conjunction with BAPI, and our code was so familiar to Microsoft that it felt like family.

It was a good presentation, and we could tell that they liked it, liked what we had to say. But Microsoft had other ideas. They said they were talking about creating their own biometric authentication system. I thought that was crazy, and I told them so. They would be reinventing the wheel. But I was stuck. After doing our big presentation, what more was there to say? I asked them at least to let us participate in the development of any new system they might come up with.

It's important to remember what was going on at this time. In the 1990s, Microsoft was involved in an escalating series of conflicts with other companies and the U.S. government, culminating in 1998 in an antitrust lawsuit—*United States v. Microsoft*. This was a new step for a software company, getting sued by the Department of Justice. It became a huge media circus: the world's richest man (Gates) was forced to come out of seclusion to testify in Washington, judges who could not operate a Palm Pilot had to listen to hours of exposition about software code, and every taxi driver who had ever watched *Law and Order* got to weigh in on the fine line between innovation, competition, and monopolistic behavior. Op-ed pieces around the country suggested that Microsoft had become too big and too out-of-control for its own good, and one court ruling proposed a legal mandate to break up the company into smaller parts. Gates, who had never put much stock in either personal or corporate PR, much less Washington lobbyists, discovered that Microsoft-bashing was quickly becoming the new national pastime.

None of this directly affected anyone outside Microsoft, but if you were trying to talk to the company about new and potentially game-changing software with global ramifications in 1998–1999, you had to deal with the fact that Redmond was a city under siege. I spoke directly to that mentality as I continued to meet with their biometric people. I told them that we chose your architecture for BAPI because we support it. We think Microsoft has actually done a big service for the whole computer industry. Your OS allows different hardware to play with different software all over the world. Because you created this single, standardized platform (Windows), you made it possible for this industry to grow quickly. Thanks to you, different programs and peripherals can work together seamlessly, agnostically. To me, that's an open system in the most important sense of the term. Yes, you control the plumbing that connects everything, but so what? That's business. What's important is that you are enabling connections, allowing companies to develop hardware and software secure in the knowledge that as long as it runs on Windows it can connect to just about anything else on the planet.

I said that long ago I had a vision that one day we'd be having this conversation, and I told our BAPI team that we had to take a page out of your play book; that is, create an architecture that works with everyone. Our guys were against it at first, but I knew that this was the way to go. The biometric industry will only take off when it gets past its limited, proprietary infancy and finds a common platform, like the Windows OS, that allows everything to link to everything.

No surprise, they liked that a lot. Half the world seemed to be saying, "Down with Microsoft!" and we were telling them that we wanted to be based on their architecture; we wanted to use their business model; we wanted to work with them in the future. They responded very positively. They could see that we got it; we understood the Microsoft culture and the Microsoft vision. That helped a lot.

Something else was going on in Redmond besides hunkering down and waiting for the DoJ storm to pass. The new OS, originally called Windows NT 5.0, was still under development with release aimed for the turn of the millennium. Late in 1998 the name was officially changed to Windows 2000, and beta versions were sent out for testing. This was the highest-profile project within Microsoft at that time, and it was devouring plenty of resources. Through my contacts in Redmond, I discovered that development of their own biometric authentication system was not speeding ahead. In fact, it seemed to be on a back burner. I figured it was a good time to remind them about I/O Software and all the things we brought to the table. I called Microsoft and spoke with their network security people again. This time they said that I'd caught them at a very good time. Their big new OS was getting ready to ship, and they were looking seriously at new features to build into future versions of Windows.

That opened a door to a whole new round of discussions. They already understood the importance of having top-class authentication as part of their OS. That feature would be absolutely essential for their enterprise (big corporate) clients, but would also be of growing importance to individual PC users. Gradually, they came to understand and appreciate BAPI. They saw that it really was device agnostic, that it could be used anywhere, with any sensors or applications that might come along in the future, and they saw right away that it was largely based on the Windows architecture. In other words, BAPI and Microsoft were a natural fit. By the end of 1999, we were engaged in serious talks about how they might incorporate BAPI into future versions of Windows.

Of course, the ANSI meetings were still dragging on, and I/O Software was still pushing for a standard. In fact, we actively contributed big chunks of text to the BioAPI specifications document that was beginning to take shape. The first BioAPI specifications, which ran over 100 pages, were liberally laced with information we had supplied. While all this was going on, however, we were working just as hard behind the scenes to bypass the political infighting and interminable committee meetings and find some way to close a private deal with Microsoft. By the dawn of the new millennium, that deal was done.

It's easy to forget what a different market we lived in around 2000. Obviously, Microsoft is still a very powerful company these days, but it is nothing like the unstoppable juggernaut it appeared to be just a decade ago. Today, a very large percentage of the world's servers run on Linux, and all the top supercomputers run Linux. But back then Microsoft products seemed to run everything that had a CPU (which was the background for the DoJ's antitrust case). Microsoft was not merely *the* major player in the software industry, controlling both the world's favorite operating system and the leading applications that ran on that system, but the company's global mind share was even bigger than its market share. Many people assumed that if new, powerful, well-accepted consumer products were going to appear, they would most likely be developed by or in conjunction with Microsoft. If you'd asked people on the street about the possibility of a pocket-size digital music player appearing, a lot of them would have guessed that it would come from Microsoft. What about an online store to sell music, or a radically new smartphone that would also combine a web browser and this digital music player? Again, a very large number of people around the world would have guessed that those products would come from Redmond. Sure, everyone knew about a company called Apple, but it was a minor PC maker with an insignificant market share. There was no iPod, iTunes, or iPhone, and the firm was still recovering from a painful shake-up in the boardroom. Some Wall Street analysts doubted it would even survive as an independent company. Just to reassure investors, one of Steve Jobs' first major acts after returning as CEO was to announce a large capital injection from an ongoing business tie-up with...Microsoft! Jobs really shocked the faithful by having Gates (still a nemesis in the minds of many Mac loyalists) speak at Macworld via video link. In short, Apple was not the company it is today, and on the other side of the seesaw, Microsoft was not the company it is today. Microsoft's dominant position inside the world's computers, big and small, and its influence on both the hardware and software industries was hard to overstate.

In practice, that meant that once Microsoft adopted an internal standard, it would become the new standard for the world—not because ANSI or the ISO declared it so, but because Microsoft said, "It's what we're going to use." In a very real sense, Microsoft decided standards simply by adopting them, which then became de facto standards for the industry. So, as long as the firm chose to sit on the sidelines at the BioAPI Consortium and wait for ANSI to decide a BioAPI standard, everything was okay. The various players in the biometrics industry could battle it out until one of them achieved supremacy and then see its code adopted as the ANSI standard.

But I knew that wasn't going to happen. We were going to do an end run around the whole process and deliver the strongest, cleanest API on the market directly to Microsoft. Once they announced that they would be using BAPI, it was Game Over for the standards race.

The Shot Heard Round the World: Microsoft Licenses BAPI

As the new millennium got under way, ANSI began shuffling toward releasing their first BioAPI spec. Several members of the committee I chaired were important clients of ours; many of them were there because I had invited them to join. As I began to hammer out the details of how our tie-up with Microsoft would work and when and how we would make the public announcement, I also realized that I could not blindside our clients with this news. They would feel, and justifiably so, that we'd double-crossed them by talking up the ANSI standard and then turning around and doing a secret deal with Microsoft. It looked as though we were stabbing them in the back, and that's not what I had in mind at all.

Even as the ANSI specs were being drawn up in February and March of 2000, I had private meetings with companies like Compaq and HP to brief them on the coming changes to the landscape, changes that were now set to become public at the beginning of May. It's a bit of an understatement to say that some of these firms were not happy with the news, but there was nothing they could do about it. The deal with Microsoft was done, and once it hit the papers there was no option for them except to throw in their lot with our BAPI group. As you can imagine, I had a lot of discussions with our client firms, explained how and why this had come to pass, and tried to make them understand that we were not anti-ANSI; we had not been planning this move from the beginning. I told them how frustrating it had been to sit for months listening to endless ranting from various firms, all intent on getting their own way with this new standard, and none of them offering a product as good as ours in the first place.

The first BioAPI spec, with a lot of our work included in it, came out on March 30, 2000. A month later, several of our clients, the companies we had lobbied hard about our reasons for doing the deal with Redmond, agreed to become founding supporters of our BAPI group.

On May 2, 2000, the *Wall Street Journal* reported:

> Microsoft today will announce it signed a licensing agreement with closely held I/O Software Inc. of Riverside, Calif., which has a proven "application programming interface," or API, for biometrics technology....
>
> Microsoft's move...may surprise some participants in a consortium of technology companies that have been working on a separate API. Yet that consensus-based effort has been slow, and many within the consortium privately said they welcome news of I/O's deal as something that will speed the development of a broader market for biometric devices.

In the biometrics industry, that was the shot heard around the world. The 100+ companies involved in the ANSI consortium were very, very unhappy. We had made all their squabbling and their self-promotion, as well as all the time and resources they had spent developing their own APIs, completely irrelevant. In this particular instance, even ANSI was irrelevant. When it came to global standards in the computer industry (at least back then), there were only three organizations that mattered: ANSI, which promoted U.S. standards; the ISO, which promoted international standards; and Microsoft, which set de facto standards just by adopting certain technologies. To be fair, Japanese standards were somewhat important then, too. We even received funding from the Ministry of International Trade and Industry (MITI), predecessor to the current Ministry of Economy Trade and Industry (METI), to help part of BAPI become a Japanese Industrial Standard (JIS).

To be commercially viable, everyone had to be compatible with the Microsoft Operating System (OS). That meant if Microsoft chose to adopt some new technology without waiting for the rest of the industry or some bureaucratic standards organization to make a decision, there was no point in debating what might or might not become the official standard. To put it another way, as long as Redmond sat quietly, looking over the field of entries, ANSI had a horse race, but once it laid a bet on the winner, the other horses might as well stop running.

Needless to say, a lot of horse owners were angry, many of them at us, but probably even more at Microsoft. Over the years, Gates and Co. had angered many in the industry by doing things their own way. In one famous instance, they said they were working with IBM to develop a new operating system called OS/2, while in reality the programmers in Redmond were cooking up Windows, which would relegate OS/2 to the Software Museum. The deal with our firm looked to many people like a repeat of that episode. I knew better, but thinking back on it, there were enough people angry at us that I was happy to let Microsoft take some of the heat. For one thing, they were used to it, and they could handle it better than we could, and for another, we were so excited about the BAPI announcement that we didn't care all that much about whatever criticism was coming our way. Just a few months back people had been dumping on us for being too weak, too dumb, and too insignificant, essentially getting in the way of ANSI business. Now the same people were criticizing us for being too smart, too clever, and by-passing them all on a private highway to success.

I took it all in stride. Upset as I was about all the insults, both to me and to my company, I never set out to intentionally sabotage the ANSI process or to get back at specific companies in the biometrics community. That's not my style. Yes, I was upset, but insults are part of the game; I got over those pretty quickly. What really motivated me was that generations-old part of my DNA that says, "Pause briefly at a red light, but if it doesn't turn green real soon, start looking for a shortcut."

I knew that my deal with Microsoft was just a response to the frustration of sitting too long in that ANSI traffic jam. Part of me was actually grateful to all those people who had looked down their noses at us and, in effect, told me that our little jalopy of a company wasn't even good enough to be in the same traffic jam with them. They were the ones who opened my eyes to the need to find a better way.

Microsoft wasn't looking to buy BAPI from us; they simply licensed it and announced that it would be included in an upcoming Windows release. That's all it took. If BAPI was going to be part of Windows, and Windows ran most of the computers on Earth, that meant that sooner or later BAPI would be everywhere, pre-installed in most machines when users bought them. How many individuals or companies would decide *not* to use the API included with Windows and instead pay extra to install some other package that might or might not be as seamlessly Windows-friendly as BAPI? It was a purely theoretical question. No one really wanted to use a biometric API that wasn't supported by Microsoft. It was possible, but for almost all users, it was just not practical. In fact, more than one company that was heavily invested in developing biometric software saw their stratospheric share price, which had been climbing steadily on the back of the Internet stock bubble, stall and begin to fall to earth immediately following the Microsoft announcement.

So, after May 2, 2000, I/O's BAPI became a *de facto* global standard (it would ultimately go on to be an ANSI, JIS, and ISO standard and be added to the permanent science and technology collection of the Smithsonian Institution). On paper, Microsoft was just another licensing client, but in reality they were *the* client. Without their support, we wouldn't be selling licenses. Because of their support, we would soon sell over 160 licenses to hardware and software makers that either had products or were developing products in this now burgeoning industry. On a personal level, my strategy of developing a single, generic biometric API and incorporating everything we knew about the field to make it the best product in the business was vindicated. Now, instead of doing customized fingerprint identification units for 50 or 100 companies, and trying to support them all, we were selling licenses to all those companies and more.

Edison famously said that genius is 1 percent inspiration and 99 percent perspiration. I think success in this business is 1 percent inspiration, 89 percent perspiration, and 10 percent luck. Don't ever underestimate the importance of luck. To this day I am absolutely convinced that my company had the best-designed API in the bio-metrics industry, but had superior technology lost out to superior marketing, corporate politics, and even fickle consumer preferences in the past? More times than I can count. Our videoconferencing software was sure enough brilliant technology, but it was years ahead of its time. So all the genius or inspiration in creating something is important, and doing the hard work to turn that inspiration into a viable product is also extremely important, but that combination still doesn't guarantee suc-cess. Nothing guarantees success—it just happens, or it doesn't. For us, BAPI was exactly the right product in the right position at the right time. Had we been six months earlier or later, had any of a dozen other variables been just a little bit different, BAPI could have become Failure Number 217, another brilliant idea whose potential we couldn't quite realize. I give credit where credit is due, and our programmers and managers and everyone did a great job, but all of that would have meant little if luck hadn't played her part as well. When the new era dawned, I/O Software was a major player in the biometric field, a major player in the security field in general, and a little company with a very healthy balance sheet.

TAKEAWAY: Don't Be Afraid to Promote Yourself

Many times, the key to advancing our strategy or getting I/O Software's products in front of a potential client or partner involved self-promotion. I don't mean hiring a PR firm; I mean calling up or e-mailing the person who was in the best position to help us. When I needed to leverage the power of Microsoft to help us hit a certain target, I e-mailed Bill Gates, and he replied right away. I've con-tacted all sorts of people—professors, politicians, business leaders, you name it—and the result has usually been positive. Lots of people think, *That guy must be really busy. He'll never even read my e-mail, much less answer it,* but that's a mistake. Important people became important by paying attention to business opportunities. No, they don't want to read a five-page e-mail from you, but if you have something compelling to say to them, keep it short and direct, and more often than not they will pay attention. Conversely, I always make it a point (and sometimes go to great effort) to reply to every legitimate e-mail I get, regardless of whom it is from.

Chapter 9

IPO: It's All in the Timing

F ollowing our joint public announcement with Microsoft on May
5, 2000, BAPI was one of *the* big stories, not just in the biometrics
industry, but in the computer world in general. Regardless of
the circumstances of its birth, the mere fact that BAPI was going to be
part of the next Windows operating system was really big news. Just a
couple of months after the announcement, Bill Gates took me along on
his annual round-the-world tour of Microsoft's Executive Briefing
Centers (EBC). The EBCs are fixed locations in a dozen different
countries where local corporate executives and government officials get a
chance to meet face-to-face with Microsoft's top brass and senior engineers to get an idea of what technologies will be shaping their world in
the coming few years. Gates always enjoyed introducing Microsoft's latest
and greatest technologies to an admiring audience of major decision-
makers, and in 2000 the big show-and-tell was BAPI, which would soon
be an integral part of the next-generation Windows OS.

We did the EBC in Korea, which was the center for Asia at that
time, and in Belgium, which was the European center, as well as

meetings in the United States. The Microsoft Office guys would demo some new wrinkle in their software suite, the hardware guys would show off some new, not yet released product, and then we'd demo BAPI. Of course, it was still an I/O Software product, not a Microsoft product, so they needed us to do the official presentation, but the message was clear: biometric authentication was going to be a big thing in years to come, and in response, Microsoft and I/O Software were working together.

All this time, even as we were taking our bows for BAPI, the Puppy was continuing to pull in rave reviews and sell strongly. Sony let us continue to sell it but allowed other distributers to get in on the action. We didn't mind losing exclusive rights to sell the product because business was booming. We didn't even care—I/O was not exactly a household name, but in our industry, we had finally arrived. A big commercial hit with Sony followed by a major coup with Microsoft. What were we going to do for an encore?

The immediate answer, of course, was to take the company public. Since the very beginning, back when Tas and I were in our teens, we had operated independently, running the company with loans or investments from what we called the 3 Fs: family, friends, and fools. We continued to grow it through internal funding, never once going outside to a bank or a venture capital company or an angel professional investor. On the contrary, our funding arrangements were so very unprofessional that Tas and I often joked that "VC" stood for "VISA card," the start-up entrepreneur's first and last recourse when it came to shoestring financing. Like most start-ups, our early years had been very lean, but once we began to get rolling the business did quite well. Many technology companies had much larger sales than I/O Software, but their impressive top-line numbers were offset by tiny profit figures, usually in the lower single digits. By the time we were selling the Puppy, we had a profit margin close to 80 percent, which is unheard of in almost any industry. We weren't exactly printing money, but we had enough free cash flow to fund our own development work and to roll with the ups and downs of the economy without ever having to resort to bank financing or vulture capital. In fact, our success in developing products for Sony led that company to make a substantial minority investment in our firm. However, I knew well enough by this time that

Japanese companies often invest in suppliers and partner companies not out of any desire to own them or control them, but as a sign of their intention to maintain a trusted, long-term business relationship. We accepted it in that spirit and that was the single big exception to our no-outside-money rule.

And yet, in 2000, I began to have a different view of our proud independence. Sure, we thought we were smart to stay away from outside financing and try to do things on our own. Unlike many venture firms we knew or knew about, we had no outside directors second to our board from VCs or investment banks or law firms. We were on our own, and we liked that. But internal funding is a double-edged sword. While it was true that we never needed to beg a bank or a VC for money, that also meant that we had no experience in the world of finance, even at a rudimentary corporate level, and that was not so good. There's an argument to be made that because we didn't use a VC, we weren't as prepared to do an IPO and do it in a timely manner as we could have been. Once we started talking seriously about doing an IPO, I sometimes wished we had a Wall Street–savvy CFO on our board.

Fortunately, in the early days of the company I had gone back to school on weekends to strengthen some of the management skills that I felt I was lacking. I enrolled in the University of California's Advanced Management Program and later on, the Executive Management Program. To be honest, I didn't join them so that I could study Corporate Finance or Accounting from textbooks, but in order to meet the successful executives who visited the program to talk to us. I met at least two dozen smart, experienced execs who had seen it all, or at least a whole lot more than I had, and that was another important part of my business education. I stayed in touch with some of those people for many years afterward, and thanks to their hands-on information and the advice of other people they introduced me to, I felt a little more comfortable getting ready to make the big leap into the public domain, so to speak.

We had kicked around the idea of doing an IPO for some time. The late-1990s were the peak of the so-called dot-com boom, when it seemed that any Internet-related company could raise roughly half the GDP of Switzerland in seed financing with just a few notes scribbled on a cocktail napkin. Looking at I/O Software objectively, we had proven technology, impressive cash flow, an incredible profit margin, and Microsoft's backing—much more than many younger companies that were inundated with VC or IPO cash, even when they were still pre-revenue. As the dot-com insanity got bigger and bigger, and the Y2K fears evaporated, otherwise sane economists and stock analysts were predicting years of robust growth ahead for the industry. In fact, many voices were now saying that the old metrics applied to stock growth were irrelevant in light of the new economy that the Internet had unleashed. PERs (price-earnings ratios, one of the fundamental mea-surements of a stock's underlying value) were said to be misleading; companies with no sales, no revenue, and mountains of debt were seen as positioned for growth. To many, the market had nowhere to go but up, even though it was already getting nosebleeds from its nearly vertical ascent of the previous year. The financial weekly *Barron's* reported, "America's 371 publicly traded Internet companies...are collectively valued at $1.3 trillion, which amounts to about 8 percent of the entire U.S. stock market." Remember that most of these companies did not even exist a few years earlier.

Crazy or not, the opening of the new millennium seemed like a good time to do our IPO. Between the Puppy's endless string of awards and the Microsoft-BAPI announcement, we figured we would be one of the more highly valued offerings that year. Investment bankers assured us that the combination of our more than 10-year track record, solid sales figures, unusually high profitability, and a tie-in to the next Windows OS would make us a stellar target for high-tech investors.

All that sounded great, and we did start the paperwork necessary to do the IPO, but as the formal Microsoft announcement drew near, we were much too busy with other things to pay much attention to the stock market. I did notice that there seemed to be a serious correction in early March of 2000, and many of the dot-com stocks dipped signifi-cantly. But we couldn't worry about that; our star was very much on the rise. However, as 2000 marched on, we did our big announcement, we did our global dog and pony shows with Microsoft, and we settled back into doing business; the realities of the stock market began to demand our attention. The NASDAQ index, where most of the dot-coms were listed, was dropping like a stone one week, then bouncing back the next, then plummeting again in stomach-wrenching drops that seemed to say that the old economics still had some surprises for overpriced Internet stocks that believed they could defy gravity. Things seemed to get a little better in 2001, but then the NASDAQ roller coaster started again, with the losses definitely ahead of the gains. Giant bankruptcies replaced giant mergers as the big media stories of the day, as high-tech businesses went bust one after another and *dot-bombs* became a new buzzword. Between March of 2000, just before our BAPI announcement, and October of 2002, something on the order of $5 trillion in market value simply evaporated from U.S. stock markets. Along the way, the investment banks that were managing our IPO started to lose their nerve. Of course they didn't want to cancel the offering—IPO fees were their lifeblood back then; instead, they wanted to rush it, which scared us even more. Tas and I looked at the market, and we talked to people who understood more about Wall St. than we did but were not involved with our listing. The only sane answer we could come up with was: the timing is bad; rushing the IPO in a failing market could be disastrous, so it's best to postpone it indefinitely. With some regret, we pulled the plug on the machinery that was going to turn us into a public company.

People sometimes ask me how things might have been different and what would have happened if we had started the IPO process about six months earlier. My answer is that all sorts of things might have been different, but looking back on it all, we were incredibly lucky right from the beginning of I/O Software, and I have no regrets. About 90 percent of all start-up companies fail within three years. We had been around much longer than that, and we were as successful as any company had a right to expect. True, our timing was off on launching a few of our earlier projects, such as videoconferencing, but the process that led from the Puppy into BAPI was like a rocket sled of personal and corporate growth. We were in exactly the right place at exactly the right time with the right technologies, just slightly ahead of the market's needs and ready to deliver solid, well-tested products as the demand for them exploded.

To answer the IPO question: Do I ever wonder what would have happened if we'd done it in late 1999, for example? Sure I do. We had a great balance sheet (a rarity among our peer companies in those days), and the Microsoft announcement was right around the corner. The stock would have listed high and shot up from there. Maybe I/O

Software would have become a household name. And maybe the shareholders would have thrown me out and hired some high-profile, media-savvy CEO who could get his face on the cover of *Forbes*. Who knows? All I can say is that things would have been different; I don't know if they would have been better. And it doesn't matter, because all of that is behind us now. The bottom line in my mind is this: by and large, throughout our last decade as an independent company, we made the right decisions at the right time. What-ifs don't change anything.

Interlude: Helping the Military

I mentioned earlier how I came to work for the local Riverside, California, police department and then, later, worked on IT-related matters with the FBI—which is still ongoing. The Bureau needs to be up to date on all sorts of technological changes that pose threats to U.S. citizens, corporations, and institutions, and ways to prevent, counteract, or neutralize those threats as well as to apprehend the people who are behind them. The FBI has tremendous resources to accomplish that enormous task, but no one organization has a monopoly on information, and the FBI is wise enough to know that outside opinions are always useful. I also mentioned before that in the process of developing I/O Software's security software products, I had become an expert on various types of digital security, and I continued to keep myself up to date on trends and practices related to this field. As a result, I could be of service to the FBI and other organizations in discussing potential problems and planning practical responses.

I suppose that sounds extremely vague, but it's intended to be. My work was very undramatic and not entertaining for Hollywood movies. An even less action-packed, 007-type adventure, but nonetheless important and rewarding, was my work for the U.S. Department of Defense (DoD).

There is a long-standing term in the DoD called COTS, short for Commercial Off the Shelf, in which the military could procure existing commercial products rather than pay to develop them from scratch. Of course, the DoD has often been lambasted both in the press and in Congress for spending billions of dollars to develop military-grade toilets or whatever, which led to a mandate to find workable commercial solutions for certain military needs and, where necessary, upgrade these commercial products to military specifications. One obvious area where huge amounts of budget and years of R&D time could be saved was electronics-related. There was a news article a few years ago about the U.S. Air Force buying over 1,000 Sony PlayStation 3 game consoles and linking them up to form a budget-priced supercomputer. That's one approach, although not very sophisticated. The Pentagon was thinking about all sorts of high-tech products that might be just what the military was looking for. Needless to say, not all the state-of-the-art electronic equipment was being made by American companies. A lot of it, PS3s aside, was and still is made in Japan.

The DoD needed to talk to Japanese electronics companies on a case-by-case basis to figure out how the Pentagon might purchase some of their technology. Mind you, this was a very entrepreneurial concept for both parties involved. Obviously, somebody from one branch of the government must have been having lunch with somebody from another, because my name eventually came up, and the DoD asked me if I could help. In spite of all the things going on with my business at the time, my answer was the same as it had been to the Riverside Police Dept. ages ago: How can I be of service?

Among the long list of things the Pentagon was interested in was optical equipment—video cameras, still cameras, night vision glasses, and so on. A number of Japanese companies had excellent equipment, and some of it was pretty durable, but in the end it was still commercial grade, which meant good but not up to military specifications (or mil-spec). The DoD wanted to see if the Japanese firms might be willing to partner on specific products so that the next time they upgraded those products the Pentagon could help pay for extra features in order to boost their specs beyond the normal consumer level. The entrepreneurial thinking was, "You'll get a much better product for no out-of-pocket development costs, and we'll save a bundle by buying from you instead of trying to build it all from scratch."

This sounded like a win–win situation for public sector-private sector cooperation, and in the United States it would be. But the very idea of military cooperation is an extremely sensitive issue for Japanese companies. The possibility that their products could be used for military applications overseas would cause most firms to veto a plan without even looking at it. Aside from providing support for Japan's own military (the carefully named Self-Defense Forces), domestic companies are strictly prohibited from engaging in any commercial activity that will support military activities. This situation grew out of Japan's Constitution, sometimes called the MacArthur Constitution, as it was drafted by American Occupation forces rather than the Japanese themselves. Article 9 of that Constitution specifically forbids Japan from engaging in any kind of aggressive acts, making it to my knowledge the only major country in the world to be legally prohibited from going to war. Article 9 has stood for well over half a century, and it is still considered sacred by a majority of the Japanese people. As far as the government is concerned, it is the law. Woe be to any company that wants to sell military goods to support a foreign war or even ordinary products that are being repurposed by a foreign military for martial applications.

I actually went to visit many companies and laid out the basic DoD proposal to purchase and test their high-end technology to see if it might have appropriate uses in military operations. Not surprisingly, a lot of companies said thank you, but no thank you. It just wasn't a good topic for discussion.

However, there were a couple of firms that were exceptionally proud of their technology and understood that the equipment in question was not in any way of a military nature. They were flattered that the United States was interested in their high-quality manufacturing and would field-test it for them in ways that Japanese companies never dreamed of. One item in particular was a high-resolution camera. Considering its performance, it was relatively compact and portable. With it, a ground commander could clearly see a target 10 miles away or identify a particular individual in a crowd from a similar distance. It wasn't a weapon by any stretch of the imagination.

Needless to say, the negotiations were kept very quiet. If word got out that a Japanese company was supplying equipment to an active military force, it had the potential to ignite a scandal. Of course, the Japanese firms knew that the technology was not directly military in nature, could not be used to kill anyone, and in many cases was merely a refinement of prior technology anyway (for example, the camera in question was just an updated, portable version of the kind we have put in spy satellites for decades, so it was hardly a radically new device). Still, in the minds of many Japanese executives, it contravened the Japanese Constitution, and that threatened to scuttle some very important negotiations at the last minute.

Perhaps this was another example of how I react when someone says, "Oh no, you can't do that." After working to bring the DoD and a limited number of Japanese manufacturers right up to the point of final agreement, I was not about to walk away and let the whole thing go down the tubes because some senior executives thought the transaction might be interpreted as unconstitutional. If it was indeed against Japanese law, I did not want any company to violate the law, and whether we could keep the transaction secret or not was irrelevant. If it was wrong, then we wouldn't do it. But if there was room for a more flexible interpretation of the law, we needed to discover that quickly. Japanese are too fast to say something is impossible, especially if there is no precedent for it, and even more so if the government is involved. The idea of talking to the officials in charge and asking for an interpretation would not occur to most people.

The Japanese government, it has been said, is really a government by bureaucracy. The prime minister is a political functionary who cuts ribbons, sits through interminable sessions of the national legislature, and smiles occasionally for TV cameras while unelected officials (the ministry bureaucrats) get on with the work of managing the country behind closed doors. The ministries are huddled together in the center of Tokyo in an area called Kasumigaseki. I knew that the only way to find out what would or would not be deemed acceptable behavior (i.e., constitutional) in this case was to get over to Kasumigaseki and ask the relevant ministry to hand down a ruling. Not only is this possible, but actually very practical. Despite their image as bastions of dark-suited, regulation-spouting officials, graduates of the same university and mainly concerned with climbing the promotion ladder, most of the people you are likely to encounter in a ministry are surprisingly helpful. They are often genuinely pleased to have a Japanese-speaking foreigner come in to ask for help, and I was determined to make my visit pleasant for them and productive for me.

In this matter, involving business dealings with overseas governments rather than companies, the Ministry of Foreign Affairs holds sway.

I took a cab to Kasumigaseki one day and went in, sans appointment, to ask for clarification on this point. I ultimately met with some mid-level officials, and I explained the situation in detail. They understood, and they said there was certainly no precedent. They wanted some time to discuss it within the ministry. When I went back for a subsequent meeting, we talked about the various aspects of the situation— I emphasized that the Japanese equipment would not be used as part of any weapons system, they were selling cameras and related equipment, not bullets or missile guidance systems; the sale would help the ailing Japanese economy and establish good relations between the U.S. government and the Japanese electronics industry. Ultimately, after a close review of the wording of the Constitution and all relevant cases they could find, the Foreign Affairs officials determined that nothing like this was clearly defined in law, nor was there any precedent to refer to. I was dejected; to me, that sounded like a bureaucratic No Way. But I had underestimated Japanese officialdom. They explained that "no precedent" did not mean "illegal" or "impossible," only that there was no prior case to base a ruling upon. Furthermore, a key tenet of the bureaucracy is that anything that is not specifically prohibited is deemed legal, at least until a new ruling appears to render it not so.

Because of my debating and reasoning skills, I became adept at thinking of creative analogies, so in this particular case, I came up with some existing uses for cameras that were similar. The bureaucrats were comforted to have ammunition they could use, so they soon became helpful.

The result was that I received official Ministry approval on behalf of my clients to conduct business along the specific lines we had discussed. Knowing how Japanese companies think, I persuaded the Ministry to issue written statements to the effect that the companies I had mentioned, with their names clearly stated in the documents, were not contravening the Constitution of Japan by engaging in the nonmilitary business pursuits specified in our discussions. Call it an emergency Get Out of Jail Free card in case any scandal should ever result, but it was exactly the kind of thing that helps risk-phobic Japanese executives sleep well at night. Needless to say, the electronics companies were astonished at my success, but quite delighted with the results. The Pentagon received their full cooperation, and American taxpayers saved a small fortune in the process.

I continued to do this type of advisory work for the DoD off and on because I was happy to help and also to continue building connections with Japanese companies. Moreover, I enjoyed exploring new and entrepreneurial ways of solving long, vexing problems. That probably would have been the extent of my involvement with the Pentagon had unusually dramatic events not unfolded one day while I happened to be visiting the building.

TAKEAWAY: Luck Is Always Part of the Game

It would be nice to think that we all get the just rewards for our labors, but it isn't so. As my company found out time and again, we could create the best damn product anyone had ever seen, but that didn't mean it would sell. Success is not just about what *you* do. Of course, you can't expect to achieve success without working your tail off, but all the great technology, smart strategy, and expensive advertising in the world cannot guarantee you'll get the brass ring. Timing is a key element, and you do not control the pace at which the market shifts or grows. A thousand small factors come into play, a thousand things that you have no control over, but which will work together to make things happen for or against you. Call it blind luck or dumb luck or whatever, but the bottom line is that you don't control everything. Luck always plays a part. Get used to it.

Also, it's important to remember that luck isn't for the lucky. It comes to those who create an environment where luck is more likely to occur. It's the ability to take appropriate risks to make luck a reality.

Luck also means your success is unpredictable. The bad side is that you can do everything right and still fail. The good side is that when you finally do succeed, you may do so beyond your wildest dreams. It's an old saying, but "expect the unexpected."

Lucky people naturally create situations that they recognize as unique opportunities to take advantage of.

Chapter 10

Using My Japanese Connections to Fight Terrorism

Much has been written about how the events of 9/11 changed the American political and economic landscape, and undoubtedly more will be revealed in the years to come. Certainly, for I/O Software, the consequences were predictable: the nation, its corporations and government organizations, became hyper-security-conscious, which meant that our security products and biometrics in general were more in demand than ever. Fingerprint identification was only a stepping stone to voice recognition, facial recognition, palm and iris scanning, and other tools that had been introduced earlier but whose development suddenly took on a new sense of urgency. And yet, even as the benefits of our post-Microsoft announcement began to accrue, and our internal discussions of the pros and cons of doing an IPO continued, our minds were not wholly on our work. Like most Americans, we were caught up in the war effort, and due to the nature of our business, looking for ways that we could contribute to its successful conclusion.

If you remember my emotional reaction when I discovered that a couple of criminals had broken into my Riverside office, and how that led me to volunteer my services to local law enforcement, then multiply that anger a hundredfold, you will begin to understand my feelings in the aftermath of 9/11. To put it bluntly, I was angry at the terrorists. I was angry, and I wanted to do something to get back at them. What I could do immediately was to offer my services, my knowledge, and experience to help thwart terrorism somehow.

The first step was to continue to step up my activities as an intermediary between the Pentagon and Japanese electronics companies, helping to source a variety of products and components that could be important to U.S. interests without contravening Japan's ban on selling weapons.

Prior to the Allied invasion of Iraq, the DoD was looking for some way to bypass the normal telecommunications networks, which were controlled by Saddam Hussein's government, and communicate directly with Iraqi citizens to advise them about the coming conflict. In another era, the air force would have dropped millions of paper leaflets on urban areas, warning civilians of impending bombing runs and the need to evacuate their families. In a desert environment, that didn't make much sense. Instead, what the DoD wanted was an open channel to the populace, an alternative source of information that Saddam could not block. The answer was to airdrop not leaflets, but radios—small, incredibly lightweight, paper-based radios that could be dropped to the populace and not break on impact.

Needless to say, when it comes to taking an existing technology, such as radio receivers, and making it smaller and lighter than anyone believed possible, no one outdoes the Japanese. So I helped to connect Japanese electronics firms with the military planners who were designing the specs for these items. The project sounded almost dreamlike, but the Japanese engineers agreed that it could be done. It took some time, but they delivered on their promise, developing what was called a paper radio, an unbelievably light device containing a small paper speaker, ultralight batteries, and a crystal pretuned to a specific frequency. Only a Japanese electronics group could come up with this combination of incredibly light materials and batteries, and then put the package together in a finished form that anyone would have said was impossible just a few months before.

While we're talking about radios, there was a major military-sponsored project with considerable civilian applications that I was grateful to play a small part in. The Joint Tactical Radio System (JTRS, called "jitters" in the military) initially grew out of the chaos of the Grenada invasion. If you saw newspaper reports at the time or the Hollywood version of the events later on, you undoubtedly remember the now-humorous scene of U.S. troops using their cell phones to call their base back in the States to direct tactical air support. The fact that the soldiers' radio equipment could not link up with the pilots' radios, and that all interservice radio communication ranged from poor to nonexistent was anything but humorous at the time. This situation resulted in part because for decades radios had used crystals to generate specific frequencies, and different military services, sometimes even different parts of the same service, used different frequencies. When the handheld radios on the front lines have only X-type crystals set for certain fixed frequencies, and none of them corresponds to any of the frequencies used by the fighter pilots or the AWACs command center in the air up above, situations like Grenada are inevitable.

This situation was no longer tolerable in the modern military. No one wanted to see televised news reports of some marine unit calling in air strikes with an iPhone. The answer was to develop a new family of software-based, programmable radios that could be reset as needed to connect all units from all services in any theater of battle. Thus, JTRS was born. It would not only guarantee communication links among all mission-related service personnel, but also match the advances in other areas of technology. The radios would transmit voice, video, and data, with integrated computer networking capabilities and operate over a very wide frequency spectrum. They would range in size from small, handheld walkie-talkies to helicopter- and ship-mounted equipment that could coordinate communications over a wide area. Replacing the old, hardware-based approach (crystals) with a new, software-based system also meant that the operating software could handle encryption and decryption of these sensitive communications on the fly. Last but certainly not least, the Pentagon wanted to acquire them at Walmart sale prices, not with the standard Nieman-Marcus price tags so common on new military hardware.

Once again, an important part of the solution was to source key components from Japanese makers. I was pleased to help introduce partner firms, interface between the Pentagon and the Japanese engineers, and coordinate the efforts of multiple firms to see that the project was delivered as promised. One important result was that this technology was adopted outside the military, so all the development work on JTRS ultimately benefited U.S. citizens at home, at least as much as Allied units on the battlefield. For example, 9/11 itself was a replay of Grenada: every unit of the New York Police Department was mobilized; more than a dozen state and federal agencies were on the ground before the last building had fallen; the Coast Guard and all branches of the military were on full alert; plus, fire crews and ambulance crews from all over the United States were rushing to New York to offer help. Once again, all these police, fire, military, state, federal, and local response units were operating on different radio frequencies. The result was chaos. At exactly the time when we most needed coordinated, interagency communications, everything was a wreck.

It will never happen again. FEMA (the Federal Emergency Management Agency) and other major organizations have switched to using JTRS. With programmable radios, they can communicate with anyone on any frequency, linking up ground response units with helicopters, ships, and even satellites. Voice, video, and computer data can be transmitted quickly, so that even command centers far away can get a fast, accurate picture of a crisis as it is happening and organize the response efficiently.

Following upon my role as a go-between for the Pentagon in negotiations with Japanese suppliers, I played a more active role in the war on terror in the years following 9/11. I served for a time on the Department of Defense Counter-Terrorism Task Force and Technical Support Working Group. I also worked with various groups in the Federal Bureau of Investigation (FBI), including something called InfraGard, which describes itself as "an association of businesses, academic institutions, state and local law enforcement agencies, and other participants dedicated to sharing information and intelligence to prevent hostile acts against the United States." Another entrepreneurial endeavor started in the mid-1990s at one of the FBI's field offices as a way to facilitate cooperation between the Bureau and local IT businesses. It grew quickly, and within a few years had regional chapters connected to every FBI field office. Thousands of corporations were cooperating with it, mostly in order to track down and prevent incidents of domestic cybercrime and malicious hacking. After 9/11, inquiries from all sorts of companies, not just IT firms, suddenly skyrocketed, and the organization grew rapidly. It came to represent all industries necessary to America's infrastructure, which means nearly everything: energy, chemical, nuclear, critical manufacturing, defense, banking and finance, transportation, shipping, water, public health, emergency services, IT, national monuments—you name it. InfraGard currently has more than 80 chapters across the United States and over 20,000 civilian members.

In a real sense, the program adds the resources of thousands of corporations, universities, and individuals to extend the FBI's ears and eyes and provide volumes of information that can help thwart terrorism before it happens. Every now and then, there is a report in the media about some dangerous plot that was broken up before it could carry out its plans, or some local law enforcement official comments in passing about the very small incidence of terrorism in the United States compared to the considerable threat posed by individuals and groups aiming to cause trouble. It seldom becomes big news, because news only happens when all our information-gathering fails to catch a serious threat and something happens. In short, there is a great deal of work and activity going on in the United States every day, but very little of it attracts attention. One of the main reasons that we hear so little about actual terrorist activity in the States is that the FBI is able to leverage this vast network of thousands of corporations, universities, and concerned individuals, and combine that with the resources of local law enforcement to create a virtual FBI that is much bigger and has far greater reach than any single government organization could possibly achieve and at a far lower cost—a truly entrepreneurial endeavor.

There are many interesting stories that should eventually be told about the valuable contributions that so many unseen people in our government have made to obtain vital information and to break up terrorist plots, both domestic and international. For obvious reasons, these stories cannot be told, but I hope the day will come when the hard work of all these men and women can be acknowledged and at least some of their stories revealed.

TAKEAWAY: Don't Be Afraid to Take Calculated Risks

Many people incorrectly assume that entrepreneurs are risk takers. I'd like to clarify that by saying that people who blindly take risks are simply idiots, whereas entrepreneurs are different. Before jumping blindly into a project, entrepreneurs will assess and measure the risks so they will know what actions to take to circumvent those risks. In other words, entrepreneurs take risks, but knowing from the start what those risks are and how to address them. They may not know all the risks involved or even all the solutions, but they are well aware of what they are getting into. Entrepreneurs, therefore, aren't risk takers, they are risk mitigators. Nevertheless, once in awhile, we all make mistakes. But the entrepreneur can learn from these mistakes and be in a better position to mitigate future risks. In this sense, failures become a valuable part of an education. As I have mentioned before, the opposite of success is not failure. It is not trying: You only really fail when you fail to try. People will tell you "it" can't be done, but if you give up at that point, you might miss a significant opportunity—like creating BAPI or licensing our technology to Microsoft.

Chapter 11

Last Exit: Microsoft Wants the Whole Thing

I mentioned that the Internet stock bubble began to collapse around the time we were licensing BAPI to Microsoft. That trend continued in the years that followed, and we put off any thoughts of taking our company public. It didn't matter much, as our business was booming. Obtaining the Good Mousekeeping Seal of Approval from Microsoft was all that was necessary to start the whole computer industry lining up to license our software; then 9/11 put the entire biometrics community into overdrive. Over the next couple of years we were not only licensing BAPI, but further developing our own package of applications to take advantage of its potential. Of course, many companies had created applications to work with BAPI, and many more apps were under development. Some of them were better than others, but in our opinion, none of them really took advantage of all that BAPI could do. Obviously, because we had created BAPI ourselves, we had a special vision about what its full potential should be and had more familiarity with its inner workings than any outside company was likely to achieve. When we realized that other firms were not likely to approach BAPI in the same way as we would, and that they seemed to lack the vision that we had for the product, we decided that the best thing to do was to create our own set of applications that showed BAPI to its best advantage.

Some of the first applications that we wrote to show what biometric authentication software could do were started back in the mid-1990s, when we first started developing BAPI. We had a rudimentary collection of these applications that we packaged under the name SecureSuite, and it got good reviews. As BAPI began to take off, we revised and upgraded these older programs, then added some new, more sophisticated applications and combined them all into a new SecureSuite package. This was I/O Software's showpiece, the toolkit that let BAPI work with all different kinds of software and hardware. In one sense, we were again taking a page from Microsoft's playbook: If BAPI was the core technology, our version of the Windows operating system, then SecureSuite was our MS Office, a collection of applications designed to work supremely well with that core technology, to interface with it seamlessly and take advantage of its power and flexibility. Everyone knows there are many rival programs that provide similar functions to Excel, Word, PowerPoint, and so on, yet most users seem comfortable running the house brand applications that were designed by the company that produces the operating system. The same situation applied in our case; there were many other programs out there, but a lot of companies that needed to rely on BAPI to create their authentication environments decided to use the applications that I/O Software had developed expressly for that technology.

So, in the first hectic years of the new century, we began licensing BAPI, we got Microsoft as the flagship licensee, we continued to develop and sell our SecureSuite package of applications, and we flirted with and then dropped the idea of doing an IPO. While all of this was going on, I was also helping the DoD connect with Japanese electronics companies to source low-cost, high-tech equipment and was spending more and more time advising various government agencies on cybersecurity and other issues. It was a crazy time, both for me personally and for the company. Crazy, but in both cases exciting, fulfilling, and rewarding in every sense. We had accepted the fact that it did not make sense to do an IPO at any time in the immediate future, and we assumed that our business base would continue to grow at this pace for a while. What we did not see was that the entire industry was growing equally fast and that the needs of our biggest client would make our success too attractive to resist. The results would change not only the company, but all of our private lives as well.

Selling the Company

Microsoft soon came to the realization that security and authentication would play an increasingly important role in the future of their products. BAPI was already an industry standard, and now our SecureSuite was fast becoming a standard as well. With increasing demand from government and industry for secure computing environments, Microsoft concluded that merely licensing this technology while we continued to market it to one and all—including Microsoft's rivals—was foolish. Why not simply absorb the technology and make it their own? In effect, Microsoft could improve its own security by acquiring all of our know-how and taking I/O Software off the market.

I won't bore you with the details, but in a relatively short period of time we came to an arrangement to sell I/O Software to the people in Redmond, with whom we had worked in one form or another for the past dozen years. The word soon got around that I/O was getting sprinkled with pixie dust, the term used when Microsoft decides to bring you into the hive. We had a brief moment of glory as we sold out to the giant, voracious empire up north, and then the company as we knew it was gone. Particularly for Tas and myself, who had spent almost every waking minute for the best part of two decades thinking about things from a corporate perspective—our corporate perspective—it was a shock. What venture capitalists consider a highly desirable exit strategy did not feel quite that way to us. We were happy, of course, delighted in fact, to have sold the company and suddenly become rich men. But when the primary thing that you have organized your life around suddenly disappears, it forces some serious changes.

It was 2004 when the deal was finally consummated. Suffice it to say that as CEO and major shareholder, I was well compensated for my work, and after the deal it seemed best to step away from IT-related business for a while. Thus began what I think of as my year of retirement.

Chapter 12

My Year of Retirement

Everyone has a dream about what they would do if they won the lottery or a long-lost uncle died and left them a fortune. Travel, new houses, cars, and a host of other things are probably in most people's Top 10 lists. Needless to say, those things all suddenly become accessible, almost too easily accessible. In the past 15 years or so, psychologists have been studying the phenomenon of what makes us truly happy, and one conclusion is that we most enjoy acquiring those things that we work hardest to achieve. Climbing a mountain makes arriving at the peak a peak experience, whereas taking a helicopter to the top of a bunch of mountains doesn't provide the same lasting sense of joy. I understood this intuitively. A new house or a new car is nice, but they have no intrinsic meaning. I needed to *do* things, not *buy* things.

My dream had always involved having lots of time to myself, time to do the things that I had loved most as a kid but hadn't had a lot of time for since then—fishing, cooking, traveling to other countries (to fish and cook, of course), and even gardening. Cooking was the easiest to jump into right away. Cooking had always been both fun and therapy for me, a chance to immerse myself in another world and to experiment, trust my instincts, and create new things. My new home in California was essentially built around a big, professional-grade kitchen, because that was most important to me, as important as the TV room or the garage would be to other guys. I dove into cooking again, tried all sorts of recipes, made up a few of my own, and enjoyed it immensely.

To feed my kitchen, I decided we needed a steady supply of fresh vegetables and herbs, some of which I couldn't acquire easily even at gourmet shops in our area. The answer was to bring in seeds from Japan and grow these things locally, which I proceeded to do. I probably imported 20 or more varieties of plants and seeds from overseas, and started what would become a large, varied backyard garden.

Okay, you already guessed that my back yard was a little different from other people's back yards—it was loaded with every high-tech gadget known to modern agriculture, and maybe a few that weren't. I had a regular greenhouse, stocked with all sorts of seedlings, both domestic and imported, and I grew about 30 different varieties of herbs. I also had a special hydroponics greenhouse for growing things in water (plants without dirt, as it's sometimes called), and special raised planters and computer-linked temperature and humidity sensors everywhere to control the whole thing. The biggest challenge was trying to grow wasabi, which needs cool, running water, and thus a lot of digging to lay water pipes, pumps, and plumbing. The rest of the garden was filled with fruit trees, many imported from Japan, and row upon row of vegetables. I bought tens of pounds of earthworms and tens of thousands of ladybugs. I had chickens that roamed freely and ate a lot of the undesirable bugs, so that I didn't need to rely on pesticides. I also created my own computer-controlled system to scare away squirrels, chipmunks, and other creatures that came to share in the bounty that I was creating (I believe in volunteering to help those in need, but I've never been a big fan of socialism; my vegetables are my vegetables, and the local squirrel population had better keep their paws off).

I noticed how surprised children were to discover that potatoes actually came from the ground and that eggs came from chickens, not from supermarkets. I don't know what kids are learning on TV or from their video games these days, but it was as much an eye-opener for me as for them to see the learning process in action when we walked into the garden, saw the chickens running around, picked fruit from our trees and vegetables that we had grown. As a matter of fact, I don't think I bought a single vegetable for a whole year, and remember, I was cooking like a madman, creating recipes that would have earned me my own TV show. And needless to say, all the leftovers and throwaways from my exploits in the kitchen were turned into compost to fertilize my high-tech garden.

But life is not all cooking and gardening. A great sage once said, "Give a man a fish and you feed him for a day; teach a man to fish and you can get rid of him all weekend." No truer words were ever spoken, although in my case it was sometimes more than a weekend. I combined my love for travel with my love for fishing and took off around the world, sometimes making a trip to a specific place just to sample the local streams. My father and I had spent a lot of weekends driving to favorite fishing holes in the California mountains, so when my ship came in, so to speak, I was ready to pack up and go fishing wherever there was an airport.

One day I was passing through a big passenger terminal, I don't remember where, catching a flight back home. For no reason I can give a name to, I picked up a computer magazine at the newsstand and decided to read it on the plane. It had been a long time since I had even looked at one, and even longer since I'd been reading them regularly, looking for reviews of the Puppy and our old SecureSuite software. I smiled as I turned the pages, looking at all the new, somewhat unfamiliar equipment and seeing ads for all sorts of products that weren't around just a few years before. I skimmed over some of the articles and kept running into terms I didn't understand. What was an ASP, and why was it *such* a big deal? I started turning the pages faster and faster. The first gnawings of doubt crept up my spine. Was I going stupid? Had I forgotten all this stuff, or was there that much new information out there that I wasn't aware of? And if so, why should it matter? After all, I was retired.

But it did matter. I tossed the magazine down and looked out the window at an ocean of clouds floating by beneath me. The simple truth was right there: I was out of touch. The world was changing without me, and I didn't like it one bit.

I had plenty of time to think about what to do, but discovered I didn't need any more time. The old impatience to be doing something and getting somewhere in a hurry was starting to gnaw at me again. Before we touched down in LAX, my mind was made up. Growing vegetables was nice, and my year off had been a great break from the nonstop hectic pace of I/O Software, but now my break was over. I didn't know exactly what I was going to do, but I knew for sure that I was meant to do something else with whatever talents I possessed. I was going to get back into the world again and back into the world of business.

I looked at my options. I had pretty much lived the American dream, or at least the Silicon Valley version of the American Dream. Where do you go when you've already reached the top? I thought about starting over, but starting over in the U.S. market, which I knew too well, was just not enough of a challenge. What about going somewhere else? I had all this knowledge of Japan and Japanese business, I spoke the language, and I felt comfortable with the culture. None of those assets were worth a whole lot in the United States anyway, so why not put them to use in Tokyo. In spite of all my work with Japanese companies, I hadn't really lived in Japan or tried to survive on my own in Japan since that summer internship way back when. Here was my chance.

TAKEAWAY: Be Curious and Always be Learning

Formal education will make you a living; self-education will make you a fortune.

— John Rohn

A person should constantly be learning and changing, because the alternative is to become irrelevant. Change continues to take place at an accelerating pace—in economics, politics, society, technology, and the environment. Task forces, cross-functional, and multidisciplinary project teams are replacing the cumbersome hierarchical organizational structures of the past in many organizations. Learning from and cooperating with team members enable the organization to be nimbler, more flexible, and better able to respond swiftly and creatively to the challenges of today's competitive business environment.

Teaching is also a good way to keep learning, since you always study a lot more about the subject when you know you are going to be grilled with questions from students. Learning another language can also give you a new and different perspective and teach you how to think outside the box. If you know your own weaknesses, you can easily figure out a way to overcome them and create a course of study that will help fill in the gaps in your education.

I'm reminded of a quote I heard once that I truly believe in, "The mediocre teacher tells, the good teacher explains, the superior teacher demonstrates, and the great teacher inspires." Try to be a teacher who inspires not just students but your employees, friends, and family as well.

With regard to learning, it has been said that we remember 10 percent of what we read, 20 percent of what we hear, 30 percent of what we see, 40 percent of what we hear and see, 50 percent of what we say or write, 60 percent by discussing, 70 percent by collaborating, 80 percent by what we do, and 90 percent by teaching others.

Chapter 13

Back in the Game

In 2005, I packed up and moved to Tokyo. I had never worked for any company but my own, so I decided to see how the rest of the world does it. I'm not very well versed in things like sales and finance, so I looked for companies that were sales-force driven with lots of reporting, lots of numbers, and plenty of financial data to review. I had also never run a public company. It was important for me to get out of my old comfort zone and make my first postretirement experience in Japan as educational as possible. I took a position as executive vice president and CTO with a Japanese company that fit that description, and put myself to work developing interesting new Internet-based strategies for them. Within that first year it was already obvious to me, and probably to them, that things weren't working out.

One of the biggest problems involved my serving on the board of directors. In addition to my executive role, I had accepted an appointment as an outside director. I thought this would not be very time-intensive and would give me an education about how things work in a Japanese corporate boardroom. After my years of developing products with and for Sony, and all my business negotiations with various Tokyo firms, I thought I knew a lot about Japanese companies and Japanese management. It turned out that I knew something about how policies were carried out within a corporate structure, but I had no clue about what goes on in the boardroom. Which was probably just as well: The old saying that you are much better off not to witness the birth of sausages and new laws is even more true for the inner workings of a Japanese corporate board.

The one thing I already knew was that in Japan the CEO runs the board of directors, not the other way around. Of course, in the Western model, the president is often a hired gun, a professional administrator who has proven her skills in other firms and is brought into a company to do a job. The president is hired by and responsible to the board of directors. The board may include members of that company, but it almost always has several outside members whose job is to impartially review the performance of the president and other company executives and decide what is best for both the firm and its stockholders.

In Japan, everything is upside-down. There is one long promotion ladder, starting from the day you enter a company and rising up through the position of general manager (*bucho*), which is what most men (there are almost no women) hope to achieve in their fifties. Among the ranks of *bucho*, a select few are promoted to the next rank, director (*torishimariyaku*). That's right, a corporate director is just another rung on the company's promotion ladder, one that only a few men in any firm can aspire to, and a title conferring great status in Japanese society. Among the directors, there are also several ranks (executive director, senior executive director, etc.), so there could still be more rungs on the promotion ladder. Finally, one man among these directors will get the ultimate promotion and become the company president (*shacho*). In that position, he is a virtual king. The former president will likely retire to the chairmanship of the board of directors, where in most cases he must defer to the wishes of the current president. In the normal scheme of things, it is the president, not the board, who makes decisions. The president not only controls the board, but has enormous influence over who becomes a director and which of them will be promoted to replace him when he decides to retire.

Although it is true that more and more companies are beginning to add outside directors, that trend is very new, and a quick look at who gets to be an outside director will reveal that a large number of these outsiders actually come from sister companies within the same group. In other words, these are outside directors who know their place in the company hierarchy, understand the way the company does business, and will basically jump when the president says jump. God forbid an outside director should come on board who didn't understand the corporate culture and had independent ideas about how the company should be managed. Imagine a really, really outside director, like a young American guy who knew nothing about the company, nothing about the CEO, and had all sorts of weird, idealistic views about corporate governance and what he thought a director's responsibility should be. Enter Director Saito.

I actually took up director positions with two different companies, but the experience was essentially the same at both. I quickly discovered that in spite of what the standard organization chart on the company's website looked like, the board of directors was in fact completely subservient to the CEO. My frustration with this structure began almost immediately and deteriorated rapidly, and I'm sure the companies felt the same. To me, if the board of directors only exists to rubber-stamp the CEO's decisions, what's the purpose of having a board in the first place? Why not skip the pretense and admit that a company is essentially a little kingdom; the king gets to do things his way until he steps down and a new king takes over. It's not very democratic, but almost no companies, either in Japan or the United States, are democracies. The Japanese need to maintain the fiction of corporate governance seemed strange to me.

Within the first month the companies on whose boards I sat must have been asking, "Who *is* this guy and how do we get rid of him?" You can easily imagine why. I asked blunt questions. I brought up issues that no one else wanted to talk about. In one glorious instance I refused to go along with a board vote and insisted on voting my conscience. Looking back on it now, I have to laugh. I was incredibly naive, but in some ways so were they. I knew perfectly well that my lone dissenting vote would change nothing, but I felt it was symbolically important, like a minority Supreme Court judge wanting to write a dissenting opinion just to put it on the record. If ideals are important, symbols are, too, at least to me. Of course, for the Japanese side, a very different kind of symbolism was also important.

I was informed that it was essential for us all to vote as one. The appearance of unanimity is essential in Japanese companies, even today, as it helps to preserve an illusion of harmony. You must never underestimate the importance of harmony. *Harmony* is to the Japanese corporate mind what *Profit* is to its Western counterpart. Without it the company cannot exist. So I was asked several times, at first politely and then in increasingly apoplectic tones, to change my vote. Not to change my thinking, of course, but to vote the same way that everyone else was voting; that's what Japanese companies mean by *unanimity*. I was told in no uncertain terms that *all* board votes were unanimous and had always been unanimous since the founding of the company. And everything was discussed among the voting directors (but without the auditors) *before* the official board meeting. Surely I was not thinking of becoming the first director in the company's honored history to destroy the harmony of the board of directors?

Actually, I was. I stubbornly stood my ground. I even pointed out that because of my dissent the vote would be 6–1, so my vote would change nothing. The CEO would still be able to accomplish what he wished to accomplish, and my solo nay vote would only matter to me, so even I would get a little symbolic satisfaction out of it. See? It's a win–win, sort of, and isn't that good for everybody?

Logic and reason are among the strongest weapons in the Western arsenal, but when they encounter Japan's group-think kryptonite they suddenly lose their power and are rendered limp and useless. My rational arguments had all the force of clubbing them with wet spaghetti. To the other directors, I was not standing up for my own ideals, but being both unreasonable and selfish. How could I be so blind to the company's need for unanimity and harmony? Why could I not understand that this was one of my responsibilities as a director? Why couldn't I think about the group good and the needs of others instead of always thinking about what I wanted to do?

Whatever. I stuck to my guns all the way, the final vote was recorded as 6–1, and both sides knew that it was time for Mr. Saito to move on. Directors normally serve a two-year term, which is then automatically renewed, but I'd had it. I was disgusted. The kind of dysfunctional operations I had seen and the total lack of any kind of meaningful corporate governance was too much for me. I wanted out. When my terms expired at both companies, I did not even ask about renewing my status for the next term, and come to think of it, I didn't hear any chorus begging me to reconsider. Reflecting back on the experience after several years, I'm glad I did it. Despite all my frustrations and the pain of the interminable board meetings I sat through, I think it was a priceless crash course in the fundamental problems of Japanese corporate management. I still tell people that I got to see the good, the bad, and the ugly sides of Japanese corporate governance, and that education will not go to waste.

TAKEAWAY: Don't Avoid Learning Hard Lessons

Some lessons are often learned the hard way, for example:

- Don't make too many enemies; the world is much too small.
- Say only what you mean, and don't believe everything you hear because someday the story will be about you.
- Think of others. Always say thank you. Respect everyone and anyone, especially those less fortunate or younger.
- Be modest, because everyone stands on the shoulders of others.
- Know your weaknesses and know how to overcome them.
- Understand the essence of the problem before solving it.
- You are the company you keep.
- If you like to be alone, join a group. If you hate being lonely, try something new. Balance your life.
- Don't panic.
- Be prepared, but not overly prepared.
- Know the difference between "big" and "small." People often make "penny-wise and pound-foolish" decisions.
- Take care of things when you have the opportunity (e.g., e-mails, to-do lists). In other words, if you are traveling abroad and there is an ATM nearby, use it, and the same goes

for bathrooms, making phone calls, running errands, and so on. Because Murphy's law can also mean they don't accept credit cards (ATM), the meeting runs long (bathroom), and the difference between confusion and clarity (the phone call).

- Time is the most precious commodity. Use it wisely and try not to repeat the same mistakes. Learn from history.
- Don't waste your time on jealousy. Sometimes you are ahead, sometimes you are behind. The race is long and, in the end, it is only with yourself.
- "Anyone who has never made a mistake has never tried anything new." –Albert Einstein

Chapter 14

From Todai into AIST

Back in the 1990s, when I was working on authentication technologies related to the Puppy development, I was engaged in a project involving Japanese authentication programs. To complete this project, it was important to visit the dean of cryptography studies in Japan, Professor Hideki Imai at the University of Tokyo, the most prestigious school in the nation. Professor Imai was the god of crypto in Japan, and well known around the world for his expertise in coding theory, block cipher design, and public-key cryptography. In 1977, he and a partner developed a coded, multilevel signal modulation scheme that is still famous today, called the Imai-Hirakawa code. As is my usual style when I don't have a personal introduction to someone, I sent Professor Imai an e-mail, and he responded in a friendly way, so I went over to visit him. Gradually, I got to know him and received his blessing for my project, and in the process we became friends. Years later, when I had come to live in Japan, Professor Imai had to leave Todai because he had reached the mandatory retirement age. He moved to a METI-sponsored (Ministry of Economy, Trade and Industry) organization known as AIST (it was then officially the Agency of Industrial Science and Technology, now called the National Institute of Advanced Industrial Science and Technology). AIST is a large, research-oriented organization based in Tokyo but with offices around the country. Its mission is to integrate science and engineering specialties to develop multidisciplinary solutions for both industrial and social needs. In 2005, Professor Imai moved from Todai to AIST to take up a position as head of its Research Center for Information Security (RCIS), and he invited me to join AIST/RCIS as a Visiting Researcher. I traveled around Japan a lot, giving keynote speeches at various cryptography conferences and lecturing frequently on the current state of research, and later worked on innovation and entrepreneurial development with another part of AIST. More on that later.

Super Creators

When I was in California, I had done a lot of speeches and other work for the LA office of the Japan External Trade Organization (JETRO), which is an arm of the very influential trade and industry ministry (called MITI back then, METI today). I had several friends at JETRO, but one in particular was just about to transfer back to Japan after serving his time in LA when I mentioned that I was thinking about going to live in Japan. Makoto Yokota said he was on his way to Tokyo shortly, and he kindly offered to use his contacts to help me get connected over there. Yokota was a reasonably senior person in MITI, so his personal Rolodex was like a thousand cables plugged directly into important nodes in Japanese business, industry, academia, and the bureaucracy. I knew already that everything of any consequence in Japan happens through personal introductions, so this offer was extremely valuable and not something he would make lightly.

True to his word, Yokota-san introduced me to several interesting organizations. One of them, the Information Technology Promotion Agency (IPA), fell under the purview of his own ministry. It's what they call an incorporated administrative agency, which means it looks like a corporation but functions like an extension of the government, which is not necessarily a compliment. IPA was designed to nurture Japan's most promising software engineers, providing both grant money and various types of advice and assistance. It's a bit like a business incubator, which was a very popular model in the United States back when IPA got started in 2000.

From the hundreds of people selected to work in IPA, a tiny handful, the best of the best, are chosen as Super Creators. Yokota introduced me to some senior people at IPA, and the next thing I knew I was named a program manager for the Super Creator program. Since I love identifying and helping sharp young entrepreneurs, this was right up my alley. What a great way to transition from the United States to Japan, I thought. I already knew one of the biggest problems facing Japanese entrepreneurs—and they have so many problems that it's hard to list them all—is that IF they can get set up in the first place, and IF they can get funded, and IF they can get to a point where they have something reasonably good to sell, they are left high and dry by both the Japanese government and the local venture capital (VC) community. Japanese institutions are amazingly good at taking ideas and projects right up to the last mile and then leaving them there, just short of becoming commercially viable. I saw my participation in the Super Creator program as an opportunity to prove that Japanese entrepreneurs could go that last mile to International Success—providing they had a little help.

We started with a group of about 17 Super Creators. They were young, smart, and energetic, and they were anything but eloquent when you asked them to explain their technology in English. Not only couldn't they speak much English, but they'd never set foot outside of Japan. This is typical of the problems I see, even today: Japan's best and brightest want to create technologies that will be accepted worldwide, but they have no experience of the world outside Japan and no communication tools to help them explain their ideas. This is part of what I mean by going the last mile to success. The Japanese educational system gives these people the knowledge to develop technology, but no way to get it out of the box and show people. So I volunteered (an ever-increasing activity) every week for three months to teach these young people how to make an English PowerPoint presentation, how to deliver it in coherent, persuasive terms, how to stand, how to move, and so on. I wanted them to be able to function on a world-class stage, to talk intelligently about their companies, and to look and sound as smart as I knew they were. I was playing Henry Higgins, in effect promising the IPA and the Japanese government that, with the right training and the right opportunities, smart young entrepreneurs could hold their own in a competitive international environment inside or outside Japan. The rubber would meet the road when I took them to Silicon Valley and put them face to face with some American venture capitalists.

I helped set up the trip, and I worked hard to help these Super Creators get their presentation skills up to par in a foreign language (if only my elementary school teachers could have seen me teaching other people how to speak proper English! A couple of them would probably have had heart failure). Then we were off to California. On our first day we visited Stanford University, which has an idyllic campus that even the bleary-eyed, culture-shocked Japanese could appreciate. But they were obviously tired and falling back on old habits, like mumbling or just not saying much of anything when people spoke to them. The next day I took them to see a couple of venture capitalists. Nothing too scary at first, but the jet lag was still dragging them down, and they weren't really firing on all cylinders. I kept taking them around to different places, shepherding the group like a tour guide, pointing out important companies and telling them about the history of places and firms that we were going to see. We visited a lot of companies, and I think the kids were all happy and very impressed but also a bit overwhelmed. When I offered to take them out for beers one night, they were so tired that all they wanted to do was go back to the hotel and crash.

The fourth day was the big finale. I'd arranged for a group of over 120 VCs to gather for a big group presentation. These were people who skim business plans before breakfast, and there were a lot of them, so it was the kids' last chance to look good and sound good and deliver what they came to deliver. If they couldn't, the whole trip, in fact, the whole program and all my months of effort were for nothing. Much to my surprise and delight, they snapped out of their previous torpor, shook off whatever fears they had about speaking to a large, professional crowd in English, and they went on, one after another, just the way they'd practiced scores of times back in Tokyo. They stood up straight, they went through their presentations smoothly, used the hand gestures I had taught them, explained the unique features and potential applications of their technologies, and outlined their capital needs succinctly. They didn't look like scruffy college students; they looked and sounded grown up. It was damn impressive, and I felt like a proud father, well, uncle of sorts. After all the time I'd spent teaching them to walk and talk and sound like people you might want to invest in, I was hugely relieved to see them accomplish exactly that.

Before that meeting was over, a few of the VC companies expressed serious interest in some of the technologies they'd just heard presentations about, and in the months to come four of the Japanese entrepreneurs would get funding from America to further develop their products. The kids were happy; just like the famed examination hell they had to survive to get into prestigious colleges, they had studied hard with IPA, survived the trial by fire in Silicon Valley, and emerged victorious—or at least came home with their dignity and a new sense of confidence in their abilities. It was a privilege to help some young entrepreneurs make their marks in a much larger world than they had ever experienced. On another level, I had also proved my point that Japan's best and brightest were being poorly served by both their government and the domestic VC community, left by the side of the road with just a short last mile of assistance needed to raise them up to international standards and give them the opportunities they deserved. At the time of writing this book, all the companies that presented at the event are still in business and doing well, which is a phenomenal statistic if you think about it. Some have even been acquired by both domestic and international firms.

Chapter 15

Starting My Own Company, Version 2.0

A year after I arrived in Japan, when I was finishing my education as a Japanese corporate director, I was contacted by a well-known consulting company in New York City. Giuliani Partners was founded in 2002 by former mayor Rudy Giuliani and staffed by many ex–New York City officials and former FBI managers. The company does both management and security consulting, and they wanted to set up a security operation in Asia. I was asked to serve as co-chairman and CEO of Giuliani Security and Safety Asia (GSSA) and to become the CTO for the parent company. In my role at GSSA, I worked with a number of clients in Japan, including the Tokyo Metropolitan government. Working together with the government, we helped to develop a high-level academic security and crisis management system for Tokyo Metropolitan University, one of the largest public schools in Japan. My relationship with Giuliani Partners continued for several years. It gave me a good opportunity to travel throughout Asia, meeting with both heads of state and senior government officials in several countries to discuss security issues.

About this time, I was contacted by the Agency of Industrial Science and Technology (AIST). Of course, I had been working with a branch of AIST, Professor Imai's Research Center for Information Security, but AIST is a large organization, and the group that reached out to me was not connected with the Research Center for Information Security (RCIS) in any way. I think they were surprised at our first meeting when I seemed to know all about their organization and then mentioned that I had an office just down the hall. They had heard about my work in the Super Creator program and wanted to talk about promoting innovation and entrepreneurship through AIST. As a result, I became a Startup Advisor at AIST's Venture Support Center, a position that again brought me into contact with many young, talented scientists who needed help taking their ideas to the next level. I am always interested in talking to creative people with new ideas and big dreams about realizing those ideas. I enjoy helping entrepreneurs of all kinds, not only in technology, although that is my forte, but anyone who has an idea that is worth developing and a drive to develop a healthy business.

In fact, after a while I decided to put my money where my mouth is and invest in some of these small start-ups. Not just throw money at them, but get involved with their business and actively help them to grow and to anticipate and overcome problems along the way. This philanthropic/venture business of my own would not be done through AIST or the Information Technology Promotion Agency (IPA), so I decided it was time to create a new platform of my own.

Starting up my first company as a teenager in the States was not really a big deal at the time, and starting up my Japanese company was much the same. It wasn't that I had a dream to accomplish something as a corporate entity, but simply a need to have a legal structure that would give me the freedom to advise, manage, and invest as I felt like. Of course, I could have tied up with any Japanese VC firm or any con- sulting firm, but I knew that would only lead to more frustration. I'm not the world's best Employee-of-the-Month type to begin with—I'm way too independent and impatient with just about every kind of procedure—and I'd been my own boss for too many years. My brief stint as a corporate employee in Tokyo had shown me that it was time to go back to doing things the way I wanted to do them. Making mistakes doesn't scare me, but suffering from someone else's mistakes or having to put up with someone else's mistakes and being powerless to correct them is not a good feeling. I needed to be back in charge of my own little business. So, roughly 20 years after starting my first company, I started my second.

In principle, InTecur K.K. is a management consultancy that helps both private companies and government organizations to take advantage of the rapid technological changes in their fields. It also has a certain personal significance for me.

Framing for Softbank

One of Japan's biggest telecommunications companies is a relative newcomer called Softbank (founded in 1981) that has grown rapidly and built a strong brand image. I knew of the company long ago, because they had bought COMDEX, the big computer show where I/O Software introduced the Puppy in what now seems like another lifetime. Softbank asked InTecur to help them develop a new product. Now, why would a big, successful telecom company like Softbank want to consult with an outside firm about new product development? The answer is that people in big Japanese organizations quickly become adjusted to that company's style, its products, its image, and its way of doing things; they start thinking the way everyone else in the organization thinks, and that means innovation will only come along a narrow channel. So, if a company like Softbank proposes developing new products, its staff will think along predictable lines: we're Softbank, we're a big cell phone company, we should create some new cell phone; let's come up with a new phone that's radically different from the Hello Kitty line but just as attractive. You see where this leads. So going outside the organization for ideas allows for a much broader perspective.

Our approach was to set aside the company's focus on its cell phones and look instead at its network. When we looked at the company, we did not see the pretty handsets for sale in the stores, but rather, a national network of cell towers, digital switching equipment, giant servers, and other infrastructure that the public doesn't see. Softbank is basically a digital data transmission network that happens to use cell phones as its commercial terminals. If they want to develop a new business, we thought they needed to leverage both their existing customer base and their network infrastructure. The challenge was to devise a new product that would substantially increase monthly revenue without having to retool or expand their infrastructure (cell towers are very expensive) and also without overloading the network with hugely data-intensive requests, such as video. Our idea was to create a product that was essentially a dumbed-down cell phone that could leverage the existing infrastructure without overburdening it and still look like a cool new product that was visibly different from a cell phone.

What we came up with was the digital picture frames that sprang up everywhere in Japan (this was several years ago). Now all the phone companies and electronics companies have their own versions out, but back then it was an interesting idea, and we had our own wrinkles to make it much more interesting. It just so happened that I had been involved in digital picture frame technology many years earlier and had some knowledge of the business. One thing I knew was that people tended to buy these picture frames, load up a bunch of photos into memory, and leave them like that. The frames would sit on a countertop or tabletop and grow old. Yes, you could wire them into the Internet, which was tedious, and some frames allowed wireless connections with the Internet, although back then very few people had WiFi routers in their homes. The result was that people bought the frames, used them for a time, and then forgot about them. Not good for consumers and, because they were one-off sales, not very attractive for the vendors. I recall what a wise Sony manager once told me: "Anyone can sell anything once. The trick is to sell it twice." So our challenge was twofold: How could we make these digital picture frames more functional, and how could we turn them into an ongoing service business instead of a one-time purchase?

It didn't take us long to find the solution. Thanks to the growth of smart phones, such as the iPhone, that Softbank was selling, PC usage in Japan was declining but cell phone use was going through the roof. The phones were getting smarter and faster every few months. I had to admit that I couldn't keep up with all the functions in my phone and wondered how Japanese housewives coped with it. One of the ways that the cell phone companies competed in their advertising back then was in the ostensible quality of their in-phone cameras. First, they were all one or two megapixels, but that soon jumped to three, and then four, and five, and then up and up. The cameras, once a meaningless add-on feature because it looked good on a checklist of features, were suddenly becoming important parts of the phone. Consumers were really starting to use their cell phone cameras, and not only for snapshots of each other or portraits of their pet poodle. You would see Japanese pull off to the side of the road in front of Mt. Fuji; everyone would get out of the car, open up their phones and start snapping pictures. The phones were coming to be seen as genuine substitutes for pocket-sized cameras.

The problem, as we saw it, was that people stored hundreds of photos in their phones but seldom if ever downloaded or printed them. The convenience stores started offering printing services for cell phone photos, but even that seemed too inconvenient for most people. The result was that everyone had a personal archive of digital photos, sometimes going back a year or more, on their phone, but if they wanted to look at the photos they had to display them on those tiny three-inch screens. Now the light bulbs went on over our heads, and we knew what had to be done.

We put a 3G chip into the digital picture frame, which allowed users to upload pictures from those high-resolution cameras directly to the frame, and even better, the frames would auto-refresh themselves as you took new pictures. The whole thing was incredibly simple: you just plugged them in and everything worked, no set up necessary. Just as we'd expected, when customers bought a new Softbank phone, they began to order a digital picture frame to go with it, and because the frames were now live, constantly updating devices, it made sense to sell them as a service rather than as a dumb device. Consumers paid a small monthly fee for the photo frame service, which meant a significant uptick in our client's ongoing monthly revenues.

What we discovered later was that the products were even more successful than we had initially imagined. People were getting the photo frames, and then giving them to their parents or grandparents. Kids would take pictures and send them to the grandparents late at night, when the rates were ultralow; the grandparents would have new snapshots of their grandkids when they woke up in the morning. From Softbank's point of view, this meant that more and more photos were being sent at off-peak hours, which meant the new service taxed the network even less than projected. And grandparents liked this easy, no set-up service so much that they would offer to buy photo frames for other members of the family and often get them new Softbank phones to match. We had tapped into what is probably the richest demographic on Earth: elderly Japanese, a group with literally trillions of dollars of savings available for things they feel are worthwhile. The picture frames just kept selling and selling, and InTecur's idea ultimately added a lot of new monthly revenue to our client's bottom line.

This is just one simple example that shows what happens when you bring in an outside team to rethink your strategy. If Softbank had tried to start a new business with only internal resources, they would undoubtedly have developed some new kind of cell phone, perhaps smaller than others or with more features, but that is their main business; that's what they're going to do anyway. Our approach was to step back, critically examine what the company's true assets were, and then come up with a product that could maximize the value of those assets at the least cost to the client. Digital picture frames may not be rocket science, but I'm always happy when we can show a big company that thinking outside the box is the best way to go.

Investing in the Future

I sometimes tell people in a half-joking way that InTecur is a holding company to manage my investments. What I really mean is that it's my platform to help deserving young start-up companies get the funding and hands-on assistance they need to realize their goals. In some sense, the inspiration to do this came while I was chaperoning those young entrepreneurs around Silicon Valley, helping them to meet and impress American venture capitalists. I realized then that Japan is awash with potential—there is no lack of extremely smart, hard-working people with good ideas that could become good businesses IF they got the right kind of help. But neither the Japanese government nor the Japanese VC industry is reaching out to help them, to take them that "last mile" to success. You'd think that helping young companies get started on the road to international success would be seen as a big plus for an economy that's been stagnating for over two decades, but for some reason this perspective has eluded the Japanese government. Suffice it to say that I could not stand to see all that young potential going to waste, and I made up my mind then and there to do something about it, even if it meant investing my own money. Besides, my company's humble beginnings and ultimate growth was thanks to Japan. It was my turn to give something back.

So that's exactly what I did. I began investing relatively small amounts in young companies that caught my eye. I not only invest in them, but I sit on their boards; I take an active interest in their management, and I try to help them in any way I can to navigate that last mile to success. I have personally invested in over a dozen companies as of this writing, and of course, as soon as I tell anyone what I do, the questions start flowing. "What do you invest in? What kinds of companies are you looking for?" and so on. I used to give them a glib answer that really wasn't very far from the truth: I invest in things I like. No, I don't invest in a restaurant because I like the food or a clothing shop because they made me a nice suit; there has to be some truly novel idea or approach and a business model that is scalable. To put it succinctly, I look for small companies, usually start-ups, that have an unusual idea or technology and need both capital and guidance to raise their businesses to the next level.

I have four basic investment criteria. The first is that the technology or business model around which the company is based must be globally applicable. That alone eliminates 85 percent of the ideas I see in Japan, because many of them are, intentionally or not, copies of things that already exist in the U.S. market. Yes, it's true that in some cases you can copy an American idea, develop it in Japan and make millions of dollars, but that strikes me as a strategy for the innovation-challenged. Anyone with a brain in her head should be able to come up with a new idea, something that's not just new for Japan but new for the world market.

Second, the company must have been formed by a team. I don't trust firms with a single founder/owner who knows everything about the business. Companies need leaders, not gods, and good leaders are people who understand and admit their own weaknesses. A good leader knows the value of surrounding yourself with highly talented people and leveraging their strengths to compensate for your own weaknesses. This stems from my own experience, not just in developing I/O Software, which I could never have done without Tas and others, but in looking at dozens of other start-up companies in California two decades ago. Even more, it comes from looking at thousands of business plans worldwide in my role as a judge for the Entrepreneur of the Year program. I have always believed it to be true, but now I have incontrovertible evidence that in almost every case companies based on effective teams of highly capable people will outperform one-man shows. By the way, this doesn't always sit well with the companies I talk to. Many a young CEO imagines himself as the next Mark Zuckerberg, and I can see it in his eyes when we talk. It comes as a rude shock when I tell him, "*If* I invest in your firm, the first thing that goes is your CEO title. If you're lucky, you may be the new CTO, but there is no way you'll run the company. That requires an experienced team, and your company doesn't have one. Yet."

Third, if a core technology is involved, the business must not rest on some temporary advantage of that technology, meaning a function like faster CPU speed, inexpensive data storage, or higher bandwidth, because these are now commodities where the eventual cost will approach free. To me, new technologies that assume and leverage the availability of unlimited transistors and free wireless communications are more forward-looking and interesting.

Fourth, the founders of the business should have experienced failure somewhere along the line (and I don't mean a lemonade stand they had at age six). Largely through my work as a judge for the Entrepreneur of the Year program, I have had an opportunity to review close to 10,000 business plans. One thing I can tell you for sure: I have never seen one business plan or one set of financial projections work out according to plan. An entrepreneur is really someone who is willing to push himself into taking intelligent risks, not afraid of failing some of the time, and ready to learn from those failures, get right back up, and try again. A successful business is not based on a perfectly thought-out business plan, but on the ability of the principal(s) to continually adapt, revise, improve, and try again.

You can probably guess that most people who ask about what kind of companies I invest in are disappointed with the answer. I don't really think about what "kind" of companies to look for. To put it another way, I don't invest in companies; I invest in people. Companies change, business models change, the commercial environment can change radically while you're having breakfast. Everything changes, so betting on anything static, like a rigid business plan, is a waste of time. I bet on people, generally smart people with really good ideas, but more than that, people with drive and passion and an ability to communicate their passion to others—because that is one of the keys to becoming successful. Passion is one of the key characteristics I look for in a company leader. In addition, I look for certain intangibles, call them human qualities, that seem to have nothing to do with business. For example, before I invest in a company, I might take the founder or founders out to dinner. I'll watch how they order, how they treat the waitress, how comfortable they can be in an uncomfortable situation, and so on. I'll go to their offices and snoop around. People don't expect to see a venture capitalist (because that's how they view me) poking around in their closets or in the company bathrooms, but I do. Little things tell you a lot about a company and its management.

An important point for me is that I expect the founder of a company to have had some sort of failure in his or her life and be able to talk about it meaningfully. What happened and why, I ask. What did you learn from it? What were your weaknesses and how would you address them in the future? How will that failure affect your thinking in the future? What will happen if this next venture is a failure? What will you do then? And so on. Japanese are taught to abhor failure and to shun those who fail at almost anything. The consequences for the nation's entrepreneurial spirit are predictable. I feel just the opposite—failure is a necessary step on the way to·success. I am inspired by the story of Abraham Lincoln, who failed at almost everything he tried until he succeeded in becoming one of the greatest presidents of the United States. Failure can be a badge of shame, as it is in Japan, or a badge of pride, as it is in Silicon Valley. "If you don't fail, you don't learn" is a common belief in the U.S. entrepreneurial world, and one that I share. Of course, that doesn't mean that people need to bankrupt a company in order to get my attention. It means that when I look at a potential investment target, I naturally respond to any company founder who has failed at some important task and then regrouped, rethought what went wrong, and found the strength to start over again. In America, that's something that deserves respect; in Japan it requires a level of guts and determination that is hard to explain. There is an old Japanese saying, "Fall down seven times, get up eight," which should be inscribed on every entrepreneur's forehead. Unfortunately, both the social and financial systems in Japan think differently, and those who stumble even once seldom get a second chance. All the more reason why I look for people who can talk unashamedly about previous failures and what they learned from them.

TAKEAWAY: Create Diverse, Passionate Teams

- **Team:** a small number of people with complementary skills who are committed to a common purpose, set of performance goals, and an approach for which they hold themselves mutually accountable.
- **Teamwork**: the process of people actively working together to accomplish common goals.

Teams are a blend of competent individuals, with a strategic mix of key competencies and skills that meet the complex needs of global business in today's increasingly diverse marketplace.

When I show my students a list of the top 25 innovative companies in the world, it is easy to see that most of the successful companies were started by a team. No one person can do everything it takes to build a business. Success requires alliances, partnerships, and collaborations to meet the demands of an around-the-clock global marketplace. Sophisticated, culturally diverse employees are needed to deal with unfamiliar cultures, languages, and customs, and sensitivity to moral, religious, and ethical choices and preferences becomes a necessity.

Everything you need to do to run a business requires team-work. Doing it passionately makes it interesting, and doing it together with an equally passionate team makes it more fun and profitable. Teamwork enhances success, helps your group excel at whatever it is doing, and boosts its chances of winning. Teamwork promotes creativity and builds synergy.

Create teams of people from diverse backgrounds, with differing points of view, and then listen carefully. It is sometimes more important to hear what is not being said when working together as a team. Diverse opinions colliding is a key ingredient of out-of-the-box thinking, which is an absolute necessity when problem solving. Your customers will be amazed when your team presents innovative solutions to their problems and needs.

Team members must have: (1) a shared purpose and mission; (2) the same goals and passion; (3) a balance of key competencies; (4) a balance of relevant skills (four goalkeepers do not make a good team); (5) deep, mutual respect for each other; (6) mutual identity and cohesiveness; and (7) a leader, but with shared leadership roles.

Team-building skills may be the most important quality an entrepreneur can have. Teams that have passion (not just intensity) for an idea can get other people excited, including investors, workers, customers, and partners.

T.E.A.M. = Together Everyone Achieves More.

Chapter 16

Consulting around the World

Another thing that InTecur allows me to do is to travel and consult. I think when people hear the word *consulting* they imagine some team of expensively suited professionals whisking into a corporate boardroom, pulling thick sheaves of documents from their designer briefcases, dispensing high-level advice to a group of C-suite clients, and leaving a million-dollar invoice on the table. I don't know, maybe those people really exist, but that's not me, and that's not the way I work. To me, offering strategic advice is a lot like teaching, which is something I've enjoyed doing for a long time. I have two main areas of expertise—IT-related security issues and nurturing entrepreneurship—and I am happy to offer what I have learned from my own experience to interested parties. Fortunately, not only companies but a few national governments are interested in what I have to say. So I am able to travel quite often to talk about things that matter to me.

I don't want to list all the places I've been to or the organizations I've worked for, but I will offer just a few simple examples. Russia is a good one. The government there has become acutely aware that their economy is hugely dependent on the energy sector, mostly oil and gas. That skews the economy in certain ways that are not necessarily desirable. A few years ago the Russian government began planning the Skolkovo Innovative Center, a high-tech facility modeled on Silicon Valley, that would spring up just outside of Moscow over the next few years. Some in the government are calling Skolkovo the "locomotive that will pull technologies for modernizing the economy."

To give you an idea how important it is, Russian President Dmitry Medvedev visited Silicon Valley in the summer of 2010, meeting with the CEOs of Apple, Cisco, Twitter, and other firms to discuss cooperation. Google co-founder Eric Schmidt signed up to be one of the project's advisors. Later, the Renovo Group, one of the largest private corporations in Russia and a key member of the Skolkovo development effort, invited me to visit Moscow to share my views on the reasons for Silicon Valley's success and how some of that might be replicated in the suburbs of the Russian capital.

I have also visited the UK often, though not to talk about entrepreneurship, and occasionally other nations in Europe. However, one of my most memorable visits was to Africa, where I had an opportunity to talk to the government about how to diversify their economy away from its reliance on minerals (diamonds) and toward more innovative and technical fields that could help to provide new jobs and new income for their people. It is this kind of work, where strategic advice has an immediate, tangible, humanistic element, that I find most rewarding.

Nowhere have I found a more receptive audience for my various, disjointed lectures on everything from primary education to state-of-the-art communications technology than in Japan. Not surprisingly, I like Japan as a nation and as a culture, but like so many other outsiders who go there, learn its language and its customs, I find certain things incredibly frustrating. So when I have an opportunity to speak in public, I never hesitate to combine my compliments about the strength of the Japanese character, social, and industrial achievements with a good dose of criticism for some of the things that seem most anachronistic or self-defeating. More often than not I'm criticizing some aspect of the bureaucracy that manages everything from education to trade to the space program.

It is often said that the entrenched bureaucracy is the real government of Japan and the politicians are merely window dressing. I don't want to get into that argument, but there is no question in anyone's mind that the bureaucracy is immensely powerful in almost every aspect of Japanese life. Being older, extremely conservative, and defensive of their position and privileges, you would expect the ministries to react very negatively when someone like me criticizes them in public. And yet, in my experience just the opposite is true: Whenever I give a speech and lambaste some policy by one of the ministries, it's almost a sure bet that my phone will ring later that week, and the very same ministry will invite me to come in and share my thoughts face to face with senior policy makers. They are surprisingly open to honest, constructive criticism and positive suggestions about how things might be done better.

One result is that I have become both a gadfly and an adviser to many of the ministries. They understand that I'm not running around bashing Japan but rather, offering a valuable viewpoint as an outsider who cares about Japan and has responsible, often useful things to say. In just the past few years I've served as an advisor to the Cabinet Ministry on the topic of innovation and entrepreneurship, and from time to time I advise the Ministry of Economic Trade and Industry (METI) on similar topics. I've talked to the Ministry of Internal Affairs and Communication (MIC) about communications technologies, the Ministry of Education, Sports, Culture, Science and Technology (MEXT) about K–12 education and scholarships, and the Ministry of Land, Infrastructure, Transport and Tourism (MLIT) about things like electronic toll systems on highways. The prime minister and various senior members of the government are all deeply concerned with the future of the nation and the challenges presented by everything from modern education to developing a culture of innovation and entrepreneurship. I am extremely honored to be asked for my opinion by these people, and I will continue to do my best to advise the Japanese government as well as other foreign governments when called upon. The common theme is that many countries are now interested in not only science and technology but in how to create an entrepreneurial system that will convert inventions and innovations into products and new industries.

Chapter 17

Teaching (United States and Japan)

As I noted before, my grandparents in Okinawa were both well-known educators. From the time I was very young I saw my grandmother working in a classroom, and I could see that she loved to teach. Her daughter, my mother, also loved to teach, and as soon as she was able to get away from raising her children and keeping house full-time, she took a job at a local university. When I was in grade school, there was no formal ESL (English as a Second Language) program, but my teachers donated a lot of their own time to teach me. So I grew up thinking of teaching as not just a natural and proper thing for people to do, but also a good way to give back to society. For many years, I've tried to find opportunities to teach, partly as my own effort to give back to society for all that I have received, and partly for a more selfish reason: Because I learn so much whenever I teach something.

Over the years, I have lectured and taught at several universities, both in the United States and in Japan, and I find it very rewarding. People say that teaching helps you to clarify your own thinking, which is true, but it also brings you into contact with new questions and new points of view that are intellectually stimulating. You certainly learn more from teaching. And it also gives you the opportunity to guide younger people and help them to make important decisions in their own lives.

Back around the time we were developing the Puppy, I was a paid lecturer at the UCLA Anderson School of Management. This is when Sony ran its own executive MBA program by sending their really bright guys to that school. Sony would choose their smartest, up-and-coming young guys and ship them off to do a one-year MBA program at UCLA. I was asked to teach a few classes, which I enjoyed, and through that program I got to meet even more Sony engineers, which expanded my connections with the company even further.

Later on, I taught a course in computer science at my alma mater, University of California at Riverside. This was ironic, of course, because I've never taken a course in computer science in my life, but it seemed interesting. My course was called Commercial Software Development, which meant I could teach students the practical aspects of real-world programming. The students all thought I would be a pushover because I didn't come from a teaching background, and I was obviously just working there part-time. But I surprised them (and I think myself) by being quite strict. I divided the class into teams because they were about to step out into a world where you don't get to design software on your own—you are part of a workgroup or a team that is jointly responsible for completing a specific part of a larger project. And this is what I tried to show them. Working in a corporation, big or small, means working together to create a specific project based on clearly defined specifications. So my course was project-based—they had to work with a virtual customer to create a commercial program—and they had to approach it as teams. Of course, they didn't get to choose the teams, and that meant they had to work with people they didn't necessarily know or even like. Just like the real world, right?

It turned out that a lot had changed in American education since I was in school. My students all wanted to be judged as individuals, and they wanted praise for their efforts rather than their results, neither of which I saw much of in the business world. In a sincere effort to help them understand what work was all about, I graded the teams much as I would in a business setting: those that performed well got high grades, those that did not got low grades, and some even got failing grades. I was then assailed by a chorus of, "But we tried really hard..." or "I did my work, but Fred didn't do his share" or "Joe was sick all the time, and I don't think he was trying all that hard anyway...." I was amazed. This wasn't kindergarten. In a year or two these "kids" would all be working for real companies that wouldn't even listen to their excuses. As I tried to explain to them in class, you have a project; if you succeed in writing your code so the project works, you succeed; if your project fails, you fail. And you succeed or fail as teams. If you fail in my class, you get a D. If you fail in a software company, you'll probably get fired. Where do you want to be making your mistakes and learning how to do it right?

Of course, the students who got poor grades all complained to the university, and of course the academic board said that this isn't a company, it's just a classroom situation and everyone should be evaluated more generously. I saw their point, and I learned a valuable lesson about respecting the individuality of different students. Everyone is different, they all have different expectations, and so on. All the same, I wondered what would happen when those students who were much more concerned about their self-esteem than their programming skills went to work for real, bottom-line–driven companies.

My bottom line was that the university continued to ask me back again and again to teach, so I must have been doing something right. Even when I became so busy with other things and could no longer teach regularly, I remained an adjunct professor at UCR for a very long time.

In Japan, I've had many more opportunities to teach, and I have moved far away from computer science. I am convinced that university students hold the key to Japan's future, and if we can somehow lead them to take an interest in certain things and to question certain values that have been beaten into them since they learned to talk, we could bring about remarkable changes in this country. Japan is a land brimming over with potential, much of it going to waste. University students are at exactly the point in their lives where they need to understand this situation and decide if the road less traveled holds more attraction for them. For that reason, I enjoy teaching about innovative thinking and entrepreneurship, things I believe these students are ready to hear about, and which some of them are ready to accept and experiment with in their own lives.

Unlike the United States, Japan has a clearly defined pecking order when it comes to universities. First come the nationally sponsored universities, with Tokyo University and Kyoto University being the number one and number two schools in the nation. Then come the most elite of the private schools, such as Keio and Waseda, and then several tiers of regional schools; in addition, there are many highly ranked specialty universities, including technical institutes, agricultural colleges, and so on. The first place I ever lectured in Japan turned out to be the most famous in the land, the University of Tokyo, universally referred to as Todai. Later on, I received a position as a regular lecturer at Keio University, a private institution with a history going back to 1858 and more company CEOs on its alumni list than any school in Japan. Keio was kind enough to ask me to talk to their students about entrepreneurism, new ways of thinking, and so on. I have enjoyed that experience immensely and have acquired great respect for university students in the process. My students often challenge me, forcing me to analyze my own positions and clarify my thinking, so that I can present my ideas more convincingly. I often bring in interesting guest speakers to give the students a break from having to listen to me talk all the time. In addition to Keio, I've lectured several times at Todai, at the Tokyo University of Agriculture and Technology, and many other institutions.

I really enjoy teaching and wish I had more time for it. Over the years, I have become concerned with larger questions relating to education. What does it mean to learn? What is the essence of learning? What is a teacher's most important mission? There are no simple answers to those questions, but we need to think very seriously about them. I enjoy my classes, and I hope my students enjoy them, too, because I try to focus on getting people to think rather than getting them to spout correct answers to basic questions. I'm not all about rote memorization, although of course that has a place in education as well, but in Japanese education it occupies far, far too big a place. I want my students to learn to think and learn to learn. I like to ask students—and new hires at companies I'm involved with—some very challenging questions (see Appendix B for samples). Many of them have no right answer; the challenge is to figure out how to approach the problem. Some of the brightest students at some of the very best universities in Japan have the most trouble with these types of questions. They overthink, they take a long, super-logical route to find a solution when a simple shortcut would serve them much better. What is intuitive to one person is a brain twister to another. That's one of the things that makes teaching so interesting, the fact that students are all so different.

There is a saying that goes something like this: The mediocre teacher tells; the good teacher explains; the superior teacher demonstrates; the great teacher inspires. My goal is to be a teacher who inspires students to think beyond their usual boundaries and to realize they can make a difference in the world.

TAKEAWAY: Give Something Back—Write a Book

Because I was given opportunities as a child that even few adults are given, it is important to me to share these experiences so that others may learn to grow a successful business without making all the mistakes I made. I was a very lucky person who, because of the generosity of many others, was able to experience things that I could have only dreamed about.

My story (yet incomplete) began way before I was born. It was built by the attention and interest of parents and grandparents who created opportunities for me at a very young age, especially with leading Japanese companies. Unfortunately, many Japanese youth today do not have those same opportunities, and are not encouraged to give it a shot or to try it again as often as I was. For me, failure was not an option—it was necessary. It was a right of passage that I still learn to this day. My story was and still remains no straight and easy climb to the top. For every success, there have been failures twice as large. But the important thing is that I was allowed to get back up, learn from those mistakes, and try again.

In my classes, lectures, and speeches, I always say that entrepreneurship is not about creating a venture and being president. It is really a mind-set and way of thinking that applies to all facets of life—not just starting a business.

I have written this book with some trepidation, best expressed by a modified version of a line from Mark Twain, " 'Tis better to be silent and be thought a fool, than to write about it and remove all doubt." Nevertheless, I have attempted this new challenge in the hope that I won't be the only one to learn something from the experience. Better to try and fail than to not try at all.

Chapter 18

Turning 40

The first quarter of 2011 was a busy time for me. In addition to the usual menu of teaching, traveling, public speaking engagements, and meetings with various ministries, I squeezed in a little extra time to do some writing. Yes, I know, somebody is sure to point out that I struggled with the English language in elementary school and had no use for any written text that was not about science or math until I was force-fed Shakespeare in high school, so the idea of me doing creative writing may come as a shock. In fact, I have written many small pieces over the years, but for the first time I took up the challenge of writing a book. At the behest of a major publisher, I agreed to write a brief chronicle of my life to this point. As you can imagine, I thought anything resembling an autobiography of someone who has spent barely four decades on this planet was a bit presumptuous, but others felt differently. And so, I set aside time each morning to write about whatever seems most important in my life (well, it's true—I did set aside the time; that doesn't mean I actually wrote every morning; maybe with practice I'll turn into a disciplined writer, but not yet). The result is this book, which I promised myself to finish by my fortieth birthday in March of 2011.

Along the way, *The Economist* magazine asked me to participate in an online debate about the nature of innovation, one of my favorite topics. There was a typically well-informed and erudite moderator, Ken Cukier from *The Economist*, and a very smart, tech-savvy opponent who was a former exec at Google. The magazine wanted to contrast the benefits of disruptive innovation, such as we often see in the United States and which I, like many people in the high-tech business, believe is the lifeblood of the twenty-first-century economy, with incremental innovation, an equally important but much less drastic approach to change, which for the purposes of this debate, the magazine identified as the Japanese way.

I don't think anyone who has considered the problem for more than a few minutes would champion either side as superior in the abstract, although for the purposes of stimulating a good debate that was exactly what the magazine wanted to do. I enjoyed debating in high school, and I have lectured often about the need for more disruptive innovation in several fields, so I was happy to get involved and honored that *The Economist* had invited me. What I had forgotten was the first rule of debate: The participants do not get to choose which position they will support: the moderator chooses and the participants demonstrate their skills by defending positions that they may or may not privately support. Thus, I was given the task of championing Japanese-style incremental innovation.

All in all, I had a great time. I had forgotten how much you can learn about a subject by being forced to argue the opposite of what you believe. Like walking a mile in another person's shoes, your perspective changes. I began to see—even more than before—the merits of incremental innovation, and I came to understand that many of the great inventions of the past century that unleashed truly disruptive changes on the world were not themselves the result of disruptive innovation but rather its quieter, less visible sibling. I enjoyed the public debate immensely, although I knew the popular sentiment would run strongly in my opponent's favor, and when the final vote came in around 60-40 for Western-style disruptive over Japanese-style incremental innovation, I was not at all discouraged. After all, if someone had asked me a month earlier, I would probably have voted the disruptive ticket regardless of whatever arguments were presented in the debate. Through this process of serious debate, I now have an even greater appreciation for what innovation is. Life is still very interesting, indeed. I have even begun to incorporate what I learned in several panel discussions and in my classes. I learned a lot, not just about innovation, but also about keeping an open mind and looking at issues from multiple perspectives. If all my writing projects could be that educational, I would make time to write more.

Another big event in my life came at the beginning of March, just ahead of my fortieth birthday. I was named a Young Global Leader (YGL) and, shortly thereafter, a Global Agenda Council member by the World Economic Forum (WEF). There are over 750 active Young Global Leaders from around the world serving five-year terms, and many of them are among the most talented and visionary representatives of their various nations. I was proud, honored, and a bit stunned to be asked to join this elite body. The goal here is to work with other YGLs to bring about some real change in the world. I have always been an idealist, but never the ivory tower type—I simply want to see things happen and help to make them happen. I hope to harness the brainpower and political connections of organizations such as the YGL and WEF to find practical solutions to global problems and, trite though it sounds, to truly make the world a better place. That's always been a mission for me, not a dream.

One result of my efforts to help Japan become more globally connected is the chance to work with the Global Shapers Community (GSC). The GSC identifies outstanding future leaders who are now in their twenties and connects them to the World Economic Forum's global network. I am honored that the WEF asked me to serve as the founding curator for the GSC in Japan. This is truly an exciting opportunity. It feels like the culmination of all my years of promoting entrepreneurship and my longstanding desire to help visionary Japanese plug into the global community of opinion leaders.

Being part of the World Economic Forum and turning 40 gave me pause to reflect on my own life. In some ways I have accomplished so much, but in other ways I feel I have done very little. I believe that there is at least as much ahead of me as behind me, and maybe more. For me, Life 1.0 was all about building a company, making it successful, and then letting it go. Life 2.0, where I am now, is all about teaching, fostering venture businesses, consulting, and finding ways to give back to society in any way I can. I stay quite busy, traveling and lecturing, speaking to dozens of different groups, contributing essays to magazines, developing new book projects, and so on. All of this is good, and I enjoy it. I also enjoy meeting more and more interesting people. My personal Rolodex gets bigger, and I have a broader, more varied network to reach out to when my own abilities are insufficient for some task (which seems to happen more often these days).

And yet, this is still 2.0. In some ways, it is still a big learning phase, learning how to combine information, skills, and people I've met. I know that somewhere down the road there is a 3.0 just waiting for me. Somehow I will find a way to bring together my vast collection of experiences, interests, skill sets, human networks, and more. I have acquired a mountain of speeding tickets in my life, not because I'm a crazy driver, but because I'm impatient to get where I'm going. My sensible wife will probably tell me to slow down a bit, but I know I'm going to get a few more tickets up ahead, because I can't wait to get to the future and see what is waiting there for me. I encourage everyone to envision their own 3.0, or even 2.0. There's no telling where it will take you.

Epilogue

The Perfect Storm Hits Japan

I had set myself a goal of completing the manuscript for this book before my fortieth birthday toward the end of March 2011, and I had already achieved that goal when something happened that forever changed my life and the lives of millions of people in Japan. The massive M9.0 earthquake that rocked the eastern half of the country on March 11, 2011, and the devastating tsunami that followed were an unprecedented one-two punch for this nation. The area affected by the earthquake included the Tokyo Major Metropolitan Area, the most populous urban center on Earth, with over 35 million people in the prefecture's 23 wards and 39 municipalities. Miraculously, there was very little damage in this area. The Japanese building codes take for granted the tremors that constantly shake these islands and assume that a big quake is coming sooner or later. The forest of office towers in downtown Tokyo swayed and shook, but not a single large building came down. Even in places like Miyagi, Iwate, and Fukushima Prefectures, which felt the full force of the quake, there was relatively little damage from the quake. Then the tsunami came. It was far bigger and far more powerful than anyone could have imagined. The warning system in place to move people to higher ground was powerless to convey the message that the rooftops people thought of as higher ground would shortly be swept away as cars, boats, and whole buildings were picked up like so many tabletop toys and carried away, in some cases several kilometers inland.

I'm sure you have all seen TV coverage of the tsunami and its aftermath. Words cannot begin to express the tragedy that unfolded on that day. In some ways, 3/11 was Japan's 9/11, only the antagonist here was Mother Nature, and the number of casualties quickly rose into the tens of thousands. But that was not the end of the tragedy. These two mind-numbing natural shocks were soon followed by another catastrophe, this one relating to man-made technology. The Fukushima Dai-Ichi nuclear power plant was built to withstand both earthquakes and tsunamis. It had a tsunami-containment wall six meters high for such an eventuality. Unfortunately, the wall of water that hit the plant on 3/11 was at least seven meters high. It knocked down power lines and drowned the diesel generators, shutting down all power at the facility. That meant that most of the cooling systems that kept both the reactor cores and the pools of spent radioactive material at safe temperatures also went offline. The result was an escalating crisis of exposed reactor cores, vented radiation, and panic throughout the surrounding area.

It was in many ways a perfect storm—a huge earthquake buckled the roads needed to move supplies to the affected area. An unimaginably powerful tsunami wiped out power and telephone lines and nearly everything else along a broad stretch of coastline, and a combination of natural causes and human errors led to one of the worst nuclear crises the world has ever known. The Japanese have an old expression, *naki tsura ni hachi* (literally, "to a crying face, a bee"), which means a child who is already crying is then stung by a bee. In other words, when trouble comes, it comes in twos and threes. The entire Tohoku area was already crying in the aftermath of the natural tragedy when the Fukushima nuclear crisis stung the area once again.

I was in Washington, DC, on March 11. I happened to be visiting the National Science Foundation (NSF) that day and was out with some NSF staff for some after-hours discussions when news of the quake and tsunami lit up the TV screens. I was stunned. Here I was safe in the United States while hundreds of friends and colleagues had to deal with this catastrophe back in Japan. I thought of my father's family in Fukushima Prefecture, which was also hit by the tsunami (the nuclear problem had not appeared yet), and I wondered if they were okay. My first call was to the Japanese embassy on Massachusetts Ave. I asked for more detailed information than was coming in over CNN, and of course I offered my services in whatever capacity I might be of help. Then I immediately booked a flight back to Tokyo.

For obvious reasons, I didn't get much sleep between hearing the news of the big quake and arriving back in Japan. Very soon I would be getting even less.

Even before I landed, I knew that the biggest problem would not be a shortage of food or water, nor a lack of people or equipment to bring aid to the troubled area. The real problem would be the after-shocks of the quake within the Japanese bureaucracy. Although there have been serious earthquakes throughout Japanese history, and a big one tore through downtown Kobe in 1995, this double-punch of a giant earthquake plus a devastating tsunami was an event beyond anything in living memory. That meant that in many parts of the government, officials had no precedent, no rule book to fall back on. More than that, the constant news stream of increasingly horrific death tolls and frightening video footage of whole towns being wiped out would have short-circuited government responses to any crisis.

As I have noted before, Japan is largely run by its central bureaucracy, and the ministry officials are basically smart, hard-working, decent people who genuinely wish to serve the nation. But bureaucrats in any country operate by rules, guidelines, and precedents, and where none of the existing ones apply, the ministries are sometimes subject to a kind of administrative paralysis. I am not in any way criticizing these officials, only noting that each ministry has a tried-and-true cookbook about how to deal with any given situation. If the situation at hand matches a recipe in that book, the ministries handle it with machine-like precision, and the results are guaranteed. However, when something new appears, something that is not in the cookbook and has no specific recipe to follow, that's when the paralysis sets in. It may be temporary, but when tens of thousands of lives are at stake, even a short lapse can be crucial.

Of course, with my standard ready-fire-aim approach, I saw an emergency that needed solutions fast, and I hit the ground running, literally. If this cookbook needed new pages, there were plenty of people, both Japanese and foreign, willing to pitch in and add a few new recipes even if they might need amending or revising later on. What was important was to get things moving right away.

One of the less-publicized tragedies of the Kobe earthquake in 1995 was the inability of many foreign medical teams to provide aid to the victims of the disaster. Rescue teams from all around the world tried to enter Kobe to offer assistance, but in that instance, with a relatively smaller quake far away from Tokyo, the bureaucracy went back to its cookbook. The rules clearly state that only doctors who have passed rigid local exams and obtained qualifications to practice medicine in Japan are allowed to provide medical services. Thus, many skilled medical personnel from foreign countries were turned away at the airport or only allowed to enter Japan on the condition that they not practice medicine in any form. This may sound crazy to most people—victims of the quake needed medical help, experienced doctors from all over the world were volunteering to help, but Japanese officials were reciting rules designed to ensure that only qualified doctors could practice medicine—rules established to protect people from quackery under normal, day-to-day circumstances. But these were certainly not normal, day-to-day circumstances. The foreign doctors and nurses who came to Japan were not looking to set up unlicensed clinics or cheat unsuspecting citizens out of their hard-earned cash. They merely wanted to help people in desperate need, do their job, and go home. But rules are rules.

Fortunately, I have worked with the Japanese bureaucracy many times in the past, and I've been an advisor, both official and unofficial, to most of the main ministries. I understand their thinking, and I know that they are only doing exactly what they have been trained to do. I did not want to fight with anyone; that accomplishes nothing. Instead, I went to the relevant ministries to see what could be done. I guessed that when a situation as big as this triple tragedy occurs, officials will be too shocked to know what to do, and that brief period of bureaucratic paralysis can provide a window of opportunity. Without going into a detailed description of dozens of meetings, let me cut to the chase: through the efforts of several people, including myself, we managed to obtain approval for hundreds of foreign doctors and nurses to enter Japan specifically to provide emergency medical services. I am confident that their hard work helped to save lives in Tohoku.

In a similar way, some of the world's major pharmaceutical companies donated large quantities of drugs and medicines to help the relief effort. Many of these medicines have not been formally approved for use in Japan, none of them has labeling in Japanese, and in other ways they do not meet the strict criteria for sale or distribution in Japanese pharmacies. But when people are suffering, it's time to skip the paperwork. Working with a lot of the same people who had helped to expedite the doctors' entry visas, I was able to do the same for truckloads of medicine.

There are so many stories to tell. I was working 20-hour days to help various organizations, ministries, and Cabinet offices to coordinate relief efforts and facilitate policy and regulatory changes needed to help the people affected by this disaster. I have made several trips to the tsunami area, even to the area surrounding the Fukushima Dai-Ichi nuclear plant, and worked to help all sorts of groups and companies to avoid even greater repercussions from the event.

Perhaps when these troubles are all behind us, when people's lives have been rebuilt and the nuclear danger is past, I will write about the events that I saw and the various roles played by a host of people in the great drama that has been unfolding since March of 2011.

The events in my life leading up to 3/11 have in some ways felt like a preparation for this tragedy. At no time in recent history have we been more in need of people with creative, innovative solutions to a crisis of incomparable magnitude. Breaking rules, trying the impossible, and being entrepreneurial are sometimes the only way to get things done efficiently.

As history has witnessed, many of the most successful and innovative companies in the world, especially in Japan, were formed in times of crisis. While this was a tremendous tragedy, we now need to look forward and use this as a catalyst to change Japan and to help create an environment for the next generation to thrive. Everything that I have done to date has been in preparation for this. I have never felt a stronger compulsion to try even harder—for at least the next 40 years.

April 2011
Tokyo

Appendix A

Famous Quotes and Helpful Advice

Innovation is the specific instrument of entrepreneurship. The act that endows resources with a new capacity to create wealth.

—*Peter Drucker*

Management is doing things right; leadership is doing the right things.

—*Peter Drucker*

The leaders who work most effectively, it seems to me, never say "I." And that's not because they have trained themselves not to say "I." They don't think "I." They think "we"; they think "team." They understand their job to be to make the team function. They accept responsibility and don't sidestep it but "we" gets the credit. This is what creates trust, what enables you to get the task done.

—*Peter Drucker*

Individually, we are one drop. Together, we are an ocean.

—*Ryunosuke Satoro*

Coming together is a beginning. Keeping together is progress. Working together is success.

—*Henry Ford*

Individual commitment to a group effort—that is what makes a team work, a company work, a society work, a civilization work.

—*Vince Lombardi*

We must all hang together, or assuredly, we shall all hang separately.

—*Benjamin Franklin*

In teamwork, silence isn't golden, it's deadly.

—*Mark Sanborn*

It is amazing how much people get done if they do not worry about who gets the credit.

—*Proverb*

Teamwork is the ability to work together toward a common vision. It is the fuel that allows common people to attain uncommon results.

—*Andrew Carnegie*

None of us is as smart as all of us.

—*Japanese Proverb*

Vision without execution is a daydream. Execution without vision is a nightmare.

—*Japanese Proverb*

A boat doesn't go forward if each one is rowing their own way.

—*Proverb*

A group becomes a team when each member is sure enough of himself and his contribution to praise the skill of the others.

—*Norman Shidle*

No one ever promised that the fastest horse in the race was the easiest one to ride. (on managing talented people)

—*Eric J. Joiner, Jr.*

We can't solve problems by using the same kind of thinking we used when we created them.

—*Albert Einstein*

Imagination is more important than knowledge.

—*Albert Einstein*

If you don't go fishing because you thought it might rain, you will never go fishing. This applies to more than fishing.

—*Gary Sow*

The difference between "involvement" and "commitment" is like an eggs-and-ham breakfast: the chicken was "involved"—the pig was "committed."

—*Unknown*

All truth passes through three stages. First, it is ridiculed. Second, it is violently opposed. Third, it is accepted as being self-evident.

—*Arthur Schopenhauer (1788–1860)*

First they ignore you, then they laugh at you, then they fight you, then you win.

—*Mahatma Gandhi (1869–1948)*

A life spent making mistakes is not only more honorable, but more useful than a life spent doing nothing.

—George Bernard Shaw

Success usually comes to those who are too busy to be looking for it.

—Henry David Thoreau (1817–1862)

Great people are those who make others feel that they, too, can become great.

—Mark Twain

Stay hungry, stay foolish.

—Steve Jobs

Appendix B

Creativity and Logical Assessment Test

This is an example of the kind of test I used to give people when they were applying for jobs at our company. As I've mentioned before, the goal here was not to come up with the right answer instantly, but to find creative approaches to the problem. Like many employers these days, we were looking to hire not just smart people, but creative, free-thinking, innovative people. They, not the brainiacs who can produce instant answers to complex math questions, become the lifeblood of modern companies.

Once again, this is only a sample (many of which are also available on the Internet), but it should give you an idea of the kinds of things we were looking for.

Problem 1: One train leaves Tokyo at 15 kph heading for Osaka. Another train leaves from Osaka at 20 kph heading for Tokyo on the same track. Assume the distance between Tokyo and Osaka is about 500 kilometers. If a bird, flying at 25 kph, leaves from Tokyo at the same time as the train and flies back and forth between the two trains until they collide, how far will the bird have traveled?

Problem 2: You have two ropes, each rope takes exactly one hour to burn completely. Both of these ropes vary in thickness, meaning that some parts of the ropes are thicker than other parts of the rope. Using these two ropes and a lighter, find a way to measure 45 minutes.

Problem 3: You have two hourglasses: a 7-minute one and an 11-minute one. Using just these hourglasses, accurately time 15 minutes.

Problem 4: A snail is at the bottom of a well that is 20 meters in depth. Every day the snail climbs 5 meters upwards, but at night it slides 4 meters back downwards. How many days must elapse until the snail reaches the top of the well?

Problem 5:

$$5 \quad 3 \quad 7 \quad 8 \quad 9$$
$$2 \quad 6 \quad 4 \quad 1 \quad x$$
$$8 \quad 0 \quad 2 \quad 0 \quad 4$$

What is x?

Problem 6: $(a - x)(b - x)(c - x) \ldots (y - x) = ?$

Problem 7: You have nine dots arranged like a rectangle:

$$\bullet \quad \bullet \quad \bullet$$
$$\bullet \quad \bullet \quad \bullet$$
$$\bullet \quad \bullet \quad \bullet$$

Without lifting your pen, draw four lines that cross all nine dots.

Problem 8: Using only a 5-gallon bucket and a 3-gallon bucket, put exactly four gallons of water in the 5-gallon bucket. (Assume you have an infinite supply of water. No measurement markings on the buckets, guessing or estimation.)

Problem 9: There is a room with a door (closed) and three light bulbs. Outside the room there are three switches, connected to the bulbs. You may manipulate the switches as you wish, but you can only open the door once. Determine which switch controls which bulb.

Problem 10: A man has a gold chain with seven links. He needs seven days of help at a fee of one gold link per day. However, each day of work needs to be paid for separately. In other words, the worker must be paid each day after working and if the laborer is ever overpaid he will quit with the extra money. Also he will never allow himself to be owed a link. What is the best way to pay the worker with fewest number of cuts to the chain to make payments every day?

Problem 11: Four people, A, B, C, and D, are on one side of a bridge, and they all want to cross the bridge. However, it's late at night, so you can't cross without a flashlight. They only have one flashlight. Also, the bridge is only strong enough to support the weight of two people at once. The four people all walk at different speeds: A takes 1 minute to cross the bridge, B takes 2 minutes, C takes 5 minutes, and D takes 10 minutes. When two people cross together, sharing the flashlight, they walk at the slower person's rate. How quickly can the four cross the bridge?

Problem 12: Imagine you are standing in front of a mirror, facing it. Raise your left hand. Raise your right hand. Look at your reflection. When you raise your left hand your reflection raises what appears to be his right hand. But when you tilt your head up, your reflection does too, and does not appear to tilt his/her head down. Why is it that the mirror appears to reverse left and right, but not up and down?

About the Author

W illiam H. Saito is an entrepreneurial evangelist, business energizer, policy adviser, and educator whose multifaceted activities elude attempts at categorization. An authority in the fields of encryption, authentication, and biometric technology, he has spent the past two decades shaping information security policy, establishing and selling companies, and managing public corporations.

While still in UCLA medical school, he founded I/O Software in 1991 and built it into a global leader in information security, earning recognition as Entrepreneur of the Year in 1998 by Ernst & Young, NASDAQ, and *USA Today*. In 2000, Microsoft integrated the company's core authentication technology into the Windows operating system, and the technology was subsequently licensed to over 160 companies worldwide.

After Microsoft acquired the firm in 2004, Saito moved to Japan and founded InTecur, a Tokyo-based consultancy with offices worldwide that helps companies identify and develop applications and markets for innovative technologies. Among his many activities, he is also an adviser to G-8 governments on information security policy, a serial venture capitalist, and an active university lecturer, as well as a Young Global

Leader and Global Agenda Council member of the World Economic Forum (WEF). He is also the founding curator for the WEF's Global Shaper's Community in Japan.

His hobbies include fly-fishing, wine collecting, and French cooking. You can follow William on Twitter (@whsaito) or on his website at http://saitohome.com/.

Index

3 1136 00281 7810